WESTMAR COLLE

THE NEW STATES OF ASIA

THE NEW STATES
OF ASIA

A Political Analysis

by

MICHAEL BRECHER

LONDON
OXFORD UNIVERSITY PRESS
NEW YORK TORONTO

Oxford University Press, Ely House, London W.1

GLASGOW NEW YORK TORONTO MELBOURNE WELLINGTON
CAPE TOWN SALISBURY IBADAN NAIROBI LUSAKA ADDIS ABABA
BOMBAY CALCUTTA MADRAS KARACHI LAHORE DACCA
KUALA LUMPUR HONG KONG TOKYO

First edition 1963
Reprinted 1964 and 1968

Printed in Great Britain by Fletcher & Son Ltd, Norwich
and bound by Richard Clay (The Chaucer Press) Ltd, Bungay, Suffolk

To
LEORA, DIANA, and SEEGLA
whose generation must not be indifferent to
the fate of Asia and her peoples

INTRODUCTION

Asia has various meanings. To some it is a geographical expression, the largest and most populous of the continents. And so it is, with 17 million square miles and $1\frac{3}{4}$ billion people, covering one-third of the earth's surface and nearly two-thirds of mankind.

Other people think of Asia as the home of the great religions. This image, too, is well-grounded in fact, as revealed by a glance around the 'Rimland'. From South-West Asia, better known as the Near East or Middle East, came Judaism, Christianity, and Islam. India gave the world Hinduism and Buddhism, while China contributed Confucianism, really a philosophy with the power of religion, and Japan added Shinto. No wonder that Westerners talk about the mystical and spiritual East. If one adds to the list such faiths as Zoroastrianism, the religion of the Persians before the coming of Islam, Sikhism and Jainism in India, Taoism in China, and Lamaism, a form of Buddhism in High Asia, along with a host of less sophisticated beliefs, the spiritual image becomes almost a self-evident truth.

Asia also suggests an area of coloured peoples. This too is accurate, although there is no such thing as an Asian 'racial type', except in the minds of special pleaders. All of the races of man are found there and most of the sub-races. There are Caucasians and Negroes and Mongolians. There are Aryans and Dravidians. There are white-skinned and brown and black and yellow and various shades of each. Millennia of migration and mixture have produced a *mélange* of physical types.

An important feature of Asia, perhaps the most crucial in the struggle for the minds of men, is its intense poverty and under-development. Statistics often conceal important truths but not so in this case. One illustration conveys the magnitude of Asian poverty. In 1950 the annual per capita income in North America was $1,100. For Europe it was $380 and for Latin America $170. Then came another sharp dip for Africa, $75, and finally, for Asia, $50. That is to say, two out of every three persons on earth had an average yearly income of $50! That fact, among others, has stimulated the great contest for the friendship of Asia.

The grim poverty that stalks the lands of Asia can only be partly portrayed by words and statistics. Yet the record itself is dramatic enough to convey the image. Hundreds of thousands make their 'homes' on the streets of her overcrowded cities. The slums of Calcutta and Singapore are among the foulest in the world. Millions suffer from malnutrition; the average daily consumption per person in 1958 was 2,070 calories, less than the minimum required for health; in Europe and North America it was more than 3,000, and even in Africa it was almost 2,400. The average per capita annual income today is about $60 or about 17 cents a day, and this must cover all expenses—food, clothing, shelter, medicines, and education. Millions of landless labourers have, at most, half that income.

If life in the city is a perpetual struggle for survival, life in the village is devoid of material comfort for all but a few. The typical peasant home is a windowless mud hut with a few cooking utensils and a string cot. It is almost always dark; less than 1 per cent of Asia's villages have electricity. Few village streets are paved and sewage disposal is rare. Sanitation in the village is abominable. Famine takes its toll periodically and malnutrition saps the strength of the majority. Most Asians eat only twice a day. Few get meat, fish, eggs, or fruit, certainly not in sufficient quantities. The result has been a very high death rate and the lowest life expectancy in the world; in India it was 32 years in 1941–51, raised to 47·5 by 1961.

Another image of Asia prevalent in the West was colonial rule, Western rule, white rule. A map of Asia in 1939, on the eve of the war, showed virtually the entire continent under British, French, Dutch, or American control. In South and East Asia only Japan was fully sovereign, with China in the throes of long-term civil war and Thailand holding on to a precarious independence.

War is often a catalyst to political change. The Second World War provides a dramatic example. Within five years of its conclusion Pakistan, India, Ceylon, Burma, the Philippines, and Indonesia had joined the community of independent states. The nations of Indo-China were added in 1954 and Malaya in 1957. The age of colonialism in Asia had virtually come to an end.

Asia did not cease to be important nor did it vanish from the news. During the past fifteen years it has occupied a key role in world affairs. A few examples will suffice: the struggle between India and Pakistan over Kashmir, including military hostilities in 1947–48; frequent civil war in Indonesia; widespread rebellion of communists in

Burma and Malaya; the Korean War from 1950 to 1953; protracted war between France and the Viet Minh culminating in the Geneva Conference on Indo-China in 1954; periodic tension over the off-shore islands of China with threats and counter-threats from Peking and Taipeh, and from Moscow and Washington; the Tibet uprising of 1959; and frontier skirmishes between Pakistan and Afghanistan. The Geneva Conference on Laos in 1961–62 and the Sino–Indian border war on the 'Roof of the World' demonstrated once more that Asia is a region of turmoil and travail, and of rivalry among outside Powers.

There are deep urges in these lands of transition: the urge for social welfare and economic change, for better health and housing and education; the desire for recognition by non-Asians, respect for their cultures, and, most important, for their right to seek the 'good society' without foreign interference or control. Among the leaders and middle class there is a demand for equality of status, compensation for the long night of alien rule.

Asia is important for all these reasons: because it is the largest and most populous of the earth's continents; because it has created High Cultures of lasting value; because the human family is represented in all its diverse creeds and colours and physical features; because it is a region of colonial rule recently emerged as politically independent; because this provides a great challenge to former rulers and ruled alike to create a new and more healthy relationship of co-operation and respect. Asia is significant, too, because it is the Achilles Heel of a future world society. As long as its millions are poor and hungry, illiterate and easily struck down by disease, as long as this is in glaring contrast with the more fortunate peoples of Europe and America, Asia will remain a focal point of tension and a danger. Temptations from without and expectations within can lead to serious conflicts from which no one would be immune.

Asia was virtually ignored in the West before 1945. The reasons are not difficult to find. Most Asian countries were objects not subjects of political behaviour until the late 1940s; that is to say, they were appendages of European or American Powers, economically, politically, and strategically; they did not shape their own destiny and so could be safely ignored. Their cultures were alien and complex. The religions of South and East Asia had no relevance to Western thought and experience. Their languages were not essential for Western peoples and were difficult to master. And their customs were without any bearing on Western modes of life. Still another source of our ignorance was the lack of communications, apart from colonial officials, a few businessmen, journalists, and tourists.

Awareness of Asia has grown in the past decade, largely under the impact of events. Much has been written about Asia as a whole or a specific region or an aspect of life in one or more countries. As a result, our knowledge has been enriched, and the following pages duly acknowledge my indebtedness to many researchers in this field. If there is any distinctiveness in the present volume it is the focus, the 'new states' of Southern Asia. There is an attempt to combine breadth, an area extend'ng from Pakistan to Indonesia, with political analysis in depth. One essay is devoted to a 'new state' outside this region, Israel, but this too concerns relationships within the community of newly-independent states. There is, necessarily, some overlapping, both to 'old' states in Asia and 'new states' elsewhere. But for the most part these political essays deal with the states of Southern Asia which have become independent since the Second World War. The rationale is the conviction that the future of all peoples is bound up with the course of events in those lands.

These essays, now slightly revised, were written during 1961 and 1962. The first two, dealing with the colonial epoch and its impact, and the arduous quest for internal political stability, were, in their original form, research papers prepared for the National Film Board of Canada. The third is an effort to construct a novel framework for the analysis of the international relations of Southern Asia, and the sixth provides the content for such a framework. The fourth essay concentrates on the most misunderstood feature of the foreign policy of many new states—non-alignment. And the fifth examines the role of Israel in the larger community of Afro-Asian 'new states'. The appendix is an edited version of rather lengthy tape-recorded interviews which I was privileged to have with the Prime Minister of the largest and most influential of all the 'new states'. Although seven years old, they are offered here because of their freshness and striking relevance to the essays in this volume. Excerpts have appeared elsewhere, but in their present integrated form they appear here for the first time.

I wish to thank the Editors of *International Journal* and *World Politics* for permission to reprint articles which first appeared in their pages (ch. 4 and 5 and ch. 3 respectively), as well as the Free

Press of Glencoe, Inc., New York, for allowing me to publish an essay (ch. 2) which appeared in slightly different form in their *Comparative Politics: A Reader*, edited by H. Eckstein and D. E. Apter, 1963. As on an earlier occasion, this volume has benefited greatly from the editorial advice of the Oxford University Press. A friend who read the manuscript of my *Nehru* and made valuable comments has kindly done the same with these essays. Most of all, I am indebted to my wife for constant encouragement in the preparation of these essays. As usual, she read the various drafts with much care and persisted with the theme that books, even scholarly ones, must be written 'in an intelligible style. This cannot always be achieved, but this author, for one, is grateful for the gentle persuasion. Whatever errors of facts there may be are entirely my responsibility.

M. B.

McGill University,
Montreal, Canada,
June, 1963

CONTENTS

INTRODUCTION   vii

1 COLONIALISM AND THE COMING OF INDEPENDENCE   1
   Introduction   1
   Growth of Colonial Empires   2
   Impact   15
   Nationalism—Origins and Formative Stages   21
   Coming of Independence   30

2 THE SEARCH FOR POLITICAL STABILITY   47
   Introduction   47
   Political Instability: The Record   49
   Causes of Instability   61
   The Way Out   73

3 A NEW SUBORDINATE STATE SYSTEM   88
   Definition of the Southern Asian System   95
   Structural Features   97
   Textural Features   106
   Conclusion   109

4 NEUTRALISM: AN ANALYSIS   111

5 ISRAEL AND AFRO-ASIA   123
   Images and Reality   123
   Partial Fulfilment in Asia   128
   Technical Assistance: Israel's 'Presence' in Africa   138
   Aims and Results   145

6 THE NEW STATES IN WORLD POLITICS   153
   Introduction   153
   The Dominant System and the Bloc Struggle   155

The Subordinate System : The New States and China   161
The Subordinate System : Regionalism and Bilateral Disputes   172
The New States and the United Nations   184

APPENDIX : TALKS WITH NEHRU   192

INDEX   216

1
COLONIALISM AND THE
COMING OF INDEPENDENCE

INTRODUCTION

ASIA, South and East, is a classic example of colonialism in modern history. As late as 1939, there were only four sovereign states in that vast region. Two of these, Afghanistan and Thailand, were buffer zones between powerful empires. China was still groping for unity in the face of civil strife and foreign aggression. Japan stood alone as a genuinely independent nation.

A glance at the map reveals the extent of colonial rule there on the eve of the Second World War: India, Ceylon, Burma, Malaya, Sarawak and North Borneo, and Hong Kong (British); Indo-China (French); Korea (Japanese); the Philippines (American); the Indies (Dutch); and Portuguese remnants in Macao, Timor, and Goa. Less than twenty years later the position had been transformed. In the aftermath of war and revolution, almost all of colonial Asia attained independence: the Philippines in 1946, India and Pakistan a year later, Ceylon and Burma in 1948, Indonesia the following year, and the states of Indo-China in 1954. Even before that year, Korea had been freed from Japanese rule—though qualified by partition and savage war; and mainland China had been unified by Communist power. The process was virtually complete with the grant of self-rule to Malaya in 1957. Only a few British, Dutch, and Portuguese possessions remained from the Age of Colonialism in South and East Asia, and almost all of these were to pass from the scene in the early sixties.[1]

The coming of independence to the peoples of that area will be explored in the following pages. But this requires a preliminary survey of the growth of colonial empires and their impact, for only thus will the nationalist movements be understood and the transfer of power by foreign rulers fall into proper perspective.

[1] India occupied Goa in 1961; Holland transferred West New Guinea to the United Nations and then Indonesian administration in 1962–3; and Singapore, North Borneo, Sarawak and Brunei are to merge with Malaya to form the Federation of Malaysia in 1963.

GROWTH OF COLONIAL EMPIRES

General

The expansion of Europe overseas is too large and complex a movement to be analysed in detail here. It will be sufficient to sketch the origins of this remarkable phenomenon, some general characteristics, and the consolidation of Western rule in South and East Asia. The setting was a composite of factors: the collapse of the unity of Christendom and the emergence of dynastic states in Western Europe, all interested in maximizing their Power, Prestige, and Profits; the growth of towns and a money economy in the thirteenth and fourteenth centuries, leading to a search for new trade channels; growing affluence in European courts, with a resultant demand for the spices and luxuries of the East; and the Turkish barrier to contact with the Orient—made more formidable by the Ottoman capture of Constantinople in 1453.[1]

Against this dynamic background, European expansion began in the fifteenth century; it gathered momentum in the seventeenth and reached its peak in the late nineteenth and early twentieth centuries. During a period of 450 years, the West—that is, Europe and the United States—penetrated the farthest corners of the earth, and brought all peoples and areas into some kind of subordinate relationship. There were various stages in the process: to America and Asia from 1500 to 1750; to South and South-East Asia in the nineteenth century; Russian expansion across Central Asia to the Pacific in the eighteenth and nineteenth centuries; the penetration of East Asia in the nineteenth century; the partition of Africa from 1880 to 1914; and control over the Middle East from 1919 to 1939.[2]

There were various motives for expansion, broadly summarized as religious, population pressure, prestige, military or strategic, and economic. Different motives predominated in different stages and for different colonial powers; for example, the original motive of Spain and Portugal was the crusade against Islam and the propagation of the Catholic faith; for others, it was the trade in spices; but in time the nature of the economic stimulus itself changed—to imports of

[1] Cf. M. M. Knight, H. E. Barnes, and F. Flugel, *Economic History of Europe*, New York 1928, Part I, ch. vi; Henri Pirenne, *Economic and Social History of Medieval Europe*, London 1936, Parts IV-VII; and C. W. Previté-Orton, *The Shorter Cambridge Medieval History*, Cambridge 1952, Vol. II, ch. 32–36.

[2] The most useful compilation of facts about the expansion of Europe is to be found in W. L. Langer (ed.), *An Encyclopedia of World History* (3rd ed.), Cambridge, Mass. 1952, pp. 524–8, 826–911, and 1081–1134.

silks and, later, to a desire for markets and raw materials.[1] It is also true that various states held leadership in different phases—first the Portuguese in the East, then the Dutch, and later the British and French. Despite these differences, however, there was an underlying unity and certain common features in this period, aptly termed the 'Vasco da Gama epoch in Asian history' by the distinguished Indian diplomat–historian, K. M. Panikkar.

Three aspects of this epoch stand out.[2] The first was the domination of Asian (and later, African) land masses by maritime powers. Indeed, of all the colonial powers, only Russia expanded by land; all others—Portugal, Spain, Holland, Britain, France, Denmark, Belgium, the United States, and Japan—conquered with superior naval power. To the present day, Soviet Russia benefits from this anomaly, for colonialism is identified with overseas expansion, a purely Western phenomenon, since Japanese colonialism is considered a special case. The British conquest of south India was greatly assisted by superior naval power. Similarly, it was Western sea power that forced open the door to China in 1842 and to Japan in 1853. In a broader sense, control of the seas aided the conquest of the Asian rimlands and ended a lengthy period of Chinese suzerainty in South-East Asia—and made the Middle Kingdom itself subject to Western influence. Finally, it was naval strength, ironically, Asian (Japanese) sea power, that set in motion the collapse of Western colonial empires in Asia as a result of their defeats during the Second World War.

A second general feature was economic: the Western colonial powers imposed a commercial economy, later, an industrial economy, on the predominantly agricultural, self-sufficient village communities of Asia. This had wide-ranging consequences on every facet of Asian life and ultimately revolutionized the relations between Asia and the West. The impact will be elaborated later; the essence may be noted here: the consequences were social—the formation of new classes like the intelligentsia and professional men; educational—the introduction of Western ideas, science and a spirit of inquiry; economic—the transformation of their material foundations; and political—a stimulus to unity, national consciousness, and the introduction of Western political institutions.

[1] See E. A. Walker, *Colonies,* Cambridge 1944, ch. ii.
[2] This discussion of the common features is based upon K. M. Panikkar, *Asia and Western Dominance,* London 1953, Introduction.

B

The third common element was the political domination of Asia
by Western peoples. This took various forms—direct and indirect.
British India was ruled by a private corporation, the East India
Company, until 1858; thereafter, it came under direct Crown rule;
but even then, there remained 600-odd princely States over whom
Great Britain was the suzerain or 'Paramount Power'. Cochin-
China was a French colony, but the remaining parts of Indo-China
were protectorates; so, too, were the Federated Malay States until
1957. There were also spheres of influence in China, where the con-
cessionaires, Western Powers, had considerable freedom of action.
Not only did the forms vary. The methods of rule varied, too—some
harsh, some considerate, some assimilationist, some apartheidist. And
the policies and goals varied considerably : the British, at a late stage,
directed their attention towards self-government; the French towards
assimilation and integration; the Belgians towards the perpetuation
of a benevolent paternalist foreign ruler; the Portuguese towards
exploitation and the preservation of the political status quo. But there
was a common, unifying theme amidst the diverse forms, methods,
policies, and goals of colonial rule—white, Western control over the
coloured peoples of Asia (and Africa). In some cases, political
domination produced, or was accompanied by, a feeling of racial
superiority. 'Racialism' was most conspicuous in British colonies and
was, to many Asians, the most objectionable legacy of Western rule.

Coming of the West

The Portuguese were the first Westerners to arrive in the East
(and will probably be the last to depart). Their daring and persistence in the fifteenth century, under the leadership of Henry the
Navigator, led to the voyage of Diaz to the Cape in 1487 and the
historic journey of da Gama to India in 1498. The latter's achievement meant a new link to the fabulous East, which the Portuguese
were quick to exploit. They swept the hitherto-dominant Arab and
Indian vessels from the Indian Ocean and dominated the trade of
the area throughout the sixteenth century. The pivots of Portuguese
maritime power were strategically located bases acquired by their
intrepid captains, notably Albuquerque, builder of Portugal's
eastern empire : Cochin (1506); Goa (1510); Malacca (1511), and
Ceylon (1517). Through these bases the highly-valued spice trade
was controlled.

The manner of acquisition of control over Ceylon and the shifting

fortunes of that island illuminate the haphazard Western involvement in Asia in the early stage. The beginning of Portuguese trade
dates to 1505, when one of their vessels was blown by a gale into
Colombo harbour! In 1517 an expedition visited the island and
established a trading fort at Colombo. The island was not formally
incorporated into Portugal's empire until 1602—though at no time
did Lisbon control more than a few coastal settlements. In 1656
the Dutch supported a dissident Ceylonese ruler and expelled the
Portuguese, whose power was already on the wane in the East. The
Dutch controlled the island's trade and a few coastal areas until
1796, when Holland was occupied by Napoleon, and the Swiss
mercenaries of the Dutch in Colombo deserted to the British. For a
few years the island was ruled as an appendage of the Madras
Presidency in south India. Then, in 1802, Ceylon became a British
Crown Colony, a status retained until it was granted Dominion
status in 1948.[1]

Domination of the Eastern trade passed from the Portuguese to
the Dutch, not only in Ceylon but also in the richer 'spice islands' of
latter-day Indonesia. Dutch ships arrived there as early as 1596—
even before Holland had won independence from Spain! The
Dutch East India Company was formed in 1602 to unite and consolidate commercial footholds in the East. Three years later the
Dutch seized Amboina in the southern Moluccas, and in 1619 they
established a fort at Batavia on the north-west coast of Java, later to
become the capital of the vast empire known as the Dutch East
Indies. A few years later the British abandoned the trade of the
Indies, following a massacre by the Dutch there. Finally, in 1641,
the Dutch captured Malacca, marking the end of Portuguese pretensions to power in the region. For the next century and a half, the
Dutch dominated the East Indies.

Dutch penetration was aided by rivalries and conflicts between the
inland agricultural sultanates and the coastal commercial states, the
legatees of the great Indian Javanese empire of Majapahit, which
ruled over the island in the fourteenth century. Gradually, too, the
Dutch secured control over all the sultanates by a policy of 'divide
and rule'. By 1705 they had effective political control over Java and
a monopoly in the spice trade. During the next century they ruled
indirectly, through the sultans and 'regents' drawn from the aristo-
cracy. Dutch supervisors resided in each of the states to ensure

[1] Cf. Sydney D. Bailey, *Ceylon*, London 1952.

efficient exploitation. This was accomplished through a system of forced deliveries of crops to the Company, notably of coffee; Javanese peasants were subjected to forced labour—without compensation; and the Dutch residents or controllers became 'coffee sergeants'.

That early phase also witnessed the emergence of the Chinese as the important middlemen in the economy, especially in money-lending and retail trade; this role has been an increasing source of friction—until now, as revealed by the anti-Chinese measures adopted by Indonesia in 1960. The existence of three clearly-defined groups—Malays, Dutch, and Chinese—was also recognized by the introduction of three separate judicial and legal systems.

Dutch activities in the Indies were largely confined to Java until the end of the eighteenth century. As with Ceylon, their control over Java was lost to the British during the Napoleonic Wars, but only briefly, from 1811 until 1818. More important than the British interlude was the abolition of the Dutch East India Company in 1799, by the pro-French revolutionary régime of the day. It was this act which divides the period of Dutch commercial exploitation and that of consolidation of Holland's colonial empire.[1]

While the Dutch were asserting their mastery over the Eastern seas, the British and French began to acquire footholds in India. Their technique was the same—private corporations of merchant adventurers seeking to exploit the trade in Oriental luxuries. The British were the first to arrive on the scene. Their East India Company, the 'John Company', it came to be known, was first chartered in 1600. In 1612 trading rights were secured at Surat on the west coast. In 1639 a fort was established at Madras; in 1661 Bombay was acquired; and in 1690 Calcutta was founded. These were mere trading posts, later to become the capitals of the 'three Presidencies' and, to this day, great urban centres of the sub-continent.

The Company made no claim to political power at that time; the sole interest was trade and profits. Among its rivals was the French Compagnie des Indes Orientales, formed in 1664 under Colbert's inspiration. Ten years later the first French settlement was established at Pondicherry. The next century was crucial in the struggle for Western primacy in India—though neither expected to win political control over the decaying Moghul Empire.

[1] Cf. Bernard H. M. Vlekke, *Nusantara: A History of Indonesia* (rev. ed.), The Hague 1959, ch. 5, 7, 8, 10. See also D. G. E. Hall, *A History of South-East Asia*, London 1955, ch. 15, 16.

Anglo-French rivalry in India, as in America, was but an extension of the main contest in Europe. The conflict reached a climax in the middle of the eighteenth century, amidst the Wars of the Austrian Succession (1746–48) and the Seven Years' War (1756–63). Thus, Dupleix captured Madras in 1746, but it was restored to the English in the general peace treaty two years later. French power was at its height in 1751—in both the Deccan and the Carnatic; in that year, however, Clive seized Arcot. Dupleix was soon recalled. Then, in 1757, the French were severely defeated at the Battle of Plassey. Pondicherry itself was captured by the English, though later returned. The dissolution of the French Company in 1769 left the British East India Company the sole European contender for power. By that time, too, it had begun massive economic exploitation as *Diwan* of Bengal.[1]

As a seeming consolation for their expulsion from India, the French penetrated Annam. Jesuit missionaries had been active since 1615 in this most Chinese of all countries outside China; it had been under Chinese control or suzerainty for almost two millennia. But it was not until the late eighteenth century that circumstances favoured French political influence. In 1789 French troops helped to reinstate a deposed Emperor. In gratitude, he granted France bases on the south coast and gave the Jesuits free rein. However, the lengthy period of revolution and war at home, followed by retrenchment and conservatism, arrested the expansion of French power in Indo-China —until the last half of the nineteenth century.

Colonialism Triumphant

The nineteenth century was, indeed, the age of colonialism *par excellence*. It was in that period that the Second British Empire reached its zenith: the conquest of India and Burma; the seizure of the Cape and Ceylon from the Dutch; the acquisition of Hong Kong, and the consolidation of power in Malaya. The French conquered all Indo-China, while the Dutch extended their sway over the East Indies. And in China the imperialist powers carved rich spheres of influence and extorted concessions from a declining Manchu dynasty.

The highlights in the John Company's conquest of the Indian

[1] Cf. R. C. Majumdar, H. C. Raychaudhuri, and K. Datta, *An Advanced History of India*, London 1950, Part III, Book 1, ch. i, ii; Percival Spear, *India: A Modern History*, Ann Arbor, Michigan 1961, ch. xvi, xvii; and Spear's Suggested Readings for this period.

sub-continent may be noted afresh. Two other contenders for the succession to the Moghuls remained following the expulsion of the French: Tipu Sultan in the south and the Maratha Confederacy in the west. The former was eliminated in 1799, the latter in 1818. Thirty years later the independent Sikh kingdom was destroyed, and the Punjab added to the Company's realm. The Company itself was dissolved following the Great Rebellion of 1857, and 'British India' came under Crown rule—where it remained until 1947.

The key to the Company's success was a flexible policy towards the princely States, a *mélange* of fragments from the Moghul Empire, later to be enlarged. From the initial victory at Plassey until 1813 the Company pursued a policy of non-involvement. In the next phase, from 1813 to 1819, all the States were brought into a relationship of subordinate co-operation with the Company—through treaties, engagements, sanads, and the like. The rulers were guaranteed against external aggression and internal revolt, in return for the recognition of the Company as the 'Paramount Power'. The third phase, from 1834 to 1856, was characterized by annexation wherever possible; this was the projection of the new liberalism at home, the effort to eliminate the relics of medievalism, to integrate the administration of India, and to introduce reforms in Hindu society. Its chief exponent was the Earl of Dalhousie, Governor-General from 1848 to 1856, though Wellesley and Hastings had earlier initiated the process of unification. The fear thus created in the Princely Order was a major cause of the Rebellion. With the onset of Crown rule, therefore, the policy of annexation ceased—forever. Queen Victoria's Proclamation of 1858 promised to respect the rights and dignity of the Princes; and three years later, this pledge was given formal expression in guarantees to the States. Indeed, the last phase, from 1858 to 1947, saw the cultivation of princely India as a counterpoise to the growing strength of nationalism. Apart from guaranteeing a minimum of good government, the British did not interfere in the internal affairs of the States; the Princes transferred control over foreign affairs, defence, and communications to the Paramount Power—in return for protection and internal autonomy.[1]

Relations with the princely States, about 600 in number, were

---

[1] Majumdar *et al.*, op. cit., Part II, Book I, ch. iii–vii, Book II, ch. i–iv; Spear, op. cit., ch. xviii–xxiv. See also Spear's Suggested Readings for that period. On the East India Company, the best work is Holden Furber, *John Company at Work*, Cambridge, Mass. 1948.

regulated by the Crown Representative and British Residents at the Princes' Courts, the counterparts of the Dutch 'coffee sergeants' or supervisors in Java. The Doctrine of Paramountcy and separate treaties or agreements provided the legal framework for the governance of 'Indian India', comprising one third of the territory and one quarter of the population of the sub-continent. The other category was 'British India' which, at the time of the transfer of power in 1947, consisted of eleven Provinces. Each was ruled by a Governor responsible to the Governor-General, who, in turn, was responsible to Parliament through the Cabinet. In time, representative and then responsible government was introduced in the Provinces. The unifying administrative link was the Governor-General, for he was also the Crown Representative to the States. Such, in brief, was the political and administrative system.[1]

The consolidation of British power was accompanied by changes in economic policy. From its formation in 1600 until the end of the eighteenth century, the East India Company was motivated primarily by trade and profit; political power was merely an effective instrument for more lucrative commercial relations and economic exploitation. With the coming of the Industrial Revolution, however, there arose ever-increasing pressure to end the Company's monopoly of trade and open India to private enterprise. This was done in 1813. Even before that time, the economic orientation had changed— India now became a valuable source of food and raw materials for the 'workshop of the world', as well as an ever-growing market for the products of British industry. So it was to remain till the end of the British Raj, a predominantly agrarian India attached to the metropolitan economy of Great Britain—with far-reaching consequences to be noted later.

The conquest of Burma took place in three distinct phases. The first Burmese War, from 1824 to 1826, led to British control over Assam, Arakan, and the Tenasserim coast. Pegu was added following the second Burmese War, 1852-3. And the process was completed in the third Burmese War of 1885. A British demand that Burmese foreign relations be guided by Delhi and that interference with trade cease was rejected by the Burmese monarch. In the war that ensued, Mandalay was occupied. The following year, Upper Burma was annexed. The Shan States were subdued in 1887 **and**

[1] Cf. A. B. Keith, *A Constitutional History of India 1600–1935*, London 1936, ch. x.

the Chin Hills in 1891. Boundaries were fixed with Thailand, Indo-China, and China in the last decade of the nineteenth century.

The territory of Burma was incorporated into the British Indian Empire. Burma became a Governor's Province—like Bombay or Madras—and enjoyed the gradual steps towards self-government in the sub-continent. Only after the 1935 Government of India Act was Burma restored to separate administrative status; and so it remained until the British departed in 1948. As for economic policy, Burma shared the exploitation of resources which was India's lot during the Raj.[1]

The British seizure of Ceylon from the Dutch has already been noted. Unlike the Dutch or the Portuguese, however, the new rulers succeeded in uniting the entire island under one authority; this was accomplished in 1815, when the British occupied the Kandyan kingdom in the highlands. With the Raj came a new judicial system, new forms of commerce, and the estate pattern for large-scale production of export products like coconuts, tea, and coffee. There were, too, experiments in political institutions, notably the Donoughmore Constitution of 1931, which gave Ceylon universal adult suffrage and a political system modelled on the London County Council. In a more subdued environment, Ceylon moved towards self-government with less pain than India or Burma.[2]

The great entrepôt port of Hong Kong, one of the few remaining British possessions in Asia, was acquired in 1842, following the first Opium War with China. The other centre of British commercial power in the region, Singapore, was founded in 1819 by Sir Stamford Raffles, one of the most imaginative builders of empire. Almost at once, it superseded Malacca, which had dominated the trade of South-East Asia for three centuries.

The various British settlements in Malaya were ruled by the East India Company until 1867; thereafter they had the collective status of a Crown Colony. British influence also grew among the many sultanates in the peninsula. In 1896 a Federation of four Malay

---

[1] Cf. John F. Cady, *A History of Modern Burma*, Ithaca 1958, ch. 3, 4, 8, 12. See also J. S. Furnivall, *Colonial Policy and Practice: A Comparative Study of Burma and Netherlands India*, Cambridge 1948; and Godfrey E. Harvey, *British Rule in Burma, 1824–1942*, London 1946.

[2] See Bailey, op. cit.; S. Namasivayam, *The Legislatures of Ceylon 1928–1948*, London 1951; I. D. S. Weerawardana, *Government and Politics in Ceylon, 1931–1946*, Colombo 1951; and W. Howard Wriggins: *Ceylon: Dilemmas of a New Nation*, Princeton 1960, ch. ii–iv.

states was formed, with Britain recognized as the Paramount Power. And in 1909 the remaining unfederated states joined Johore under British protection. For the next half-century these three entities existed side by side: the Straits Settlements, a Crown Colony under Governor's rule, like Indian Provinces; the Federated Malay States; and the Unfederated Malay States, with a status comparable to the Indian princely States. All but Singapore were grouped into a Federation of Malaya and given Dominion status in 1957.[1]

To the north, French power was being consolidated in Indo-China. It began in 1858, when a French–Spanish naval expedition forced open the door to Annam again and came to the defence of persecuted Christians. In the Treaty of Saigon that followed, France was ceded the three eastern provinces of Cochin-China, its first territorial foothold; it also received an indemnity and trading rights at three ports. The following year, 1863, a French protectorate was established over Cambodia. In 1867 France occupied the three western provinces of Cochin-China. Then, in 1874, French control over Annam's foreign policy was conceded. The status of protectorate was extended to Tongking and Annam itself in 1883, with the unrestricted right of French military occupation. China's objection led to a brief war and Peking's acceptance of the new state of affairs. An Indo-Chinese Union under French control was formed in 1887, comprising Annam, Tongking, Cambodia, and Cochin-China. Laos was added in 1893; and so it remained until the forced withdrawal of France, after bloody warfare, in 1954.

Of the five constituent units in the Indo-Chinese Union, only one, Cochin-China, was a colony; the others were protectorates, and three of them monarchies. The structure of government was highly centralized—in the French tradition. The head of the Union was a Governor-General, resident in Hanoi. A political appointee, with a term of only two years, he relied heavily on the permanent civil servants. The senior official in Cochin-China was a Governor; in the protectorates, Résidents Supérieurs. There was an advisory privy council to assist the Governor and a colonial council, partly appointed and partly elected, to control taxation. Similar organs existed in the protectorates, but Cochin-China was for all practical purposes a part of metropolitan France. Even in local government,

[1] See Rupert Emerson, *Malaysia: A Study in Direct and Indirect Rule*, New York 1937; Lennox A. Mills, *British Rule in Eastern Asia*, London 1942; and C. N. Parkinson, *A History of Malaya*, New York 1961.

the degree of French control was much more pronounced than in British colonies. Nor did the gradual introduction of representative and responsible government seriously weaken French control—certainly not until the Second World War and rebellion made substantive concessions urgent.

French social policy in Indo-China, as elsewhere, was assimilationist: the highest reward for aspiring natives was French citizenship, which gave them élite status. Few were admitted to the club. The principal economic goal was the exploitation of Indo-China's abundant resources for the world market, especially rice. Land tenure systems varied from peasant ownership in Tongking to absentee landlordism in Cochin-China, but indebtedness to Chinese moneylenders was everywhere to be found. Apart from rice, sizeable quantities of rubber, tin, and other minerals were produced. In all aspects of economic life, French interests were favoured—until the end of French rule.[1]

Three major themes stand out in the history of the Dutch East Indies during the era of triumphant colonialism. The first has already been noted—the abolition of the Dutch Company and the assumption of power by the Netherlands Government. The second was the emergence of a nationalist movement, to be discussed later. And the third was the transfer of economic control from public to private enterprise. It is this phenomenon which earned for Dutch colonialism the reputation of being the most ruthless and exploitative in Asia.

The British interlude in Java, from 1811 to 1818, was followed by the restoration of Dutch power and the policy of monopoly exploitation. This led to a serious revolt (1825–30) which was suppressed only with great difficulty. One effect was administrative reorganization of the island: Dutch-controlled territory was divided into districts under the nominal control of native 'regents' supervised by Dutch residents; the remaining sultanates in the interior were placed under the control of Dutch advisers; indirect rule was retained, but with more careful administrative controls. Another effect was to induce the Dutch to extend their control over the interior. But the most important consequence was the introduction of the 'culture system' (*kulturstelsel*), perhaps the most efficient method of economic exploitation devised in Asia.

[1] Cf. John F. Cady, *The Roots of French Imperialism in Eastern Asia*, Ithaca 1954; and Virginia M. Thompson, *French Indo-China*, London 1937.

This involved government contracts with the natives, crop control and fixed prices. In essence, Indonesian villages were compelled to devote 20 per cent of their land to the production of export crops determined by the government and to spend 20 per cent of their labour time on their cultivation; prices for crops and labour were fixed by government contract. The main products were coffee, sugar, tea, indigo, tobacco, and cinnamon, all in high demand in the West. The net earnings for the Dutch government—really direct plunder—amounted to 823 million guilders, or nearly one-third of the national budget, from 1831 to 1877, when remittance to The Hague ceased. Forced labour continued, however, until 1890 on sugar plantations and until 1915 in the production of coffee. Apart from this, both Dutch and native administrators acquired greater authority through the implementation of the system. Moreover, both production and population increased on Java, from 5 million to 34 million people between 1815 and 1920. And as the demands for forced labour and diversion of land to export crops increased, famine came upon the land—until the agrarian law of 1870 forbade the sale of Indonesian land to foreigners. This helped to assure sufficient land for food crops. It also induced the growth of private plantations, to replace the 'culture system'.

The plantation system, developed to a fine art, brought even larger profits, though not to the Dutch government. With their growth came banks and trading companies. It was this system, too, which led to the final consolidation of Dutch political power in the Indies. Land was plentiful on Sumatra, Borneo, and the Lesser Sundas to the east, unlike Java with its high rate of population growth. Thus, the Dutch moved to absorb the outer islands in the last half of the nineteenth century. Most of northern Sumatra was conquered in the 1870s, and the interior of Borneo between 1896 and 1900. Atjeh, in north Sumatra, was finally subdued in 1907. In the wake of this political expansion came plantations, the discovery of oil, and the mining of tin. By 1920, 60 per cent of the plantation economy was to be found in Sumatra, only 20 per cent in Java. As a system of economic exploitation, Dutch colonialism was unexcelled.[1]

China was never formally part of the colonial system. In the late nineteenth century, however, the declining phase of the Manchu dynasty almost invited foreign intervention. It started with the

[1] Cf. Emerson, op. cit.; Furnivall, op. cit.; and Furnivall, *Netherlands India: A Study of Plural Economy*, New York 1944.

Opium War (1839–42) and the remarkable Treaty System set in motion by the Treaty of Nanking. At first 5, ultimately 80, 'treaty ports' were assigned to foreign (Western) powers; there, in a separate part of the town, the aliens had their markets and warehouses, churches and clubs. Within the treaty port and, indeed, applying to all foreigners, was the principle of extraterritoriality, whereby the respective alien legal systems would apply. Other ingredients of the system of Western penetration of China were the treaty tariff—special rates for the import of European goods—the most-favoured-nation clause, which enabled all foreign powers to share whatever each could squeeze out of a faltering Manchu government, and the Concessions.

As the power of the dynasty lessened, the range of the Treaty System grew. The Treaties of Tientsin (1858) opened new ports to trade, permitted foreign legations in Peking and Christian missions in the interior, established a maritime customs service—with a Western supervisor—and legalized the import of opium. Then came the Anglo-French occupation of Peking in 1860 as punishment for alleged maltreatment of foreign envoys. In the early 1860s Western Powers intervened to suppress the T'ai P'ing Rebellion, the gravest internal threat to the Manchu Empire. As a result, Western influence was greatly enhanced—with virtual control over finance and customs, free rein to missionaries, and access to the vast Chinese market.

The pace quickened in the 1880s: recognition of a French protectorate over Tongking and the British conquest of Burma, along with the cession of Macao to Portugal. But it was only after the Sino-Japanese War (1894–5) that the *de facto* colonial system in China reached its zenith. To Japan went Formosa and the Pescadores and later, in 1910, Korea. During the last five years of the century enormous concessions were made: Russia received the right to build the Chinese Eastern Railway across Manchuria; France secured extensive commercial rights in Yunnan Province; Britain was given a wide-ranging concession in the rich Yangtse Valley; Germany extracted a 99-year lease on Kiaochow Bay, with exclusive rights to construct railways and develop mines in Shantung; Russia added a long lease to Dairen and Port Arthur, Japan another on the south coast; and Britain added a 99-year lease of Kowloon opposite Hong Kong. In 1900 came the short-lived Boxer Rebellion, followed by the Boxer Protocol, with further concessions. It was, then, nothing short

of the unofficial partition of China.[1] If one adds to this account
Spanish colonialism in the Philippines, followed by American
occupation at the turn of this century, the picture is complete. Asia
was, in truth, the continent of colonial rule.

IMPACT

The impact of colonialism may best be treated here in general
terms. It should be noted at the outset that the consequences varied
greatly in breadth and depth, depending upon: the colonial power;
the duration of alien rule; the character of the society; the size of the
colony; the level of development, and other factors. Thus, general-
izations are not universally applicable. Yet it is possible to abstract
from the historical experience of colonial rule in Asia, for this reveals
much in common. A second prefatory remark is in order: the
impact of colonialism was wide-ranging, affecting most aspects of
life in the colonial society and area—as well as the colonial power
itself; and the process has been one of mutual interaction.

The most striking consequences for the colonies lay in the economic sphere. Regardless of the level of technology—India, for
example, was very high and Laos very low—all Asian economies
were predominantly agricultural when the West arrived on the
scene. Four phases are evident in the economic impact. The first
was characterized by the 'drain of wealth', whether through forced
labour, as in Java, or through extortion and concealed taxes, as in
India, or through low prices for valuable goods, in China and elsewhere. In the domain of the British East India Company between
1765 and 1772, for example, only £9 million was remitted as taxes
to the Moghul Court, with £4 million added to the coffers of the
Company in London. Adam Smith referred to the stockholders as
men acquiring 'a share, though not in the plunder, yet in the
appointment of the plunderers of India'.[2] And two noted English
historians remarked: 'One remembers the early history of British
India which is perhaps the world's high water mark of graft. . . .
Bengal in particular was not to know peace again until she had been

[1] The story of Western penetration of China is best chronicled in W. L. Langer,
The Diplomacy of Imperialism (2nd ed.), New York 1950, 2 vols. See also John K.
Fairbank, *The United States and China* (new ed.), Cambridge, Mass. 1959, ch. 7,
and Harley F. MacNair and Donald F. Lach, *Modern Far Eastern International
Relations* (2nd ed.), New York 1955, ch. ii and iii.
[2] Adam Smith, *The Wealth of Nations* (Modern Library ed.), New York 1937,
p. 710.

bled white.'[1] The figures already quoted from the Dutch East Indies are even more persuasive. But the drain was a short-run effect.

The second phase witnessed the creation of disequilibrium in the colonial economy. More specifically, the local handicraft industries, such as weaving and spinning of cloth and silk, glassware, pottery, and iron goods, were destroyed by the cheaper machine-made products of the colonial power; the process was assisted by tariff discrimination in favour of British or Dutch or French goods as the case might be. The Governor-General of India summed up the result in 1834: 'The bones of the cotton weavers are bleaching the plains of India'.[2] No less serious was the destruction of the balance between agriculture and industry in the self-sufficient villages of Asia. Unemployed artisans in the towns returned to the land, increasing the pressure on limited resources and causing greater poverty. Moreover, as Western goods penetrated the interior—through newly-constructed railways and roads, as well as rivers—they undersold the products of village artisans; they, too, were forced back on the land, further increasing the pressure on resources. The results throughout colonial Asia, with variations, were smaller holdings, steady fragmentation, higher rents, greater indebtedness, more alienation of land to moneylenders, and the growth of a large class of landless labourers. One figure will suffice. In India, the proportion of the total population dependent on agriculture for a livelihood increased from 55 per cent in 1850 to 75 per cent in 1930. The extent of this unsettling process varied considerably, but no Asian colonial society was immune.

The third phase, really an extension of the second, was characterized by population growth and price and income instability. The establishment of law and order, combined with improved health and sanitation, brought the death rate down; but the birth rate remained the same, leading to a rapid and large-scale increase in population, further aggravating the economic problem. Java was the most extreme case, a seven-fold increase between 1815 and 1920. In India the percentage increase was only slightly less, and the absolute figures are more impressive—this despite the fact that an estimated 20 million died there of famine between 1800 and 1900. Another concomitant of colonial rule was the introduction of a money and exchange

[1] Edward Thompson and G. T. Garratt, *Rise and Fulfilment of British Rule in India*. London 1934, p. 681. See also William Digby, '*Prosperous' British India*, London 1901.

[2] As quoted in R. Palme Dutt, *India Today*, Bombay 1947, p. 71.

economy. In time, there came the stress on cash crops, like rice in Indo-China, coffee and sugar in the Indies, tin and rubber in Malaya, jute and cotton in India, tea and coconuts in Ceylon, rice and teak in Burma, etc. This concentration on staples, and their dependence on the world market, led to serious fluctuations in prices and incomes. The last to benefit from higher prices, and the first to suffer from a depression, were the primary producers. Since most Asian peasants had only a subsistence income, this frequently brought severe hardship. Moreover, these export crops expanded at the expense of food production—precisely when more food was needed for the growing population. This, along with the export of food to the 'mother country', accounted for the relatively frequent famines in India, Java, and elsewhere during the nineteenth century.[1]

There was, however, a positive by-product of the second and third phases, namely, economic integration and unification. This was one of many consequences of the introduction of advanced transport and communications systems—rail, road, telegraph, and telephone—and effective law and order. Slow to mature, and continuing into the first half of the twentieth century, this was the lasting economic contribution of colonial rule; without it, the proliferation of planning in Asia today could not have taken place. The fourth phase, then, is one of benefit to the colonial economies. A skilled man-power pool was created, made necessary by the new technology. Similarly, local industry began to arise, more in some countries (India) than in others (Dutch Indies), but a general phenomenon of the late period of colonialism. And with these came the beginnings of planning, under the impact of the two World Wars, especially the second. All of this is observable in Asian colonial economies in the decades before the transfer of power. On the whole, then, the economic effects on the colonies were more negative than positive.

The colonial powers benefited considerably in an economic sense. Enough has been said about the lucrative drain of wealth—except to note that in the case of Britain and India, the flow of silver from the latter provided much of the capital, as well as the base for expanded currency, to finance the early stage of the Industrial Revolution. So remarks Brooks Adams in a perceptive passage:

Very soon after Plassey the Bengal plunder began to arrive in London, and the effect appears to have been instantaneous, for all authorities agree

[1] For a thoughtful discussion of the economic impact, see Fred Greene, *The Far East*, New York 1957, ch. 2.

that the 'industrial revolution' . . . began with the year 1760. . . . Before the influx of the Indian treasure, and the expansion of credit which followed, no force sufficient for this purpose existed; and had Watt lived fifty years earlier, he and his invention must have perished together. . . . Possibly since the world began, no investment has ever yielded the profit reaped from the Indian plunder, because for nearly fifty years Great Britain stood without a competitor.[1]

As the Industrial Revolution gathered momentum in Europe, the role of the colonies changed. Henceforth they served as sources of food and raw materials for the metropolitan economies of the colonial powers—rubber, tin, and oil from the Dutch East Indies, jute and cotton and tea from India, tin and rubber from Malaya, etc. They also provided assured markets for the manufactured products of the 'mother countries'; among these France created the tightest control over entry of foreign goods into her colonies, though others were not much more liberal. As capital accumulated in Europe, with declining opportunities for a high rate of profit, the colonies emerged as an outlet and an assured area for profitable investment, as the Dutch plantation system in the Indies, French mining enterprises in Indo-China, and the British managing agency system in India amply revealed. In that tangible sense, the colonies certainly paid.[2]

In the broadest perspective the cultural impact on the colonies was the infusion of Western values, ideas, religions, philosophies, and conceptions of morality. Where the process had time to work itself out, the effect was far-reaching: for example, Catholicism in the Philippines, British political liberalism in India, and the English and French languages in all their colonies.[3] One consequence of the transplantation of language, it may be noted, was to separate the new, Westernized élite from the traditional society; indeed, for a time, to alienate them from their own society. Later, the two segments joined forces in a nationalist struggle against foreign domination.

One early reaction to alien culture, especially in the early phase of

---

[1] Brooks Adams, *The Law of Civilization and Decay*, New York 1943, pp. 297, 298, 300.

[2] For a contrary view, see, for example, Sir A. Burns, *In Defence of Colonies*, London 1957; and R. Strausz-Hupé and H. W. Hazard (eds.), *The Idea of Colonialism*, New York 1958 (articles by Possony, Elliott, and Linebarger and Hazard).

[3] See, for example, Eric Stokes, *The English Utilitarians and India*, London 1959.

nationalism, was to revive 'native values' in an effort to demonstrate their superiority. This provided a stimulus to popularization of the 'national' language, the use of 'national' symbols, and the elaboration of a 'national' literature. A long-term effect of the Western cultural penetration was the creation of a widespread inferiority complex among the colonial peoples, notably regarding technology and the art of modern government; this, of course, often reflected itself in assertions of superiority, by way of compensation. A very late reaction to the 'White Man's Burden' is something that can only be described as the 'Brown (or Black) Man's Burden', an assumption of a superior morality to that of the West, a decrying of its 'materialism and immorality'.

The most significant social result of colonial rule was the creation of new classes. The consolidation of power in the colonies and the growth of bureaucracy led to a need for trained colonials, that is, teachers, clerks, lawyers, doctors, and the like. A product of colonialism for its own needs, this group of Westernized classes, the intelligentsia and professional men, were to provide the leadership of the nationalist movements soon to arise.[1] In this, as in so many other respects, colonial rule bred conditions leading to its downfall.

The political consequences were positive and lasting on the whole.[2] The initial benefit was law and order, tranquillity and internal security. There followed the introduction of Western legal concepts and systems, with a stress on individual rights, the sanctity of property and contract, and the judicial process. These differed from traditional legal norms and methods, supplanting them in some areas and supplementing them in others. Thus, the Dutch retained *adat* law for the Indonesians, and the British continued to use *Shariat* law and the Hindu code for Muslims and Hindus respectively; but the Spanish eradicated the 'native' legal system in their missionary zeal. Where the experience of foreign rule was harsh, with frequent resort to coercion—in Korea for example—the long-term effect was disrespect for law. Where authority was tempered by justice—in most British colonies much of the time—there developed a respect for law and peaceful change; but this was offset in large measure by the intensity and duration of the nationalist struggle

[1] Cf. Edward Shils, 'The Intellectuals in the Political Development of the New States', *World Politics*, Vol. XII, No 3, April 1960, pp. 329–68.

[2] For discerning studies of the political impact of the colonial epoch, see Rupert Emerson, *From Empire to Nation*, Cambridge, Mass. 1960, and John Plamenatz, *Alien Rule and Self-Government*, London 1960.

for independence·in countries like India and Burma, much less so in Ceylon and Malaya.

At a later stage came the introduction of Western political institutions, practices, and ideas—democracy, representative and responsible government, elections, the parliamentary system, and the right of national self-determination. Only Korea, among the Asian colonies, suffered from total political suppression until the moment of 'liberation'—with consequences evident to the present time. Some colonial powers made niggardly concessions late in the day, notably France in Indo-China and Holland in the East Indies—Portugal is the most extreme Western case, in Asia as in Africa. Others began the process relatively early, such as the Americans in the Philippines and the British in India and Ceylon.

The general effect of Western ideas was to instil a desire, later a demand, first for autonomy and then for independence. This was true in all Asian colonies, whether these ideas filtered into the new intelligentsia through English, French, Dutch, or Spanish literature. The general effect of Western institutions was twofold: to create a habit of hostility to government *per se*;[1] and to train a small number of colonial people in the procedures of constitutional government, an experience of great value in the transition period after the transfer of power.[2] In a negative sense, these ideas and institutions gave Asian nationalists a wedge and a support in their struggle against the colonial power.

The political consequences for the colonial powers can be summed up as enhanced prestige and influence in world politics. France's status as a Great Power from 1890 to 1939, for example, owed much to the prestige of a vast empire. Similarly, her loss of colonies from 1946 (Syria, Lebanon) to 1962 (Algeria) caused a grave loss of prestige and, indirectly, a decline of power.[3]

The impact of colonialism on Great Power politics can be exaggerated, but it cannot be dismissed. For one thing, there have been wars between the colonial power and the colonial people, such as the Dutch and Indonesians (1945–49), the French and Vietnamese (1946–54), and the French and Algerians (1954–62). There have also been 'colonial' wars among the powers, such as the Anglo-French struggle over India and America (eighteenth century), and Japan

---

[1] See p. 63 below.
[2] W. H. Morris-Jones, *Parliament in India*, London 1957, ch. ii (1), esp. pp. 70–73.
[3] Cf. Herbert Luthy, *The State of France*, London 1956, Part III.

versus the Western Powers in South-East Asia (1941–45). Still another effect is apparent in the diplomatic incident and crisis. Indeed, much of world politics between 1890 and 1914 was a story of friction engendered by colonial rivalries; most were in Africa, like Fashoda (1898), Algeciras (1906), and Agadir (1911), but the scramble for concessions from China (1890s) was also important.[1] And during the twenty years' armistice (1919–39), a serious source of friction between the satisfied and revisionist powers was expressed in the controversy between 'Haves and Have-Nots', essentially a colonial issue.[2]

NATIONALISM—ORIGINS AND FORMATIVE STAGES

Perhaps the most important legacy of colonial rule was nationalism. This sounds paradoxical, but it is a cardinal truth about the impact of colonialism on Asia. The creation of law and order, along with administrative and territorial unity over fragments of empire, permitted peaceful progress and an awareness of commonality under foreign rule. Economic exploitation over a prolonged period led to mounting resentment among strategic segments of the colonial people. At the same time, economic unification and the introduction of modern communications and transport made it possible for people from distant parts of the realm to come together and kindle an awareness of common interests. The infusion of a Western language provided a medium of direct communication among the new élite of colonial societies. And through that medium came ideas, liberal ideas, especially the revolutionary doctrine of national self-determination. That idea spread among the élite and, through them, to the masses, whom they organized for political action. In short, the historic role of the colonial power was to create the conditions for nationalism and, ultimately, its own demise.

Stated in other terms, Asian independence was inevitable, the climax of a lengthy process inherent in the character of colonial rule. The key to its attainment was the creation of a common purpose; once that purpose, the quest for freedom, penetrated substantial strata of the colonial people, the transfer of power was inescapable. Two processes helped to create that purpose. In part, it was the

[1] Cf. Langer, The Diplomacy of Imperialism.

[2] See MacNair and Lach, op. cit., ch. 5, 6, 9, 11, 13, 14, 15, and Frederick L. Schuman, International Politics (3rd ed.), New York 1941, ch. ix.

inadvertent legacy of foreign rule: administrative integration and communication systems that united the territory, often for the first time in history; the penetration of a foreign language as the carrier of new ideas; and secular education, which broke down age-old barriers and facilitated common modes of thought and action. In part, it was forged by the nationalist movement and the use of traditional symbols to galvanize people into action, non-violent or violent. Periodic revolt, peaceful or otherwise, maintained a continuous focus on the goal of national freedom, welding diverse groups together in the common purpose. The participation of the peasantry at a later stage hastened the process. The success of the Russian Revolution also acted as a stimulus; so did the dramatic defeat of the colonial powers by Japan in the early 1940s; indeed, this was the *coup de grâce* for Western empire in Asia. Ultimately the common purpose spread throughout the colonial society, and the power of the foreign ruler was insufficient to stem the tide. At that point colonial rule came to an end, either by careful assessment and voluntary withdrawal, as in the case of Britain and India, or by expulsion—with international pressure—as with the Dutch in Indonesia, or by agonizing and disastrous colonial warfare, as with the French in Indo-China. It is with the nationalism of, and coming of independence to, these three colonies that we shall turn, illustrating different colonial systems in action. But in the general terms described above, it may be said that colonialism in Asia contained the seeds of its own destruction.

India

The history of Indian nationalism falls into three distinct phases: (1) 1885–1905; (2) 1905–19; and (3) 1920–47. The origins of the movement can be traced to the early part of the nineteenth century, when various Bengali intellectuals, notably Ram Mohan Roy, began to think and act in terms of reform—under the influence of European liberalism. But it was not until 1885 that the Indian National Congress was founded, ironically, by a retired English civil servant, A. O. Hume.

At its inception and, indeed, for the first twenty years, the Congress was a moderate group. Its membership was drawn from the new professions—law, medicine, teaching—and most were highly

Westernized. They spoke in English and wore morning clothes to their annual sessions. Their speeches and resolutions abounded in expressions of loyalty to the Crown. Their 'demands' were modest—increased Indian representation in the Legislative Councils and simultaneous examinations for the Indian Civil Service in England and India: in short, administrative reforms that would enable them to play a more active role in public affairs. Responsible government was beyond their horizon. Their main interest was modernization by British-type liberal reform, but within the existing, authoritarian framework of government. The Congress was, in truth, an urban middle-class club at the time, though some of its leaders were eminent men, especially Gokhale, Pherozeshah Mehta, and Naoroji.

At the turn of the century various stimuli to extremism appeared. First there was the economic distress following upon the great famines of 1896 and 1900, disasters which were blamed on the British Raj. There was, too, the growing hostility of the Viceroy and the bureaucracy, after initial friendship; Lord Curzon remarked in 1900 that he would like nothing more than to preside over the dissolution of the Congress. But most important was the (first) partition of Bengal in 1905. This act, a precedent for the partition in 1947, was motivated by the desire to appease the Muslims and also for administrative efficiency. The reaction among the Hindus was terrorism, under the leadership of Tilak in the west and Aurobindo, later the eminent philosopher, Pal, and others in Bengal. By that time the social composition of the Congress had been modified, with the addition of poor intellectuals, students, and unemployed members of the middle class. These were 'angry young men'. Their programme was to rescind the partition of Bengal, to expel the British, and to glorify Hindu culture. Their techniques were individual terrorism and economic boycott. In brief, they were aggressive, reactionary, and militantly Hindu.

The Extremists, or Integral Nationalists as they were sometimes called, pushed through a radical four-point programme in 1906: *swaraj* (self-rule) became the Congress goal; *swadeshi* (home-made goods), national education, and the boycott of foreign products became the movement's techniques. The following year the Congress split, with the Extremists withdrawing and the Moderates taking control of the organization. They were reunited in 1916 but split again in 1918 for ever; this time, however, the Congress was firmly in Extremist hands. Soon after, Tilak died, and Mahatma Gandhi assumed control of the Congress, inaugurating the third and final phase of the movement.

To return to the phase of terrorism—the Government's reaction was a typical, double-edged carrot and stick programme. There were widespread arrests, repressive legislation, curbing of the press, Congress meetings and the like. But there was also a positive element, an inducement to the nationalists, in the form of the Morley-Minto Reforms of 1909: the powers of the Legislative Councils were increased, and a majority of the members made elective; Muslims were given a separate electorate; one Indian was to be appointed to the Viceroy's Executive Council, and two to the Secretary of State's Council in London. A conscious attempt to strengthen the hand of the Moderates in the Congress, this was the third Indian Councils Act, the third instalment of representative government in the subcontinent, the others being passed in 1861 and 1892.

The special concession to Muslims was in response to a request for communal electorates by the newly-founded All-India Muslim League in 1906. In time, these two nationalist movements were to engage in a bitter political struggle culminating in the partition of India in 1947. And the most powerful weapon of the League was to be the separate electorate, injected into India by the British in 1909. There was also a concession to the extremist Congressmen, the reunion of Bengal in 1911. And as compensation to the chagrined Muslims, the capital of British India was shifted that year from Calcutta to Delhi, near the main concentration of Muslims in the north-west of India.

The First World War, like all wars, was a catalyst to change. Within India, it witnessed a rare example of Congress–League unity, notably the Lucknow Pact of 1916: the Congress accepted the principle of separate electorates and weighted representation for Muslims and other minorities in the Legislative Councils and the Services; the League agreed to co-operate in a demand for Dominion Home Rule. The honeymoon was short-lived, however. Within a few years, Gandhi's radical methods were to prove anathema to the League leaders, especially Mohammed Ali Jinnah—'ambassador of Hindu-Muslim unity' at the time, and later to become the 'Father of Pakistan'.

The British, too, took account of 'the winds of change', with a pledge of ultimate self-government for India, contained in the

Montagu Declaration of 1917; this was, indeed, a landmark in the history of the Raj. The first instalment was proposed in the Montagu-Chelmsford Report of 1918, and was formally incorporated in a Government of India Act the following year. By way of experiment, partial self-government was recommended for the provinces—the principle of dyarchy, it was termed: certain matters would be placed under the jurisdiction of a 'cabinet' of Indian ministers drawn from an elected legislature while others, 'reserved subjects', would remain under the control of the Governor and his advisory Executive Council. To the British, this was an appropriate introduction to responsible government. To most Indian nationalists, however, it was a paltry concession, far short of the expectations raised by the Montagu Declaration. Thus, the Congress demanded self-government within the Empire' and rejected the proposals. Soon afterwards, Gandhi was to launch his first civil disobedience campaign against the new Act. But that belongs to the 'Gandhian epoch' of Indian history and the coming of independence.[1]

Indo-China

Nationalism in French Indo-China differed from the nationalist movements in India–Pakistan in two respects: the predominance of violence and the crucial role of the communists. Unlike the subcontinent, too, there was active rebellion from the very outset of colonial rule. Three phases are evident in Indo-Chinese nationalism, as in India, but the time sequence differs: (1) pre-First World War; (2) the inter-war period; and (3) the Japanese occupation and its aftermath.

There was large-scale guerrilla war from 1884 to 1887 and again in 1893. The reform movements in China at the turn of the century influenced Vietnamese intellectuals. Then came the shock of 1905, the victory of Japan over a Western power, Tsarist Russia; the impossible now seemed less so. Indeed, the modernization of Japan appeared to many as an admirable model. From France itself came the most advanced revolutionary ideas in the West.

Conspiracy and rebellion marked the early years of this century. In 1908 an attempt was made to poison the French garrison in Hanoi. There were prolonged guerrilla activities in Tongking under De Tham. And in Cochin-China, nationalist agitation was linked

[1] See Spear, op. cit., ch. xxvi–xxix, xxxi, and his Suggested Readings for that period.

with Japanese agents. A major revolt occurred in 1916, under the leadership of scholars, notably Tran Cao Van, and the young Emperor, Duy Tan. The rising was suppressed and hundreds were put to death or deported to remote islands. So ended the first phase of the struggle against French rule.

Not all early nationalists favoured the path of violence. Some sought to emulate the West—the 'Free School' in Hanoi, which taught science and the humanities, and the 'Hair-Cutters', aimed at such traditions as wearing the hair long and bound at the back of the head; they, too, were suppressed by the French, in 1908. A large majority of Indo-Chinese nationalists at the time were, however, militant—and conservative. Their goal was to oust the French and restore the old order of Nguyen Emperors and the Confucian-type bureaucracy. In aim and method, they resembled the Extremists of the second period in Indian nationalism.

Not so the generation of the inter-war period. Their formative influences were war and revolution in the West; some 90,000 Indo-Chinese soldiers and workers were sent to France during the First World War, and the Russian Revolution set off a chain reaction all over Asia. From these two sources came Vietnamese communism and its outstanding figure, Nguyen Ai Quoc, better known as Ho Chi Minh, now President of North Vietnam.

Ho's career is a fascinating study in Asian revolution, but only the bare essentials can be noted here. Born in 1892, he spent the war years in France. Like many other Asians, he petitioned the leaders at Versailles for autonomy, without success. He plunged into French politics and was a founder-member of the French Communist Party in 1920, and sought support for colonial freedom. In 1923 he went to a peasant conference in Moscow and remained for over a year, becoming the first Vietnamese to study at the Stalin School for revolutionaries. He then went to China in 1925, where he worked at the Soviet Consulate—until 1927, when the communist–nationalist split in China forced him to flee, to Hankow and back to Moscow. From there, he inspired and directed revolutionary movements in his homeland.

The efforts of moderates to organize in the 1920s were frustrated by French rigidity. There was a short-lived Constitutionalist Party in Cochin-China in the early twenties and an abortive Vietnam People's Progressive Party in 1926. In Tongking and Annam all political activity was forbidden. The beneficiary was the conspiratorial Left.

In 1929 the Ho-created Revolutionary Youth Association met in Hong Kong and issued a manifesto calling for a dictatorship of the proletariat, nationalization of the land, and sweeping social reforms. Almost at once, factionalism arose—there were three communist groups in 1929—until Ho reunited the fragments into the Indo-Chinese Communist Party in 1930. The following year, when it officially joined the Comintern, the ICCP had a core of 1,500 members and 100,000 affiliated peasant supporters. Ho Chi Minh remained its acknowledged leader from abroad, where he doubled as chief of the Southern Bureau of the Communist International.

In the meantime, a powerful non-communist rival had emerged, the VNQDD or Vietnam Nationalist Party, founded in 1927 by a young teacher in Hanoi, Nguyen Thai Hoc. As the ICCP looked to the Soviets for aid and modelled its organization on the CPSU, so the VNQDD was linked with the Chinese Kuomintang, on which it was modelled, and sought Chinese aid. Its membership was mainly teachers, students, and civil servants, with financial aid furnished by wealthy Tonkinese. Various terrorist acts were followed by an uprising in the frontier town of Yen Bay in February 1930. Within a few months French reprisals had decimated the party. It survived in Chinese exile for a decade, with a Kuomintang subsidy, until world war created an opportunity for revival at home.

The Indo-Chinese communists filled the void by leading a large-scale peasant revolt in the summer of 1930. For a time there were Soviets in two Annamese provinces. The French responded with an equally violent 'White Terror' in 1931. Thousands were killed—communists, liberals, and nationalists—and even more were arrested. Ho vanished after brief detention in Hong Kong and was presumed dead.

The present President of South Vietnam, Ngo Dinh Diem, made a brief appearance in 1933 as chief minister to the Emperor, Bao Dai. His efforts at moderate political reform met French intransigence and he resigned. At the same time, the left-wing movement in the south gathered new strength, communists under Tran Van Giau, and Trotskyites under Thu Thau. The two joined forces in 1932, though the 'October' faction of Trotskyites remained opposed. The new coalition even secured two seats on the Saigon city council. All this was in Cochin-China. Elsewhere, communist fortunes were at a low ebb until the Macao Conference of the ICCP·in 1936. The new anti-fascist line of the Comintern came to Indo-China. And with a Popular Front Government in Paris, political prisoners were freed.

Beyond minor reforms, however, the French Left was not prepared to go; indeed, the Vietnamese were still denied freedom of assembly and the legal right to organize trade unions. The result was agitation on the Left, but the coalition of Stalinists and Trotskyites was sundered in 1937. In 1939 the latter won 80 per cent of the votes for the Cochin-China Colonial Council. And with the coming of war, the Communist Party was outlawed, in Indo-China as in France. But its underground organization remained intact.[1]

Indonesia

Nationalism in the Dutch East Indies was characterized by a multiplicity of parties and groups ranging from extreme Marxist to conservative Muslim. As in Indo-China, the 'great divide' was Japanese occupation, but the story can be treated in three broad phases: (1) 1908–20; (2) 1920–42; and (3) 1942–9—the coming of independence.

Nationalism began as a cultural force, the first formal expression being the *Budi Utomo* (High Endeavour), founded in 1908 on Java and Madura. Its primary purpose was to promote Indonesian culture and Western education so as to strengthen the claim to greater participation in public affairs. Within a year there were 10,000 members, mostly civil servants and students. The momentum was short-lived, however, and a new, more popular organization took the lead.

This was the *Sarekat Islam*, founded in 1910 and destined to play a major role in the Indonesian nationalist movement. Its origins were psychological and economic, a reaction of Javanese merchants to the aggressive and effective competition from Chinese traders; resentment was compounded by concessions of the colonial government to the Chinese in the first decade of the century. As such, it acquired religious, political, and nationalist dimensions and became a rallying ground for Indonesians. By 1916 it had 360,000 members, and at the end of the war 2½ million, with an openly declared goal of independence. It had been suppressed briefly in 1912, following anti-Chinese riots in Soerabaja and Soerakarta the previous year, but rapidly regained ground. In 1914 the authorities tried to arrest its growth by denying legality to the central organization of Sarekat Islam. The result was to facilitate radical left-wing infiltration of the

---

[1] Based upon Ellen J. Hammer, *The Struggle for Indo-China*, Stanford 1954, ch. 1–3.

branches and to weaken the moderate leadership. By 1917 it was pushed to a condemnation of 'sinful capitalism' and an uncompromising call for complete independence—partly under the impact of the Russian Revolution and local radical-socialist penetration.

A decisive split in Sarekat Islam occurred in 1919 when the far left group, the Social Democratic Association, withdrew. The following year this faction became the Communist Party of the Indies, PKI, and joined the Comintern almost at once. During the early twenties the two groups engaged in a fierce struggle for control of the branches of Sarekat Islam. The communists triumphed, but at a heavy price—the evaporation of peasant support. This was accentuated by the PKI stress on the trade union movement, in line with Comintern direction. Increasing militancy led, in November 1926, to communist insurrection in West Java and Sumatra. The leadership had split over the wisdom of an uprising, Tan Malaka opposed and Musso and Alimin in favour. Some 13,000 were arrested, many being detained in remote New Guinea.

The vacuum thus created was filled by non-communist groups, notably the PI or Indonesian Union, an organization of Indonesian students in Holland, founded in 1922, and its creation, the PNI or Indonesian Nationalist Party, the party of President Sukarno to this day. The latter was formed in June 1927 under Sukarno's chairmanship, but essentially under the ideological influence of PI and its outstanding leader, Mohammed Hatta, later political friend—and enemy—of Sukarno. The aim was complete independence, to be achieved by non-co-operation, though not exactly of the Gandhian variety; labour unions, co-operatives, and 'national' schools were promoted as instruments of 'liberation'.

The PNI grew rapidly—10,000 members by 1929. It had also formed a federation of six nationalist groups. Then the Government struck: Sukarno was given a three-year prison term, and the party was outlawed. For a while its membership was fragmented among the Indonesian People's Party, a moderate group prepared to co-operate with the Dutch, the Indonesian Party, and others. Upon his release, Sukarno galvanized the latter into attaining a mass membership, but in 1933 he was again arrested and detained until 1942, when the Japanese released him. Hatta and the Socialist leader, Sjahrir, followed him into exile in 1934, also until 1942.

The middle and late thirties were years of dilemma for Indonesian nationalists, as for those in India, Indo-China, and elsewhere in the colonial world. The menace of fascism impelled them to moderation and to co-operation with the colonial rulers; but the response of those rulers caused frustration and anger. Thus, in 1936, the Soetardjo Petition requested a conference to plan progress towards 'Dominion Status' in the next decade. The idea was rejected outright, even though passed by a majority of the Volksraad, the People's Council. That body had been established in 1918, in response to war-created pressure for a measure of representative government. Originally it had 39 members, the majority European, with advisory functions only. By 1928 there were 60 members, half of them Indonesian, and a majority of the total elected. By the late 1930s it had acquired substantial legislative power, especially over the budget, though the Governor-General retained a veto in case of disagreement.

The initial result of Dutch intransigence was the formation of a new nationalist group in 1937, the *Gerindo* or Indonesian People's Movement. This party tended to co-operate in the work of the Volksraad. In the spring of 1939 eight nationalist groups were united in *Gapi*, the Federation of Indonesian Political Parties, on a programme of self-determination, national unity, democracy, and anti-fascism. At the Indonesian People's Congress later in the year, they adopted a national language, flag, and anthem. Another demand for self-government followed in 1940. The reply was a vague pledge of some constitutional change after the war, which resulted in a swing of nationalist opinion away from the anti-fascist theme to that of immediate independence. Thus it was into a relatively sympathetic atmosphere that the Japanese made their entry at the beginning of 1942.[1]

COMING OF INDEPENDENCE

India

The third phase of India's struggle for independence, 1920 to 1947, was dominated by Mohandas K. Gandhi, India's greatest son since the Buddha. Out of the sands, out of lethargy and fear, the Mahatma created a mighty national movement and fired the imagination of millions. The tone remained militant, but this time it was based on the novel creed of non-violent non-co-operation.

The essence of Gandhi's concept of *satyagraha* was revealed in

---

[1] The definitive work on Indonesian nationalism, on which this account is based, is George McTurnan Kahin, *Nationalism and Revolution in Indonesia*, Ithaca 1952. See ch. i–iii.

his remarks on the Amritsar Massacre of 1919: 'The Government went mad at the time; we went mad also. I say, do not return madness with madness, but return madness with sanity and the whole situation will be yours.' In practice, too, Gandhi and the Indian National Congress adhered to this creed. Four times they engaged in civil disobedience—in 1921-2, 1930-4, 1940, and 1942. Sometimes it was individual in form, sometimes collective; in some cases it was partial, in others total. But on all occasions Gandhi eschewed violence. In 1922 he called off the first campaign at its height because of a single act of violence in a remote village. During the early years of the Second World War he opposed active Indian participation in the conflict, even if independence were granted. During the last, abortive, 'Quit India' campaign of 1942, he repudiated violence in any form. And in the time of trouble, 1946-7, when riot and murder were on the rampage, the Mahatma performed miraculous acts of healing in his endless walking tours and his pleas for non-violence; his followers, like his opponents, were not always devoted to this ideal. Ultimately, the Mahatma himself fell victim to the madness he decried—assassinated by a Hindu fanatic in 1948.

The third phase was not only militant and, in the last years, increasingly violent. It was also characterized by greater mass action, as peasants and workers were galvanized by Gandhi's magic wand. At the very outset of this era, in 1920, he transformed the Congress from an upper-class urban club into a nation-wide mass organization capable of penetrating to the grass roots, to the village, to the heart of Indian society: 1920, therefore, represents the 'great divide' in the coming of independence—the emergence of a new leader, a new method of political action, a more advanced goal, and a mass party.

There is almost a cyclical character to the story of the third phase. The first civil disobedience campaign, a high point, in which many Muslims participated, was followed by years of passivity and frustration—and a recurrence of Hindu-Muslim tension. Gandhi was in prison from 1922 to 1924 and the Congress was engaged in acrimonious debate, between the 'pro-changers' and the 'no-changers', those who advocated deviation from, and total adherence to, the Mahatma's programme. The Congress was truly in the doldrums during most of the twenties; the Muslim League was still a microscopic minority.

Another upswing began in 1928-9 and reached its peak in the second civil disobedience campaign. It began in typical Gandhian fashion, a march to the sea from his *ashram* (spiritual retreat) and a violation of the law imposing a tax on salt. The very simplicity of the issue was its greatest strength as a focus for political action; and to dramatize the goal, he chose the technique of a long march from village to village, the only means of transport for millions of peasants. It took twenty-four days to reach the sea. The spark was ignited when the Mahatma picked up salt lying on the shore; the explosion followed with devastating effect—a nation-wide violation of the Salt Law. By early summer the 'revolt' had assumed mammoth proportions. Before the year was out, some 90,000 persons were arrested and sporadic incidents of violence occurred in the North-West Frontier Province and Bombay; a boycott of foreign goods was widespread, the peasantry was aroused, and women joined in the fray. It was the first truly mass political movement in Indian nationalism.

A truce with the Raj was reached in the Delhi Pact of March 1931. Most political prisoners were released; in return, the Congress agreed to participate in the Round Table Conference in London, with Gandhi as the sole representative. The Mahatma returned to India empty-handed at the end of that year and, at once, the campaign was resumed. This time the Government was prepared. Sweeping decrees, covering almost every aspect of life, were promulgated for India as a whole. Taken together, they constituted a 'catalogue of absolutism' and the fabric of a police state. As in 1930, thousands were arrested. By the spring of 1933 civil disobedience was at its lowest ebb; the wave of enthusiasm had vanished, though the campaign continued in a desultory fashion for another year. Once more, nationalist agitation had reached a low point.

Once again, too, the Government responded to the demand for change—with another instalment of constitutional reform. It had taken eight years to produce the Government of India Act 1935. In essence it provided virtually complete responsible government in the provinces of British India and the framework for a loose All-India Federation of the provinces and as many of the 600 princely States as wished to join. Much care had been taken to ensure the ultimate authority of Great Britain in the affairs of India, through an array of special powers vested in the Viceroy and, to a lesser extent, in the Governors of the provinces. Over 90 articles conferred 'discretionary powers' on the Viceroy. There were, as well, 'reserve powers' which gave him exclusive control over defence, external affairs, ecclesiastical affairs, and certain frontier areas. Finally came the 'safeguards' or 'special responsibilities' which were all-embracing; for example, 'the prevention of any grave menace to the peace or tranquillity of India or any part thereof', the prevention of discrimination against British imports, protection of the rights of Princes, etc. Moreover, representation in the federal legislature was to be heavily weighted in favour of the Princes—40 per cent in the Council of States and $33\frac{1}{3}$ per cent in the Federal Assembly, compared with their numerical representation of 24 per cent of the total population of India at the time.

This Act, suitably amended, served as the constitution of the Dominion of India from 1947 to 1950 and of Pakistan from 1947 to 1956. It is in fact the basis of India's present constitution. But in its original form the federal part of the Act was hedged by so many 'safeguards' as to deny complete self-government to India as a whole. Such was the view of most Indian politicians and of many Englishmen. By contrast, the provincial part of the Act was a far-reaching concession to self-government. Apart from some general safeguards, which were not intended to be used except in rare circumstances, daily administration was to be entrusted to a Cabinet selected from the legislature, all of whose members were to be elected, and by a much larger proportion of the population than at any time previously.

It was this temptation of power which attracted many Congress moderates. In the provincial elections of 1937 the party won a spectacular victory, an absolute majority in five of the eleven provinces, and a plurality of seats in three others. By contrast, the Muslim League, which was to be triumphant in its quest for Pakistan ten years later, won only 5 per cent of the Muslim votes.

After a sharp internal squabble, the Congress took office in seven (later eight) provinces. The experiment in constitutionalism lasted $2\frac{1}{2}$ years, until October 1939, when all Congress governments resigned because of the cavalier way India was brought into the war. Apart from various social and economic reforms, valuable experience in administration was acquired by many Congress politicians, men who assumed total responsibility in independent India.

In the long run, the most significant effect of the 1937 Congress victory at the polls was a widening of the breach with the Muslim League. Flushed with success, the Congress adopted an imperious attitude to all political parties. More specifically, it violated a tacit understanding with the League in the United Provinces to form a coalition government and substituted conditions amounting to an ultimatum for the League's self-destruction. Jinnah took it as a declaration of war and replied in kind, crying 'Islam is in danger'. Here were the opening shots in the calamitous Congress–League war which was to envelop north India in flames and ultimately result in partition. Congress haughtiness was to prove a 'Himalayan blunder', though few anticipated the consequences.

As elsewhere in Asia, the Second World War hastened the coming of Indo-Pakistani independence. It also influenced the struggle for the succession, a united India versus partition. Most of the details may be ignored lest the main themes be obscured. There are two broad periods: 1939–42; and 1942–5. The first year of the war witnessed a fruitless exchange between Viceroy and Congress, with the latter insisting that Britain's war aims be clearly stated as a condition of Congress co-operation in the war effort. The replies were vague, with minor concessions towards greater Indian representation in the highest councils of Government. At the same time, the Muslim League was assured that no constitutional changes would be made without its approval. The Congress replied initially with the resignation of the provincial ministries and, in October 1940, with individual civil disobedience. The campaign was designed to inflict the least damage on the war effort while dramatizing Gandhi's dictum that war was evil. It lasted until Pearl Harbour, when another exchange between Congress and Raj occurred.

As the Japanese marched through Burma, London dispatched Sir Stafford Cripps in an effort to break the deadlock. The Cripps Plan of 1942 offered Dominion status after the war with right of secession from the Commonwealth. It also pledged British acceptance of a constitution framed by a constituent assembly—subject to the right of any province to remain outside the Dominion; such non-acceding units would receive a status comparable to that of the projected Indian Union—the opening wedge for Pakistan, which was proclaimed the goal of the Muslim League in its Lahore Resolution of 1940. There were to be no constitutional changes during the war. Both parties rejected the offer, though for almost diametrically opposed reasons; and the negotiations ended on a note of acrimony, especially between the Viceroy and the Congress.

Bitterness mounted swiftly in the Congress. After months of agonizing discussion, the course was charted. 'Quit India', demanded the Congress in a resolution of 8 August 1942. But before its planned campaign of mass civil disobedience could be launched, most of its leaders were arrested and detained until the end of the war. The reaction was swift and spontaneous—the August Revolt, it is called, or the Rebellion or the August Movement. Here was the climax to the first stage of the war period. By the end of the year the Congress organization was smashed, many thousands were in jail, and the campaign was suppressed.

Most important were the long-range political consequences. The Congress was outlawed for almost three years, its leaders were in prison and its funds seized. In this political vacuum the Muslim League was able to build a mass party, by appealing successfully to religious emotions and genuine Muslim fears. Between 1942 and 1945 the League increased its membership to two million, with the result that by the end of the war it was able to put forward a strong claim to Pakistan. The Congress paid dearly for its 'Quit India' resolution; unwittingly it paved the way for Partition.

The pace quickened with the end of the war. The Congress leaders were released, and an acceptable formula was unsuccessfully sought at the first Simla Conference in the summer of 1945. The polarization of politics was startlingly revealed in the elections to the central Assembly and the provincial legislatures in the winter of 1945–6. The lines were now drawn, as it became evident that the Muslim League did represent the vast majority of Muslims. Then came the three-member Cabinet Mission, which laboured long on a formula to satisfy the Congress demand that the British quit India and the League insistence that the British split India.

Theoretically, all the warring parties could have been satisfied by the Mission's complex plan. There were to be three sections for British India, one consisting of the Muslim-majority provinces in the north-west, another consisting of Bengal and Assam in the north-east, and the third comprising the rest. The Sections would meet to form Groups and to draft the provincial and group constitutions. Each province would have the right to opt out of a group by a majority vote of its legislature after the first elections under the new constitution. Thus the League was offered a *de facto* Pakistan. The Congress could find in the scheme a united India and an assurance of provincial autonomy. The plan also provided for the lapse of Paramountcy, thereby granting freedom of action to the Princes. The basic drawback of the plan was its cumbersome procedure. The three-tier scheme was an intellectual *tour de force*, but

D

it was impracticable in the environment of a deadly struggle for power. The proposal would have brought Pakistan in through the back door and would have maintained the façade of a united India. Both parties accepted it on paper, with serious reservations. Finally, in July 1946, Nehru virtually rejected the Mission's proposals and then Jinnah responded in kind.

There followed a year of tension and conflict, brutality and inhumanity, and mass misery. It began with the 'Great Calcutta Killing' in August 1946, when 4,000 were killed and an equal number injured in the streets of India's largest city. This set in motion an irrevocable chain reaction, in Bengal, then Bihar and the United Provinces, and finally, and most disastrously, in the Punjab, the 'land of the five rivers'. There the tidal wave of communal madness reached catastrophic proportions.

All communities share the blame for that black record in modern Indian history. As it became evident that partition would ensue, tension reached boiling point. Insecurity and the desire for revenge were everywhere. The alternatives appeared to be death or flight. People reacted with blind instinct and set out for the 'Promised Land', Pakistan for the Muslims, India for the Hindus and Sikhs. In remote villages members of the minority community were mercilessly killed, for no other reason than the accident of birth. Rumour, fear, and the desire for vengeance maintained the momentum of communal fury. Many were killed en route to larger centres. No quarter was given—torture, mutilation, assault, conversion by force. It was nothing less than a war of extermination. The battlefield was everywhere, in village, town, road, temple, and mosque. Trains going from Amritsar to Lahore and vice-versa were considered fair prey; eyewitnesses reported incidents where up to 2,000 were killed in one train. The less fortunate began to trek by foot in a frenzied search for security. In sheer numbers, it was the greatest trek in history, probably about twelve million, equally divided between Hindus and Sikhs fleeing from West Punjab and Muslims from the East. Before the year was out half a million people died, or were murdered. In such an atmosphere did India and Pakistan become independent and the British Raj vanish from the stage of history.

The formalities of the transfer were conducted under the leadership of Clement Attlee as British Prime Minister and Lord Mountbatten, the last of the Viceroys. Soon after his arrival, in March 1947,

Mountbatten concluded that Partition was the only way out. The momentum of riot and violence only strengthened his conviction, based on conversations with the Big Five of Indian politics—Gandhi, Jinnah, Nehru, Patel, and Liaquat Ali Khan. With a sense of urgency he produced the final plan.

In essence, it provided a procedure for ascertaining the will of those people living in areas claimed for Pakistan. In Bengal, Sind, and the Punjab the issue was to be determined by the provincial legislatures. But in Bengal and Punjab the vote was to be in two sections, Muslim majority and non-Muslim majority, each with a veto, thereby assuring partition. In the Frontier, there was to be a referendum. The plan also indicated a willingness to transfer power earlier than the specified final date of June 1948.

Congress and League accepted the plan early in June. The Act was hastily pushed through the British Parliament. And on 14–15 August 1947 India and Pakistan joined the family of independent states—amidst carnage and disorder in the Punjab. Thus was the promise of independence fulfilled.[1]

Indo-China

As elsewhere in Asia, the Second World War undermined the colonial order in French Indo-China. The fall of France had major repercussions in the East—a new, Vichy Governor-General and, in September 1940, surrender to Japan's demand for military control of the peninsula. The following summer all Indo-China was occupied by the Japanese, though the French administration was retained almost to the war's end.

French–Japanese collaboration eased the task of Indo-Chinese nationalists. A communist-led uprising at the end of 1940 was crushed, but in May 1941 a broad-based united front was organized in south-west China, the Vietnam Independence League, the Viet Minh as it came to be known. Ho Chi Minh emerged from a decade of obscurity to become its General Secretary. The programme was relatively moderate, modelled on Mao's 'New Democracy' and stressing independence. All classes and groups were welcome in the struggle for a free and democratic Vietnam, with individual rights,

[1] This account is based upon the author's *Nehru: A Political Biography*, London 1959, ch. iii–xiv. See also Spear, op. cit., ch. xxxii–xxxviii; V. P. Menon, *The Transfer of Power in India*, Princeton 1957; Khalid bin Sayeed, *Pakistan: The Formative Phase*, Karachi 1960, ch. ii–v, and Spear's Suggested Readings for that period.

including private enterprise, and land reform occupying a key place in the manifesto.

Peasants and workers, intellectuals and businessmen rallied to the movement. At first, however, the Chinese Nationalists were wary. Ho was imprisoned and a rival coalition organized, the Vietnam Revolutionary League. By 1943 the superior organization of the Viet Minh was recognized; Ho was released and took over the Revolutionary League, with his Viet Minh a crucial affiliate. Chinese subsidies and arms enhanced its influence, as did American aid in the last year of the war. Effective guerrilla operations in Tongking got under way at the end of 1944 and soon a 10,000-man army was forged under the brilliant leadership of Vo Nguyen Giap, later the victor over the French in the prolonged civil war.

In the spring of 1945 the Japanese belatedly took over direct control from the French. As a parting gesture, puppet régimes were established in Vietnam, Laos, and Cambodia. At the same time, the only real native force, the Viet Minh, was consolidating its power. Non-communists were attracted by a liberal post-war programme— representative assembly, minimum wage, eight-hour day, etc. A National Liberation Committee was formed, with representatives of various political hues, and the Emperor of Annam abdicated voluntarily. Then, on 2 September 1945, the day Japan formally surrendered, the Democratic Republic of Vietnam was formed in Hanoi with Ho as President and ex-Emperor Bao Dai as 'Supreme Political Adviser'. In Cochin-China conditions were more fluid, with diverse groups such as the Cao Dai, the Hoa Hao, Trotskyites, and pro-French elements contending for power; but there too the Viet Minh established control—through a National Committee of the South.

The South-East Asia Command dispatched British troops to Saigon to accept the Japanese surrender south of the 16th parallel, and Chinese troops to Hanoi. The policies of the two occupying powers differed markedly and shaped the coming struggle for power. General Gracey went far beyond his instructions—to disarm the Japanese. On 23 September 1945 the French were restored to power; the Vietnamese press was curbed; demonstrations were banned; interned French soldiers were armed, and left-nationalists detained. It was a veritable *coup d'état,* concurred in by the British Labour Government. By the time the British withdrew, in January 1946, French control was re-established in the cities and rubber plantations

of Cochin-China. In Cambodia, too, the British paved the way for
the French return. Under an agreement at the beginning of 1946,
Cambodia's 'independence' was recognized, some concessions were
made, but effective control over finance and external affairs remained
with French 'advisers'. A similar agreement was later concluded
with Laos.

In north Vietnam, however (i.e., Tongking and Annam), the
position was different. There, the Chinese followed their traditional
policy of support for Vietnamese nationalism. French soldiers were
disarmed and French fortifications dismantled, while Vietnamese
were allowed to keep their weapons and the Viet Minh régime
allowed free rein. The Chinese were mainly interested in control of
the railway to, and the port at, Haiphong, the status of 400,000
Chinese in Indo-China, most of them in the south, and in the ter-
mination of French rights in China. These concessions they were
able to extract before allowing French troops to return in February
1946. In the nine months of their occupation, however, the Chinese
enabled the Viet Minh to consolidate their republic in the north.

Ho Chi Minh took advantage of the Chinese presence to broaden
his base of support. In November 1945 the Indo-Chinese Communist Party was abolished and replaced by a Marxist Study Group.
The governmental structure was also reorganized, with People's
Committees at every level and non-communists added to the cabinet.
Many taxes were removed, social evils eradicated, special legislation
passed for workers, women, and children, a militia organized, etc.
So successful were these measures that all the Vietnamese bishops
and a majority of the two million Catholics rallied to the cause of
independence.

Throughout the uneasy transition period Ho conducted negotiations with French delegates in Hanoi. The outcome was an agreement on 6 March 1946 whereby France recognized the Democratic
Republic of Vietnam as a 'free state with its own government,
parliament, army and finances, forming part of the Indo-Chinese
Federation and the French Union'.[1] A referendum was promised in
Tongking, Annam, and Cochin-China on the question of reunifica-
tion. The Vietnamese agreed to the return of the French army. The
army was fixed at 15,000 Frenchmen and 10,000 Vietnamese under
French command. Apart from French troops at special bases, all

[1] It was through these larger frameworks that the French hoped to retain effective
power, a model for the Dutch attempt in the Indies three years later; both failed.

French troops were to be withdrawn in five annual instalments, i.e., by 1951. It was this which made the agreement more palatable to Vietnamese extremists.

French reaction was mixed, with the colonial army and civil servants openly hostile—and back in control. There followed conferences at Dalat and at Fontainebleau to determine the distribution of power between the Indo-Chinese Federation and its constituent units and the relationship of Cochin-China to Vietnam; the French wanted the Federation to have major economic and financial controls; and on Cochin-China, they reneged on the pledge to hold a referendum, installing a puppet régime instead. The result was stalemate in the negotiations and the resumption of hostilities.

By the end of 1946 the break was complete, following the French bombardment of Haiphong and the killing of 6,000 Vietnamese in the city. Ho was still the voice of moderation, but things had gone too far. Open war broke out on 19 December 1946, in Hanoi and elsewhere. It was to last almost eight years. During most of that time the French controlled the cities and the coastal areas; the rural districts were held by the Vietnamese.

The French now sought a political alternative to Ho Chi Minh. They found him in Bao Dai, ex-Emperor who had also served Ho. He, too, sought concessions, which the French could not fully resist. Thus, in the Elysée Agreements of March 1949, they recognized the 'independence' of Vietnam as an Associated State within the French Union, yielded to his demand for a separate army, and accepted the inclusion of Cochin-China in Vietnam. Although these concessions were hedged by safeguards, the principle of independence and the unity of Vietnam had been formally conceded. There was no turning back for the French. Bao Dai never succeeded in freeing himself from the stigma of being thought a French puppet, but the Viet Minh were able to build on his verbal triumph.

The struggle for power crystallized early in 1950, when Indo-China became enmeshed in the cold war. The Viet Minh régime was recognized by the victorious Chinese communists and the Soviet Union, while Bao Dai and the Elysée Agreements received the backing of America and Britain. Arms began to flow from the Great Powers to the contending forces. The Viet Minh benefited more than its rival, for it could now engage in positional warfare. Chinese influence became increasingly paramount, as reflected in the political changes of 1951 which created a Vietnam League of

National Union with Mao's 'New Democracy' as the model. Ho now abandoned all hope of winning non-communist support abroad and moved irrevocably into the 'communist camp'. At home, the old Indo-Chinese Communist Party was reconstituted as the Workers' Party, the core of the League of National Union.

Cambodia and Laos had also become Associated States of the French Union under the Elysée Agreements; but in both states opposition arose—Free Laos and Free Cambodia movements, which later became attached to the Viet Minh. In the meantime, American aid strengthened the French forces and American pressure led to a slight increase of Vietnamese autonomy. The military conflict continued, with the Viet Minh extending its control over all but the major cities and garrison towns, and penetrating Laos. By 1953 Ho's army consisted of 300,000 to 400,000 men, against over 400,000 troops of the French Union—but the latter included many unreliable elements interested in their own power. Indeed, within Bao Dai's Vietnam were religious sects with their own armies, like the Caodaists (who combined Buddhist and Christian ideas), the Hoa Hao, a Buddhist secret society, and the Catholics, all vying with Bao Dai's government and armed forces.

The climax came in May 1954, when the great fortress of Dien Bien Phu fell to the Viet Minh. This occurred soon after the opening of a conference in Geneva under the joint chairmanship of Great Britain and the Soviet Union to end the conflict in Indo-China. The military shock hastened a settlement, for a French victory was no longer possible.

The Geneva Agreements mark the end of French rule in Indo-China. Laos and Cambodia were recognized as sovereign states. And Vietnam was 'temporarily' divided near the 17th parallel, the northern half under Viet Minh control, the south under a non-communist régime. Both sides were to withdraw their troops from the other's territory, and civilians had freedom to move. Moreover, pro-communist guerrillas in Cambodia and Laos were to be withdrawn. Two years later, that is, in 1956, a general election was to be held in Vietnam for a united government over the entire territory. None of the successor states was to be allowed to join any military grouping. In this protracted manner did independence come to the fragments of former French Indo-China.

The scheduled elections and unification of the two Vietnams have not taken place. In the north, Ho Chi Minh consolidated a typical communist state. With more than half the population and a powerful army, including guerrillas all over the south, the Democratic Republic of Vietnam remains a formidable state. In the south, the Republic of Vietnam, Ngo Dinh Diem gradually consolidated his power. The dissident armies of the religious sects were destroyed, as was the corrupt Xuan sect. American military and economic aid have stabilized South Vietnam, replacing the French as protector and provider. Yet the transfer of power from France did not lead to stability in Indo-China.[1]

Indonesia

The fall of Holland in 1940 seriously undermined the Dutch position in the Indies. And when the Japanese assault came, it was swift and sharp. South Sumatra was overrun in mid-February 1942. All of Java followed in March, the surrender coming within eight days of invasion; many Indonesians suspected an attempted Dutch deal with Japan, like that of the French in Indo-China. In any event, Dutch prestige in the colony crumbled.

The initial reaction to the Japanese was enthusiasm. Almost all Dutchmen and many Eurasians were interned; political prisoners were released; and a paucity of personnel led to heavy reliance on Indonesian civil servants—who rose abruptly in rank. In time, however, Japanese exploitation and offensive behaviour bred antagonism. Hence, a year after the conquest, Tokyo promised self-government and permitted the establishment of the Centre of People's Power, or *Poetera,* an all-inclusive nationalist organization. Then, in September 1943, Central and Local Advisory Councils were created in the Residencies; Sukarno presided over both the Poetera and the Central Council. To strengthen their military position, the Japanese backed a volunteer army of Defenders of the Fatherland, or *Peta*; by the end of the war its 120,000 men provided the core of the new Indonesian army, for while the Japanese saw it as an auxiliary defence against allied invasion, Indonesian nationalists moulded it to their own purposes. By tacit agreement some, like Sukarno and Hatta, worked together with the Japanese, while others like Sjahrir and Sjarifuddin organized underground forces, of which there were many. Poetera was replaced in March 1944 by *Hokokai,* a more pliant organization, but the growth of nationalism continued unabated.

[1] See Hammer, op. cit., ch. 4–12, and D. Lancaster, *The Emancipation of French Indo-China,* London 1961.

As in Indo-China, the Japanese left the former colonial power the problem of an aroused and potent nationalist movement. In March 1945 they formed a special investigating committee for the preparation of independence. As the allies advanced, the date was pushed back. Finally, on 17 August 1945, just two days after the Japanese surrender, Sukarno and Hatta proclaimed the independence of Indonesia. Already the pillars of the new state had been erected by Sukarno—the *Pantja Sila* or Five Principles: nationalism; internationalism; representative government; social justice; and belief in one God. As President, Sukarno ruled with the aid of a cabinet and a Central National Indonesian Committee.

British troops arrived in October to accept the Japanese surrender; by that time the Republic was the only organized power in the Indies; as such, it received *de facto* recognition from the British—to the consternation of the former colonial ruler. The Dutch returned in late 1945 determined to re-establish the old order. During the following year they regained control of most of the Java coast. Under British and American pressure they engaged in leisurely negotiations with the Republic, culminating in the Linggadjati Agreement on 25 March 1947.

Certain broad principles were laid down. The Republic was recognized as the *de facto* authority on Java and Sumatra. This was to form one of three states (the others being Borneo and the Great East State) in the United States of Indonesia. Moreover, this federal state was to be tied to Holland and the Dutch West Indies through a Netherlands-Indonesian Union, headed by the Queen of the Netherlands, to be formed by the beginning of 1949. The Union was to 'regulate' matters of common interest such as foreign affairs, defence, and aspects of economic and financial affairs.[1] There was also an arrangement for the reduction of armed forces by both parties and the gradual evacuation of Dutch troops from Republic territory, along with the recognition of the claims of foreigners and existing property rights; here was the mutual *quid pro quo*—recognition of the Republic in exchange for participation in a Dutch Commonwealth and protection for Dutch property. There remained the problem of working out the details. Before it was settled there would be two wars and much bitterness.

[1] The three-tier structure was almost identical to that in the Indo-China Agreement of 6 March 1946, with the Republic of Indonesia occupying the same position as the Democratic Republic of Vietnam.

The Dutch pursued an indirect political strategy, setting up 'friendly' régimes in the outer islands as a counterpoise to the Republic. They also imposed an effective economic blockade on the Republic, allegedly to protect the rights of private owners but, in reality, to slow down exports from Republican territory and imports of arms. Then, a Catholic Government in Holland advocated a strong line— a demand for an immediate interim federal government to include the Republic and the pro-Dutch states. When the Republic refused, the Dutch launched their first 'police action', in July 1947. During the six months of hostilities, the Republic's territory was sharply reduced to the hill country of central Java, despite guerrilla tactics and scorched-earth destruction of Dutch property. The United Nations intervened and appointed a Committee of Good Offices. The upshot was the Renville Agreement of January 1948.

The truce terms were even more favourable to the Dutch than Linggadjati, for they retained control of all their territorial gains. There were also twelve Dutch political principles which virtually ignored the Republic, though they did contain a pledge of free elections within a year based on the right of self-determination; and the Committee added six principles of its own, assuring 'fair representation' to all units in the projected United States of Indonesia, the transfer of sovereignty from Holland to the U.S.I., and a plebiscite in Java and Sumatra to determine the relationships of territories on those islands to the Republic.

Tension remained, however, for the larger political issues were still unresolved. Dissatisfaction with the moderate line of the nationalist leaders increased, and a communist *coup d'état* was attempted; the Republic withstood the shock. Soon after, in December 1948, the Dutch launched a second 'police action' in an effort to crush the Republic completely. The capital, Jogjakarta, was taken and the key Republican leaders—Sukarno, Hatta, and Sjahrir—imprisoned. And yet the Dutch success was short-lived. For one thing, the Republic's army remained intact and turned to guerrilla warfare, promising a long and costly campaign. For another, Asian opinion was outraged. In January 1949 a special Asian Relations Conference was summoned to Delhi and strongly urged the United Nations to intervene. Finally, the United States abandoned its ally in the U.N. General Assembly. Even in Indonesia the pro-Dutch federalists became alarmed at the extent of Dutch violence and their destruction of the Republic. Confronted with these pressures, the Dutch released

Sukarno and others, restored the Republic to Jogjakarta and its surroundings, and resumed negotiations at a Round Table Conference.

The climax in the struggle for independence was The Hague Agreement of 2 November 1949. Most important was the provision for the unconditional transfer of sovereignty by the end of that year to the Republic of the United States of Indonesia (R.U.S.I.), a federal state comprising the Republic of Indonesia and fifteen pro-Dutch units in the Indies. As anticipated at Linggadjati, this federation was linked to Holland in a Netherlands–Indonesian Union, similar to the Commonwealth—i.e., with the Dutch Queen as 'Head of the Union' but without real authority and power. Three organs were created in the loose Union structure: a Conference, meeting at least twice annually as the principal channel of co-operation; a Secretariat; and a Court of Arbitration, with three judges each from Holland and the R.U.S.I., to settle legal disputes arising out of the Union Statute, and empowered to add a judge from the World Court in case of deadlock. Dutch troops were to be withdrawn as soon as possible. Existing rights and concessions were to be guaranteed, property restored to rightful owners, and confiscation or nationalization to take place only after consultation and due indemnity. Moreover, the special interests of Dutch nationals and corporations were recognized by the R.U.S.I. But the greatest Indonesian concession was the assumption of the public debt of 1·2 billion dollars and agreement to prior consultation with Holland on all financial and economic matters. The only problem unresolved was control over Dutch New Guinea, or West Irian. The Indonesians claimed the territory on the grounds that it was part of the Dutch Indies. The Dutch countered that its people were ethnically unrelated to the Indonesians. They agreed only to discuss the disposition of the territory a year later 'without prejudice'.[1]

Such in essence were the terms for the transfer of Dutch power to Indonesia. Despite the façade of the Union, real sovereignty now passed to the Indonesian people. Moreover, the federal structure itself proved unviable. Almost as soon as the ink was dry on The Hague Agreement, all the states voted for their own abrogation and unification with the Republic of Indonesia. Some uprisings occurred,

[1] The administration of West New Guinea was finally transferred to Indonesia in 1963, after a brief period of United Nations control, under the terms of an American-devised plan.

but the process was irrevocable. It was completed in the summer of 1950 and, on 17 August, the fifth anniversary of the Declaration of Independence, a new constitution for a united Republic of Indonesia was promulgated. The coming of independence had been fulfilled. The final link with Holland was severed in 1954, with the dissolution of the Netherlands–Indonesian Union.[1]

Of the three 'case studies in Asian colonialism' briefly examined, the British withdrawal from India-Pakistan was the most 'peaceful' and voluntary. The Dutch withdrew under pressure from the international community, but salvaged much for a few years. The French were ignominiously defeated in battle and were ejected from Indo-China. Among the remaining Asian colonies the process was relatively peaceful. The coming of independence to Ceylon (1948), Malaya (1957), and the Philippines (1946) was almost blood-less; and the transfer of power to Burma (1948) was marked by goodwill.

The variations in tone were due partly to the aims and attitudes of the colonial powers and partly to the character of nationalism in the different societies. British policy was directed towards the attainment of self-government, however slowly, and at times painfully. The French aimed at assimilation of their colonial subjects, a *mission civilisatrice* which did not think in terms of independence from France. And the Dutch were paternalist, concerned with economic advantage and without a conscious goal of independence.[2] Among the nationalist movements, the Ceylonese and the Malayan were the most placid. The Indian movement was militant but non-violent for the most part. Others were less constrained to abjure violence. Despite these differences, however, the climate of world politics in the aftermath of the Second World War hastened the confluence of concessions by colonial powers and demands for self-government by colonial peoples in Asia. In a dozen years the great drama of the coming of independence unfolded on a vast stage. The historic relations between Asia and the West had been transformed.

[1] Kahin, op. cit., ch. iv–xiv.
[2] See Emerson, *Malaysia;* Furnivall, *Colonial Policy and Practice*; Luthy, op. cit.; and Strausz-Hupé and Hazard, op. cit. (articles by Saxe and Kloman).

2

THE SEARCH FOR
POLITICAL STABILITY

INTRODUCTION

GOVERNMENT in contemporary Asia has taken many forms—constitutional monarchy, absolute monarchy, republic, military régime, and communism. In practice, too, there has been diversity, with three general types of political system—democracy, communist dictatorship, and non-communist authoritarianism.

'Democracy' in this context refers to a political system based on the Western model—more precisely, the Anglo-American models. Its principal components are: a parliamentary or congressional form of government; a representative legislature; periodic secret elections based on universal adult suffrage; the rule of law, guarded by an independent judiciary; individual rights effectively guaranteed, such as freedom of speech, press, assembly, religion, and organization; respect for minority views and protection of minority rights—religious, ethnic, political, cultural, and economic; and more than one political party competing for influence and power, with circulation in the political élite. A system so defined may be found, with deviations from the pure model, in India, Japan, the Philippines, Malaya, and, precariously, in Ceylon.

The Soviet or communist model is evident in three Asian governments—China, North Korea, and North Vietnam. There, a constitutional façade masks the monopoly of power in the hands of the Communist (or Workers) Party. State organs are subordinate to the party; the legislature is hand-picked; elections are unfree—that is, without any choice; the courts lack tenure or independence; individual rights are subject to party-government decision and revision; minority rights may or may not be protected, depending upon the needs and plans of the party; and the political process is frozen—under one-party control, a domination exercised by a variety of techniques involving persuasion and coercion.

All other Asian states reveal some form of authoritarianism. It may be mild, as in Pakistan since 1958, or severe, as in South Vietnam under Ngo Dinh Diem since 1955 and in South Korea under Syngh-man Rhee. It may be military rule, as in Thailand, South Korea, Burma, and Pakistan in 1958–62; or civilian dictatorship, as in South Vietnam; or an uneasy blend of civil-military control, as in Indo-nesia; or absolute monarchy, as in Afghanistan, Nepal, and Cam-bodia. In all of these cases, the indices of 'democracy' are absent in whole or in part. In some, the disregard for civil liberties is as great as in communist lands, and the instruments of control are no less oppressive. In most, the army has become a major political force, either exercising power directly (Thailand, South Korea, and Burma) or standing in the wings ready to seize control from a faltering civil authority and acting as guardian of the political order (e.g. Pakistan and Indonesia). But in none of these states is authoritarianism total; this is one vital distinction between communist governments and those of 'the middle zone'. Another difference is the commitment in principle to 'democracy', though this has lessened in recent years; but even among those who seek alternative paths to a stable political system, there is acceptance of the idea of change in the political élite, protection for individual and minority rights, the notion of choice by the governed as to who shall be the governors, and other com-ponents of 'democracy'. Because of these commitments and the possibility of change in the political system, these authoritarian régimes are potentially closer to the substance of 'democracy' than to the rigid, closed political system of communism. For the present, however, they remain almost as far removed from 'democracy' as is communism; and many are less welfare-oriented than either of the polar models.

All three types of political systems in Asia today are 'Western' in the sense that they are legacies of the Western epoch in Asian history. 'Democracy' is the direct intrusion of colonial rulers. Communism is the product of Western ideas and the example of a non-Asian state. And the 'middle zone' of authoritarianism uses Western-derived techniques and political forms to maintain power. No system is tradition-oriented, though some current experiments, notably in Pakistan and Indonesia, draw inspiration partly from the pre-Wes-tern period of their history.

One further introductory comment is in order. The three types do not correspond to the three major colonial empires—British, French, and Dutch; nor can they be correlated with former colonial areas and independent Asian states. All former British colonies began as 'democracies', but Pakistan and Burma turned to authoritarianism. In former French dependencies there are examples of communism and civilian dictatorship, along with absolute monarchy. And in the former Dutch Indies, non-communist authoritarianism holds sway. Among the few Asian states which escaped direct Western domination, all three models are evident—democracy in Japan, communism in China, and military rule in Thailand.

POLITICAL INSTABILITY: THE RECORD

The dominant feature of politics in the new states of Asia is instability. The range is wide, from near-constant flux in Pakistan and Indonesia to relative calm in India. But no Asian state has been free from threats to a stable political order. The record is emphatic on this theme.

Pakistan. In the first eleven years of statehood Pakistan had four Governors-General (and President) and eight cabinets. If one excludes the lengthy tenure of the first Prime Minister, Liaquat Ali Khan, there was an average of one cabinet a year. The turnover in the provinces was almost as rapid—six Governors of the Punjab and six of the North-West Frontier Province between 1947 and 1955, and seven Chief Ministers of Sind during the same period. On three occasions the normal process of constitutional government broke down in the provinces and Governor's rule was imposed—in the Punjab from 1949 to 1951, in Sind from 1951 to 1953, and in East Bengal in 1954–5. Despite sincere intentions and frequent pledges, no national election was ever held, the members of the Constituent Assembly (which doubled as a legislature) having been elected to provincial legislatures *before* independence. Three provincial elections were held but two were marred by official interference and bias; and the third, in East Bengal in 1954, was followed almost at once by severe disorders and Governor's rule.

Political instability in Pakistan appears in bold relief when one glances at the sequence of leadership at the centre. The first year was dominated by the creator of Pakistan, Mohammed Ali Jinnah, who held three key posts simultaneously—Governor-General, President of the Muslim League, and President of the Constituent Assembly. His death in 1948 was a severe blow to the new state. Fortunately his right-hand man, Liaquat Ali Khan, remained as Prime Minister—to whose office Jinnah's power as Governor-

General was now effectively transferred; a moderate, religious Bengali leader, Kwaja Nazimuddin, succeeded to the Governor-Generalship. Another blow befell Pakistan in September 1951 with the assassination of Liaquat Ali. Thereafter, the vacuum of leadership was never adequately filled. Nazimuddin stepped down to the Prime Ministership, and an able civil servant, Ghulam Mohammed, became Governor-General. Another crisis occurred in 1953, with severe religious riots in the Punjab, proposed concessions to *mullah* control over the Constitution, and a serious food shortage. Without awaiting a vote of no-confidence in the Assembly, the Governor-General dismissed Nazimuddin and appointed another Bengali, Mohammed Ali, as Prime Minister.

Perhaps the gravest constitutional crisis took place eighteen months later, in the autumn of 1954. An attempt to curb the powers of the Governor-General led to his abrupt dismissal of the (first) Constituent Assembly, the nullification of its enactments since 1947, and the formation of a 'cabinet of talents' under the discredited Mohammed Ali. A test before the Supreme Court vindicated Ghulam Mohammed's action, but it insisted that a new Assembly be formed. The cause of stability and respect for authority were not enhanced. In the meantime, too, the election in East Bengal had swept the Muslim League Ministry from power with a resounding victory for a leftist United Front, seeking greater autonomy for Bengal. A month after the election, however, widespread riots led to the dismissal of the United Front and the imposition of Governor's rule.

To satisfy the Bengali demand for equality with the western region and to calm Punjabi fears of Bengali domination by virtue of a larger population, Ghulam Mohammed forced through the 'One Unit Scheme', creating the province of West Pakistan to replace the *mélange* of provinces, tribal areas, etc. He then induced the formation of a new Constituent Assembly, indirectly elected and with equal representation for East and West Pakistan. All the old Assembly's laws were revalidated, and a constitution for the Islamic Republic of Pakistan was finally passed in March 1956.

By that time, a physically disabled Ghulam Mohammed was replaced by 'strongman' Iskander Mirza as Governor-General, later Acting President. Like Jinnah and his immediate predecessor, the new Head of State played an active role in politics; indeed, he manipulated politicians and parties to suit his aspirations. Thus, he backed Dr. Khan Saheb of the Frontier Province in his newly-formed

Republican Party which held power in the province of West Pakistan. He also helped to bring another civil servant, Chaudhri Mohammed Ali, to the Prime Ministership in the summer of 1955. A year later, the Bengali leader of the Awami (People's) League, H. S. Suhrawardy, became Prime Minister. A clash between President and Prime Minister led to the latter's dismissal without a vote of no-confidence, a measure of the adherence of Pakistani leaders to constitutional procedures. The President then appointed I. I. Chundrigar as Prime Minister in 1957; and, within a fortnight, still another pliant politician, Firoz Khan Noon, succeeded to the post.

The dismal game of Pakistani political musical chairs came to an end in October 1958 when President Mirza abrogated the Constitution, imposed martial law, dismissed the central and provincial governments, and outlawed political parties. Within three weeks Mirza himself was ousted by General (later Field-Marshal) Mohammed Ayub Khan, commander-in-chief of the army. The experiment in parliamentary government, bedevilled from the outset, had come to an end; and with it the chronic instability of Pakistan's political life. The 'club' of 150 men who controlled politics for eleven years and made a mockery of 'democracy' were swept aside, a few into jail, many barred from public life for a long time. The military took power and rejected the British institutions as unworkable in the Pakistani environment.

There is no better description of Pakistan's prolonged crisis of instability and political malaise than that contained in General Ayub Khan's statement of 8 October 1958 : [1]

. . . there was no alternative to it [the imposition of martial law] except the disintegration and complete ruination of the country. . . . These chaotic conditions . . . have been brought about by self-seekers who in the garb of political leaders have ravaged the country or tried to barter it away for personal gains. . . . Their aim is nothing but self-aggrandizement or thirst for power. Meanwhile weak and irresolute Governments looked on with masterly inactivity and cowardice and allowed things to drift and deteriorate and discipline to go to pieces.

Ever since the death of the Quaid-e-Azam [Great Leader, referring to Jinnah] and Mr. Liaquat Ali Khan, politicians started a free-for-all type of fighting in which no holds were barred. They waged ceaseless and bitter war against each other regardless of the ill-effects on the country, just to whet their appetites and satisfy their base motives. There has been

[1] Text is in *Dawn* (Karachi), 9 October 1958.

E

no limit to the depth of their baseness, chicanery, deceit and degradation. Having nothing constructive to offer, they used provincial feelings, sectarian, religious and racial differences to set a Pakistani against a Pakistani. . . . The country and people could go to the dogs as far as they were concerned. . . .

The result is total administrative, economic, political and moral chaos in the country. . . .

The General was an interested party, but no objective observer of Pakistani politics during the first decade would disagree with this harsh critique.[1]

Indonesia. The crisis of instability was no less severe in the successor to the Dutch Indies. There were seven cabinets from 1949 to 1958, when 'democracy' gave way to 'guided democracy'. Violence has been endemic, starting with the acquisition of weapons from the departing Japanese in 1945 and the lengthy war of independence against the Dutch. Banditry has never been stamped out. Nor has guerrilla war, beginning with a force led by the Dutch Captain 'Turk' Westerling in 1949. A fanatic, orthodox Muslim group, Dar-ul-Islam, has never ceased terrorist activities in West Java in support of a theocratic state. But the main area of disorder has been the 'outer islands'. There, regional loyalties and the fear of 'Javanese imperialism' have led to four major insurrections: in the Moluccas, Macassar and Amboina on two occasions, in 1950–1 and 1954–5; in Sumatra in 1956–7; and a complex series of revolts in Sumatra, Borneo, and the Celebes in 1958–60.

In the political arena, too, fragmentation has been the keynote. Dozens of groups engaged in the struggle for power. Three parties held the centre of the stage—the Nationalists, Masjumi, and the Communists—but none was strong enough to establish a firm

---

[1] Pakistan's politics before the military *coup* are ably dissected in K. Callard, *Pakistan: A Political Study,* London 1957, and *Political Forces in Pakistan 1947–1959,* New York 1959; Mushtaq Ahmad: *Government and Politics in Pakistan,* Karachi, 1959; and Khalid bin Sayeed: 'Collapse of Parliamentary Democracy in Pakistan', *Middle East Journal,* Autumn 1959, pp. 389–406, and *Pakistan: The Formative Phase,* Karachi 1960.

See also: Leonard Binder, *Religion and Politics in Pakistan,* Berkeley 1961, Parts Two and Three; G. W. Choudhury, *Constitutional Development in Pakistan,* London 1959; Herbert Feldman, *A Constitution for Pakistan,* Karachi 1956; Sir Ivor Jennings, *Constitutional Problems in Pakistan,* Cambridge 1957, pp. 3–75; W. C. Smith, *Islam in Modern History,* Princeton 1957, ch. v; Richard D. Lambert, 'Factors in Bengali Regionalism in Pakistan', *Far Eastern Survey,* XXVIII, April 1959, pp. 49–58; K. J. Newman, 'Pakistan's Preventive Autocracy and Its Causes', *Pacific Affairs,* XXXII, No. 1, March 1959, pp. 18–33.

majority. Coalition cabinets, the bane of political order in other states of Asia and the West, accentuated the problem. Only in one respect, perhaps, was Indonesia more fortunate than Pakistan: the leading symbol of Indonesian nationalism, Sukarno, has been President throughout the transition period, offsetting in part the elements of disruption. But even he has been unable to create a stable polity.

The measure of Indonesia's flux and uncertainty may be gauged in the sequence of cabinets. Vice-President Hatta served briefly as Prime Minister immediately after independence. There followed a series of coalitions. First the Muslim party, Masjumi, dominated the cabinet—under Mohammed Natsir, leader of its liberal wing, in 1950–1, and Sukiman, a prominent conservative, in 1951–2. Another short-lived cabinet was headed by moderate Premier Wilopo in 1952–3. Then came the Nationalists, under Sastroamidjojo, with Presidential support, from 1953 to 1955. The Masjumi remained aloof, but parliamentary support was assured by communist backing—forthcoming because of the strong neutralist line of the Nationalists, culminating in the Bandung Conference. Real power, then as before, was in the hands of Sukarno.

A turning point in the unsuccessful quest for stability was the general election of 1955, the only genuine national poll in Indonesia's history. (Members of the Provisional Parliament (1949–55) had been appointed, in proportion to the estimated strength of the various parties at the time of independence.) The results did not augur well for the future, for a state of fragmentation was now firmly established. The Nationalists and Masjumi each won 57 seats, a more conservative Muslim Teachers Party 45, and the Communists 39. Once more, a coalition was necessary. Both Muslim parties rejected Sukarno's proposal to include the Communists, but they joined the Nationalists, again under Sastroamidjojo, in a new cabinet formed in the spring of 1956.

Tension mounted during the next year—between Sukarno and Vice-President Hatta, between Java and the 'outer islands', and among the political parties. Hatta finally resigned in December 1956—over the issues of growing communist influence, the President's 'guided democracy' plan, and excessive Javanese control. At that time, too, army commanders in north Sumatra led a revolt against the Centre. It was this continuous evidence of dissension, and perhaps his admiration for the monolithic solidarity of China, which led Sukarno to challenge the parliamentary system itself.

The President's assault gathered momentum after Hatta's resignation. The essence of his argument was contained in a speech early in 1957:[1]

I have finally come to the conclusion that the cause [of political instability] lies in our practising a system not suited to our specific requirements, in our indiscriminate adoption of every feature of the system that is known as western democracy. . . . The principles of western democracy . . . incorporate the concept of an active opposition. . . . By accepting this concept we have come to think in a manner that is alien to the Indonesian way of life [where decisions were traditionally arrived at by consensus].

To overcome the dissensions of the parliamentary system, Sukarno proposed and succeeded in creating a National Council to 'guide', i.e., direct, the cabinet on major policy issues. Parliament would remain and so would the cabinet, but ultimate power would be vested in the Council. A 43-member Council was installed in July 1957; all parties and the armed forces were represented. Thereafter, the façade of parliamentary government remained, but its substance was destroyed. Even the form itself was eliminated in 1959, and the following year Sukarno used his decree powers to restore the first and provisional constitution of 1945—which gave the President vast authority. In Pakistan, then, a decade of instability led to military rule; in Indonesia, civilian rule remained, but 'democracy' was destroyed and the army acquired considerable power, becoming virtually an equal partner of Sukarno in his 'guided democracy'.[2]

Other illustrations of instability in the new states of Asia may be treated more briefly.

[1] Quoted in George McT. Kahin (ed.), *Major Governments of Asia*, Ithaca 1958, pp. 565-6.

[2] See George McT. Kahin, 'Indonesia' in *Major Governments of Asia*, ch. xxi-xxiii, for a good, succinct analysis of that state's political travail.

See also: Louis Fischer, *The Story of Indonesia*, New York 1959, Part II; Miriam S. Budiardjo, 'The Provisional Parliament of Indonesia', *Far Eastern Survey*, XXV, February 1956, pp. 17-23; Herbert Feith, *The Indonesian Elections of 1955*, Ithaca 1957 and *The Wilopo Cabinet, 1952-1953*, Ithaca 1958; John D. Legge, *Problems of Regional Autonomy in Contemporary Indonesia*, Ithaca 1957; Guy J. Pauker, 'The Role of Political Organizations in Indonesia', *Far Eastern Survey*, XXVII, September 1958, pp. 129-42; Abdulgani Roeslan, 'Indonesia's National Council: The First Year', *Far Eastern Survey*, XXVII, July 1958, pp. 97-104; Irene Tinker and Millidge Walker, 'Indonesia's Panacea: 1959 Model', *Far Eastern Survey*, XXVIII, December 1959, pp. 177-82; Justus M. Van der Kroef, 'Instability in Indonesia', *Far Eastern Survey*, XXVI, April 1957, pp. 49-62, and 'Disunited Indonesia', *Far Eastern Survey*, XXVII, April 1958, pp. 49-63 and ibid., May 1958, pp. 73-80.

Burma.   The symptoms of disorder in Burma were flagrant, and the survival of the Union was in grave doubt for a decade. The crisis began in August 1947, on the eve of independence, when General Aung San, leader of the nationalist movement, the Anti-Fascist People's Freedom League (AFPFL), and six cabinet colleagues were assassinated by a rival group. The danger of chaos was overcome by the closing of nationalist ranks under the leadership of U Nu.

The gravest challenge came from open rebellion by various groups. Most serious was the revolt of the Karens, a militant minority of a million who sought an independent state. Two bands of communists —White Flag (Stalinist) and Red Flag (Trotskyite)—also defied the central government; so did a segment of the wartime underground PVO, People's Volunteer Organization, and extremists of other minorities such as the Chins and Kachins. Indeed, during most of the 1950s, the writ of the Union Government extended only to Rangoon and its immediate surroundings. Gradually the communists were reduced to insignificance, the PVO personnel were amnestied, and the Karens were given acceptable assurances of autonomy. During the process of consolidation the army grew in stature, as did its leader, General Ne Win.

The political process itself was much more tranquil. The AFPFL was a coalition of many interests—the Socialist Party, the Karen League, and Congresses of the Kachins, the Chins, and the Hill People. With the communists in revolt, and the extreme Right virtually non-existent, there was no one to challenge the AFPFL at the polls. Thus, in the 1951 elections, it won 220 of 250 seats in the dominant lower house, the upper house being the Council of Nationalities. In 1956 its majority was reduced to 169 out of 250. But the real danger to the party, and the crisis it precipitated, came from within.

The split became ominous in 1957–8, with Socialist and Peasants Organization members of the ruling party voting on opposite sides in the House. Violence occurred, and with it an open struggle for the party machine. Prime Minister U Nu, backed by the Peasants Organization, sought to retain his weakened position by strange tactics—an offer of statehood to dissident Arakanese and Mons, a pledge of amnesty to communist rebels in the hope of winning support from the leftist National Front in parliament, and the dismissal of treason charges against two M.P.s so that they could vote!

He thereby secured a narrow vote of confidence, but the rot had gone too far. In October 1958 the army took over direct authority—at the request of U Nu—and General Ne Win became Prime Minister. The army promised to restore civilian rule after the residue of corruption was swept away. And so it did, in February 1960, when new elections returned U Nu to power as head of the 'Clean' faction of the AFPFL. This rare example of self-abnegation was short-lived, however. In March 1962 Ne Win and the army acted in accord with time-honoured patterns; they seized power in a *coup d'état*, imposed martial law, outlawed parties, and put an end to the British-type political system in Burma.[1]

Ceylon.   No country in Asia seemed to have better prospects for a stable democracy than the island dominion. A peaceful road to independence, a high literacy rate (65 per cent), and a Westernized élite with experience in government—all this augured well for the future. And, indeed, the early years were relatively tranquil. The conservative United National Party won a substantial majority in the elections of 1947 and 1952. There were many opposition groups, including two Trotskyite and one Communist party, and two Tamil parties; but none threatened UNP control. Until the mid-1950s, Ceylon seemed an exception to the pattern of Asian instability.

Beneath the surface, however, new political forces and problems were gathering strength, notably a new rural élite of Buddhist monks, village teachers, and Ayurvedic doctors, all highly national-istic, especially towards the fermenting problems of language and the Tamils. A growing demand for 'one national language' to re-place English angered the large Tamil minority, two million out of a

---

[1] The most comprehensive and thoughtful analysis of Burmese politics since inde-pendence is Hugh Tinker, *The Union of Burma* (3rd ed.), London 1961. See also Josef Silverstein,' Burma' in George McT. Kahin (ed.), *Governments and Politics of Southeast Asia*, Ithaca 1959, ch. vi, vii.

On the crisis of 1958 see John H. Badgley, 'Burma's Political Crisis', *Pacific Affairs*, XXXI, December 1958, pp. 336–51, and Frank N. Trager, 'The Political Split in Burma', *Far Eastern Survey*, XXVII, October 1958, pp. 145–55.

For an analysis of the Army *coup* in 1962 see Richard Butwell, 'The Four Failures of U Nu's Second Premiership', *Asian Survey*, II, No. 1, March 1962, pp. 3–11.

See also Richard Butwell, 'The New Political Outlook in Burma', *Far Eastern Survey*, XXIX, February 1960, pp. 21–27; Richard Butwell and Fred von der Mehden, 'The 1960 Election in Burma', *Pacific Affairs*, XXXIII, June 1960, pp. 144–57; Alan Gledhill, 'The Burmese Constitution', *Indian Yearbook of International Affairs*, Madras 1954, II, pp. 214–24; and Josef Silverstein, 'Politics, Parties and National Elections in Burma', *Far Eastern Survey*, XXV, December 1956, pp. 177–84, and 'The Federal Dilemma in Burma', ibid., XXVIII, July 1959, pp. 97–105.

total of ten million. The cry of 'Sinhalese only' was championed by
S. W. R. D. Bandaranaike and his leftist Sri Lanka Freedom Party.
The tradition-oriented rural élite rallied to this party, and the UNP
was swept from power in the elections of 1956; Bandaranaike took
51 of the 95 seats. But his victory ushered in a period of intense law-
lessness in the country—widespread strikes organized by the far left
parties, especially in Colombo, and riots by the supporters and
opponents of 'Sinhalese only'. The clashes in 1956 and 1958 led to
1,000 dead and many more injured, with widespread arson, looting,
and assault. Only martial law restored order in the summer of 1958.
But the tension remained, as economic discontent added fuel to the
flames. In the autumn of 1959 the Prime Minister was assassinated
by a Buddhist monk.

New elections in March 1960 were inconclusive, but soon after,
fresh elections brought the slain Prime Minister's widow to power
with a bare majority, the first lady Head of Government in the
world. Once more severe Tamil–Sinhalese riots occurred, as the date
for the imposition of one national language drew near. By 1961 the
hopes for a model democracy had faded into history; Ceylon has
joined the ranks of troubled Asian lands.[1]

Laos. Nowhere is politics as confused and unsettled as in this
remote, land-locked kingdom. The French protectorate was terminated by the Geneva Agreements of 1954, but the years of
independence have seen constant violence and tension. Even before
independence, civil war raged between the Royal Laotian Government and the pro-communist Pathet Lao (Free Laos) movement—
which occupied the two northern provinces. A precarious truce and,
for a brief period, an uneasy coalition of the rivals was maintained
by the International Control Commission. By 1959, however, the
coalition was sundered, the Pathet Lao leader was imprisoned, and
the Great Powers had openly intervened; the United States backed
the Royal Government, China and Vietnam the Pathet Lao.

Disorder has been permanent since the late summer of 1959. First

---

[1] The most valuable and thorough treatment of Ceylon's politics since indepen-
dence is W. Howard Wriggins, *Ceylon: Dilemmas of a New Nation*, Princeton 1960.
See also Sir Ivor Jennings, *The Dominion of Ceylon*, London 1952; S. Namasiva-
yam, *Parliamentary Government in Ceylon 1948–1958*, Colombo 1959; Tarzie
Vittachi, *Emergency '58*, London 1958; D. K. Rangnekar, 'The Nationalist Revo-
lution in Ceylon', *Pacific Affairs*, XXXIII, No 4, December 1960, pp. 361–74;
Calvin A. Woodward, 'The Trotskyite Movement in Ceylon', *World Politics*, XIV,
No. 2, January 1962, pp. 307–21.

came an intensification of the civil war and Royal Government charges of massive Chinese and North Vietnamese intervention. A United Nations Security Council inquiry mission found no direct evidence, and tension declined. Early in 1960 a leftist paratrooper, Captain (later General) Kong Le, led a rebellion and was supported by neutralist Premier Souvanna Phouma; the Pathet Lao was brought back into the cabinet. Then came a right-wing *coup* which replaced the Prime Minister with Prince Boun Oom. Souvanna Phouma fled to Cambodia, his régime still recognized by Moscow, Peking, and Hanoi. Then, in the autumn of 1960, the civil war became ominous, as the Soviet Union airlifted supplies and weapons on a large scale, with the United States retaliating. The danger of another Korea was grave.

The struggle on the battlefield moved rapidly in favour of the Pathet Lao; by the time a truce was arranged in the spring of 1961, almost two-thirds of Laotian territory was under its control. A 14-power conference in Geneva finally reached agreement in July 1962 on the basis of a neutralized Laos. Within Laos itself, prolonged negotiations led to a delicately-balanced coalition of right-wing, neutralist, and Pathet Lao factions under the premiership of Souvanna Phouma. There remains an almost Gilbertian quality about Laos today, with grave political instability ever-present.[1]

South Vietnam. Non-communist Vietnam is more stable than Laos today, but only at the price of authoritarian rule. And in the early years, 1954–5, it seemed doubtful if the Saigon régime would survive. Indeed, only decisive action by Ngo Dinh Diem—backed by the United States—prevented utter chaos. In succession, Diem destroyed the bandit organization Binh Xuyen, which controlled the Saigon police, asserted control over the army, reduced the Hoa Hao sect to insignificance, and eliminated the Cao Dai as an autonomous force. Finally, he deposed Emperor Bao Dai, in a 'popular' referendum, and became Chief of State. Within eighteen months of Geneva, Diem was master of the South. Then, lip service was paid to the forms of democracy by having a Constituent Assembly enact a new

---

[1] See Bernard B. Fall, 'The International Relations of Laos', *Pacific Affairs*, XXX, No. 1, March 1957, pp. 22–34, and 'The Laos Tangle', *International Journal*, XVI, No. 2, Spring 1961, pp. 138–57; and Robert Gilkey, 'Laos: Politics, Elections and Foreign Aid', *Far Eastern Survey*, XXVII, June 1958, pp. 89–94.

For the negotiations at Geneva and among the three princes, from April 1961 to July 1962, the best source is the *New York Times*.

constitution. For all practical purposes, Diem is dictator of South Vietnam, aided by a small coterie, mainly of close relatives; nothing is done without his—or their—approval.

It would be wrong to assume, however, that South Vietnam is stable and secure. Parts of the country are heavily infiltrated by the Viet Cong, communists working with the North. By assiduous guerrilla warfare they have killed thousands, including many village officials, thereby disrupting administration and tax collection in the rural areas. Some 2,500 dead on both sides in the civil war was the estimate in the first seven months of 1961. Saigon itself is virtually surrounded by communist guerrillas, and few will venture forth after dark. Moreover, discontent with the rigid Diem family rule bursts out periodically, the most recent crisis being in November 1960. Three battalions of paratroops surrounded the presidential palace and demanded reforms, including free speech and a new—military—cabinet. The revolt was suppressed but the régime was nearly toppled. Thus, the surface of South Vietnam is stable but fear and dictatorship prevail, and disruptive forces are within, growing steadily. Without massive United States aid, it is likely that chaos—or communist control—would ensue.[1]

Enough examples have been cited to demonstrate a pattern of political instability in the new states of Asia. There are some notable exceptions—India, Malaya, and the Philippines. But even they are not free from grave threats to political order.

India. India is the most stable of the new Asian states. The Congress Party has held power in Delhi and in all but one of the States since 1947. Three general elections and five State contests have been free from disruption, violence, and corruption. The army is clearly subordinate to the civil authority; the judiciary is independent; political parties are free to organize and persuade, but threats

[1] See Wells C. Klein and Marjorie Weiner, 'Vietnam' in Kahin (ed.), *Governments and Politics of Southeast Asia*, ch. xix; Francis J. Corley, 'The President in the Constitution of the Republic of Viet-Nam', *Pacific Affairs*, XXXIV, No. 2, Summer 1961, pp. 165–74; John T. Dorsey, Jr., 'South Viet Nam in Perspective', *Far Eastern Survey*, XXVII, December 1958, pp. 177–82; Bernard B. Fall, 'South Viet-Nam's Internal Problems', *Pacific Affairs*, XXXI, No. 3, September 1958, pp. 241–60; Wesley R. Fishel, 'Political Realities in Vietnam', *Asian Survey*, I, No. 2, April 1961, pp. 15–23; Roy Jumper, 'Mandarin Bureaucracy and Politics in South Viet Nam', *Pacific Affairs*, XXX, No. 1, March 1957, pp. 47–58; Robert G. Scigliano, 'Political Parties in South Viet Nam under the Republic', *Pacific Affairs*, XXXIII, No. 4, December 1960, pp. 327–46; U.S. Senate Committee on Foreign Relations, *Situation in Viet Nam*, 1960, 2 Parts.

to law and order have been suppressed. Social and economic reforms have been effected within a stable framework. At no time has the existing political system been in danger of being swept away.

Yet there have been acts of disorder and sources of instability in India. The coming of six million refugees posed serious problems to the new government—as it did in neighbouring Pakistan. Kerala in the south and Punjab in the north had to be placed under President's rule on various occasions because of tension and deadlock in the political arena; so too with Orissa in the east. Fasting has triggered off disorder frequently, notably in Andhra in 1952. Regional loyalties and linguistic passions have caused widespread violence and destruction, as in Bombay during the States Reorganization period in 1956 and in Assam in 1960. Students are often in revolt against authority; major strikes are not uncommon; and a communist-led revolt in Hyderabad caused havoc and disorder from 1948 to 1950. The latest challenges to stability have been the Sikh demand for a separate state within India and the pressure for a separate South Indian state of Dravidistan, led by the DMK. In short, India has not escaped the challenges to stability afflicting all Asian states. The difference has been in the capacity of the government to withstand the challenges and the commitment to democracy. In both spheres, India has been a notable success, but symptoms of disquiet are widespread beneath the surface of Indian politics.[1]

Philippine Islands. The Philippines may also be regarded as a stable democracy. Its constitution is modelled on that of the United States, and its political process has also drawn much from the former colonial ruler. There have been six elections to the presidency, not without malpractice, but leading to orderly transfers of power to the winner. Parties have been less important than in British-type patterns of politics, resembling rather those of America. The constitutional

---

[1] For analyses of Indian politics since independence, see Michael Brecher, *Nehru: A Political Biography*, London 1959, ch. xv–xviii; W. H. Morris-Jones, *Parliament in India*, Philadelphia 1957, especially ch. 1, 2, 4, 7; Norman D. Palmer, *The Indian Political System*, Boston 1961, ch. 5–10; and Richard L. Park and Irene Tinker (eds.), *Leadership and Political Institutions in India*, Princeton, 1959, Parts 3, 4, 5, 6.

See also Margaret W. Fisher and Joan V. Bondurant, *The Indian Experience with Democratic Elections*, Berkeley 1956; M. V. Pylee, *Constitutional Government in India*, Bombay 1960; Myron Weiner, *Party Politics in India*, Princeton 1957, ch. 1, 2, 8, 9, 11, 12; Lloyd I. Rudolph and Susanne Hoeber Rudolph, 'The Political Role of India's Caste Associations,' *Pacific Affairs*, XXXIII, No. 1, March 1960, pp. 5–22; and Myron Weiner, 'India's Third General Elections', *Asian Survey*, II, No. 3, May 1962, pp. 3–18.

order has been firmly established but not entirely serene. Indeed, for almost a decade after the coming of independence in 1946, Manila was confronted with a challenge from the communist-led Hukbala-hap movement. This began as an anti-Japanese army, based on the peasantry, and mushroomed into a broad political organization for land reform and basic political change. In the early years it held effective control over parts of central Luzon. Guerrilla war continued until 1955, and the threat was only overcome by the one outstanding Philippine leader of recent times, Ramon Magsaysay. Apart from the Huk threat, Philippine politics have been relatively tranquil.[1]

Malaya. The Federation of Malaya was the last Asian state to achieve independence, in 1957. Too little time has elapsed to judge the success of democracy and the degree of stability, though on both counts the evidence is favourable. Yet it should be noted that a communist rebellion wreaked havoc in Malaya from 1948 to 1957 and has not been totally eradicated. The continued presence of Commonwealth troops has shored up Malaya's security; the threat still remains below the surface.[2]

CAUSES OF INSTABILITY

Almost all the new states of Asia inherited the forms of democracy. All but a few set out to build a political order of the Western type. The key motive seems to have been psychological—the belief of the nationalist élites that only by working a constitutional democracy would their claim to equal status with the former rulers be recognized. It was also the line of least resistance, for many had a full-blown system to ease the transition; and nationalist leaders had absorbed the idea, as well as the assumed superiority, of democracy.

[1] See David Wurfel, 'The Philippines', in Kahin (ed.), *Governments and Politics of Southeast Asia*, ch. xxiv. See also Willard H. Elsbree, 'The Philippines' in Rupert Emerson, *Representative Government in Southeast Asia*, Cambridge, Mass. 1955, pp. 82–117; Robert Aura Smith, *Philippine Freedom, 1946–1958*, New York 1958, ch. 4–8; David Wurfel, 'The Philippine Elections: Support for Democracy', *Asian Survey*, II, No. 3, May 1962, pp. 25–37; and Martin Meadows, 'Philippine Political Parties and the 1961 Election', *Pacific Affairs*, xxxv, No. 3, Fall 1962, pp.261–74.

[2] See J. Norman Parmer, 'Malaya and Singapore' in Kahin (ed.), *Governments and Politics of Southeast Asia*, ch. xiv–xvi.

See also Charles Gamba, 'Labour and Labour Parties in Malaya', *Pacific Affairs*, XXXI, No. 2, June 1958, pp. 117–30; J. Norman Parmer, 'Constitutional Change in Malaya's Plural Society', *Far Eastern Survey*, XXVI, October 1957, pp. 145–52; and T. E. Smith, 'The Malayan Elections of 1959', *Pacific Affairs*, XXXIII, No. 1, March 1960, pp. 38–47.

There was no appeal in the traditional political system; by temperament, philosophy, and experience they were committed to democracy, whether of the British, American, French, or Dutch variety.

Whatever the stimuli, most failed: within a decade of independence the elaborate framework of constitutional democracy was dismantled in much of South and South-East Asia or was robbed of content. A glance at the record has shown the environment of that area to be unreceptive on the whole to that bold experiment. Many of the states have adopted some form of authoritarian rule. Most striking, perhaps, has been the rise of the officer corps to prominence. The army exercises direct authority in Burma and South Korea. It holds a crucial position in Indonesia, Pakistan, South Vietnam, and Laos. Only India, Malaya, and the Philippines, and Ceylon with reservations, remain in the 'democratic column'. Finally, the record suggests widespread instability in the region, both in states that have 'fallen from democratic grace' (one of the causes of the 'fall') and those that persist with the task of political adaptation. It is to the reasons for these related developments that we may now turn—the causes of instability in the region as a whole, the causes of the failure of democracy, and an explanation for the growth of army influence. This will be supplemented by an outline of the obstacles to stability and democracy in specific countries.

General

The sources of instability in the new states of Asia are varied and complex. Perhaps the most disquieting—because it is certain to remain on the Asian scene indefinitely—is widespread poverty. People who live at the margin of subsistence are either indifferent or hostile to government. And in Asia there are hundreds of millions who are under-fed, disease-ridden, and uneducated. Their reaction will range from passivity to overt anger; if aroused, they will blame those in power for their ills, frequently resorting to riots and demonstrations against authority; certainly, they cannot be expected to act as 'responsible citizens' sympathetic to order and the delicate process of constitutional democracy. Where they have been receptive, special factors intrude—tradition or faith in a charismatic leader or a nationalist movement which is committed to democracy or enough material improvement to induce patience and faith in the future. Nevertheless, it remains true for most of South and South-East Asia that all-pervasive poverty undermines government—of any kind. It is a persistent cause of instability and makes democracy well-nigh impossible to practise.

To this must be added a tradition of antipathy to government, an attitude born of untold centuries of fear and resentment of the power of authority. Asia's peasants, about 75 per cent of her population, have long identified government with the tax collector and the oppressor, friend and protector of money-lender and landlord. Régimes came and went, but government remained. Foreign or native, it performed the same functions, made the same demands, imposed the same onerous obligations. Since their conditions of life did not change very much, Asia's masses did not differentiate one set of rulers from another. When independence came, it brought another change of tax collector—and often oppressor. In most states of the region it did not bring a perceptible improvement in the peasant's standard of living. Why then should he change his time-honoured distrust or antipathy to those in power. It was hard to maintain stability in the transition period, much more difficult to build the delicate mechanism of the democratic process. In short, the new régimes lacked a broad base of support in the crucial early years.

Even within the political élite hostility to government was wide-spread. This was a legacy of the struggle for independence, when almost everything done by the colonial ruler was deemed evil. It was natural to carry this attitude of oppositionism or negativism over to the post-colonial period—especially among those out of power. In most of the new states, then, obstruction became the norm of political behaviour, partly because it had brought results in the past and partly because it was familiar. The notion of a loyal opposition, one of the most significant in the democratic process, was unknown among almost all nationalist movements in Asia. Thus, both the groups now in power and those outside found the idea unappealing; all opposition seemed treason and all government seemed immoral. In most states elections were a farce and were so regarded by rivals for power. This tended to place a premium on extra-constitutional means of achieving power, the *coup d'état*, civil war, and the like. Hence the frequency of violence in the politics of the new Asian states. Weak and untried régimes could hardly flourish in this environment. Many faced permanent crisis and were toppled. Instability became the rule—and democracy an illusion.

There was, too, an unreal quality to the democratic experiment.

Asian politics had a long tradition of autocracy, whether monarchical or military, indigenous or foreign. Government was stern as well as distant, harsh and unused to criticism. This was true even after the coming of the West—and even after democratic forms were introduced. Government by decree and ukase, by political power and threat of punishment, was the recognized pattern. In some colonial areas, like Indonesia and Indo-China, autocratic rule remained to the very end, despite the constitutional façade. In others, like British and American colonies, the beginnings of democratic practice were apparent in the decade or two before the transfer of power. But the crucial fact remained that democracy was a sharp break with tradition.

This is, perhaps, another way of saying that the peoples of Asia had limited experience of democracy. The middle class was familiar with its form and substance, though few had held positions of responsibility before independence. But to the peasantry both the ideas and the institutions of democracy were alien; their contact with government was limited to the district official and an occasional glimpse of a visiting dignitary. No less important, in this connexion, was the gap between the small Westernized élite, the carrier of the new idea, and the masses. Most nationalist leaders spoke a Western language, dressed in Western clothes and behaved like the foreigner. Indeed, they stood suspended between their own culture and that of the West; some, as Nehru remarked about himself, were 'a queer mixture of the East and the West, out of place everywhere, at home nowhere'. To the extent that they became Westernized, they became alien in their own societies. No wonder, then, that the masses looked askance at their political innovation—if they looked at all. In short, the bulk of the population were accustomed to autocracy; a minority considered democracy superior but had inadequate preparation in the art of constitutional government—two further reasons for the political crisis in the new states.

There were other disturbing legacies of the recent past. One was the upheaval of war and revolution, and the habit of violence formed during the years 1940–5; political armies date to the Japanese conquest, and states like Burma, Malaya, and Indonesia have paid a heavy price. But even more serious was the attitude to politics born of that tumultuous era, with the stress on force to achieve goals. This alone undermined the precarious stability of many successor states.

Another residue was the shortage of trained civil servants to fill the needs of welfare states. Only in India, Pakistan, Ceylon, the Philippines, and Malaya was an adequate 'steel frame' left by the departing colonial power. Elsewhere the new governments had to depend upon a handful of their own people and a host of unqualified political appointees. All this occurred against a background of rising expectations of material improvement, imposing even heavier burdens on state administration. With few exceptions the challenge was not met. Bureaucracies floundered amidst the enormous strain of transition, building a welfare state, planning the economy, and maintaining law and order in the face of dissension, rebellion, and violence. The outcome could not have been different in some Asian states, given the paucity of competent, relatively honest administrators. Even where a substantial body of civil servants were available, there was much friction with nationalist politicians, who identified them with the colonial régime.

More broadly conceived, it was the inadequacy of trained manpower in a host of spheres which made the creation of a stable order more difficult. These countries also suffered from the small size of the middle class. In the West this class has been the strongest proponent of political democracy, and this system has been successful only in countries with a substantial middle class (though some states so endowed are models of autocracy). But in the new states of Asia the urban population was relatively small, and the literate, aware, comfortable middle class tiny even in terms of these islands of progress surrounded by a sea of tradition-bound peasants. The fact that this class was apart from the mass and was Western in outlook only aggravated the problem of political innovation—the creation of a democratic system on the flimsy foundations of the colonial era.

The presence and quality of leadership has played a role in the quest for stability. Nehru survives and is deeply committed to democracy; he also helps to unify the myriad of groups and interests in Indian society. Pakistan was less fortunate. Jinnah died a year after independence, and Liaquat Ali was assassinated three years later; the resulting vacuum was not filled until 1958. In Burma, Aung San was removed from the scene even before the transfer, amidst turmoil and dissension. Other lands have been less favoured with outstanding men. And in still others, democracy has been expendable, as with Sukarno in Indonesia, or held in contempt, as with Ngo Dinh Diem in Indo-China.[1]

[1] See Brecher: *Nehru*, ch. i, xx; Hector Bolitho, *Jinnah: Creator of Pakistan*, London 1954; Hugh Tinker, 'Nu, The Serene Statesman', *Pacific Affairs*, XXX,

The presence of an efficient, popular, mass party has also influenced the degree of stability. In India the Congress played a vital role, supporting the new régime, educating the masses in the benefits of democracy, and linking the middle class of the cities with the peasantry. No other party in Asia was successful in these roles. Indeed, most political parties in the new states were ill-prepared for responsible self-government, let alone constitutional democracy. For one thing, they were movements not parties, i.e., they brought diverse, often conflicting, interest-groups under the umbrella of a 'national movement' struggling for independence. None succeeded in becoming truly homogeneous, not even the Indian National Congress—though it had compensating features enabling it to exercise power responsibly. These movements were held together by the common aim of independence, but few had a positive social and economic programme, certainly not the Muslim League in Pakistan, the United National Party in Ceylon, the Alliance in Malaya, or the Nationalist Party in Indonesia. And the AFPFL in Burma never freed itself of the heterogeneous character attending its birth in the midst of war.

Political parties also contributed to instability through their ignoble behaviour. Almost all 'national movements' ceased to aggregate and articulate interests after independence. Rather, they degenerated into factional strife and corruption. The lure of power overcame scruples. Politicians switched loyalties frequently. More important, they lost touch with the masses, with the result that the political 'game' became utterly divorced from society as a whole and devoid of content and meaning. Cabinets changed frequently, but the same men in different combinations reappeared. The club was very small and functioned in a vacuum. Only when elections were held was there any pretence of concern for real issues and the people's welfare. The frequency of political turnover, the glaring gap between politicians and people, the widespread corruption and nepotism—all these undermined respect for democracy or, indeed, for any government.

The new states of Asia have also been troubled with the problem of large and vocal minorities which undermine internal unity. They may be religious groups, such as the Hindus of East Pakistan or

June 1957, pp. 120–37; Leslie H. Palmier, 'Sukarno, the Nationalist', *Pacific Affairs*, XXX, June 1957, pp. 101–19; and Vera Micheles Dean, *Builders of Emerging Nations*, New York 1961, Part I, ch. 3.

Muslims and Sikhs in India. They may be ethnic or national in character, like the Tamils in Ceylon, the Indians in Burma and Malaya, or the Chinese all over South-East Asia. And they may be linguistic or cultural or regional units, such as the dozen non-Hindi language groups in India or the Karens, Kachins, and Chins in Burma. Whatever their distinctive trait, these minorities are often unassimilable and, at best, are sources of irritation and instability.

Reference has already been made to the lengthy Karen revolt in Burma—which delayed political stability for a decade. In Ceylon, the corrosive influence of the Tamil–Sinhalese clash was no less severe, and still threatens the very unity of the island. Here is a well-organized minority, related to a giant neighbour which feels a sense of responsibility for their welfare. Ceylon has sought a mass repatriation or withdrawal of recent immigrants to Ceylon from India. Delhi has steadfastly objected, as has the Tamil community itself. Since 1949, when a special discriminatory Ceylon citizenship bill was passed, until today, the tension has been high, frequently boiling over into violence, as in the riots of 1956, 1958, and 1960. The clash has rent the new state asunder, particularly as it became enmeshed with the question of language. Until it is resolved—or reduced to manageable proportions—the stability of Ceylon will be fragile and the political system combustible.

The abrupt, discriminatory action against Chinese traders in the Indonesian countryside in 1960 illustrates the precarious and resented economic role of that minority all over the region; it also suggests that some states will take advantage of exposed minorities for other ends. In Malaya the position of the Chinese is stronger, yet more corrosive. Indeed, it is the overwhelming Chinese community in Singapore which keeps the island colony apart from the Federation of Malaya. In more general terms, the Chinese minority in half a dozen states of the area is a challenge to political stability—made more difficult by the presence of a powerful and interested mainland Chinese régime.[1] In India, according to some observers, the presence of fourteen distinct language groups represents a major threat of political Balkanization in the coming decades.[2] Even if this speculation is alarmist, it remains true that the reorganization of the Indian States in 1956 unleashed disruptive forces and left deep scars among

[1] Victor Purcell, *The Chinese in Southeast Asia,* Cambridge 1951.
[2] Selig S. Harrison, *India: The Most Dangerous Decades,* Princeton 1960.

F

some minorities—witness the Sikh agitation to the present day. Viewed in terms of the quest for stability, these illustrations reveal local loyalties which transcend a 'national' identity. When to these are added tribal, caste, family, and communal attachments, often more purposeful than that to 'the nation', the problem of stability seems overwhelming.

Some of the obstacles to democracy in Asia were noted earlier. One of the more important is an apparent clash between its principle of tolerance and the aims of the new states. An active, free opposition is essential to democracy. But democracy is a slow and divisive technique of decision-making. To the Asian élites time is short, and the crucial need is a strong government to achieve unity and modernize their antiquated economies. The gap has seemed wider with the passage of time—and democracy has been a natural scapegoat for the slow pace of progress.

It remains to note the most common explanation—Asian states do not possess the classic conditions of democracy : a high level of literacy; a general level of prosperity well above subsistence; social homogeneity; a strong and large middle class; and a lengthy period of peace. These conditions have obtained in the established Western democracies. They are also to be found in some Western autocracies. It is also true that none is found in India, where democracy has most successfully been transplanted. All that may be said is that the presence of these conditions is likely to make democracy successful and that their absence, in whole or in part, increases the magnitude of the task. A more rigid correlation seems unwarranted at this stage of the political evolution of Asia—and the West.[1]

It was this complex of factors which led to the twin phenomena of recent Asian politics—the decline of democracy and the upsurge of army influence; the climax was reached in 1958. Stated succinctly, the military rode to power on the crest of a wave of despair—despair with civilian government in general and democracy in particular. Much had been promised by the nationalist politicians and relatively little had been achieved. The spectacle of corruption and inefficiency did not endear democracy to those who pondered the future, either the middle class or the army. But the latter had distinct assets.

The army was, in most of the new states, the only disciplined and organized group capable of ensuring stability and continuity. More-

[1] R. Emerson, 'The Erosion of Democracy', *Journal of Asian Studies*, XX, No. 1, November 1960, pp. 1-8.

over, it had a reservoir of educated men, in predominantly illiterate societies, men who were aware of the enormous problems on the road to a modern state. It was likely to be less corrupt than civilians in power. And it had an *élan* to move society and the economy. For many intellectuals in Asia the army became the saviour; some officers also saw their role in this light. In any event, the army has become a vital political force.[1]

Specific

Pakistan. All the sources of instability in the region as a whole—plus some peculiar to itself—were present in Pakistan. Indeed, here is an outstanding example of the political crisis in the new states of Asia, especially the decline and fall of democracy.

Poverty was intense in the 'Land of the Pure'—with an annual per capita income of about $60. The degree of illiteracy was awesome, upwards of 75 per cent. The middle class was small, comprising civil servants, members of the liberal professions, the officer corps, and the infant business community in the cities. Peasant antipathy to government was profound, the legacy of millennia of oppression; the British Raj did not alter this basic attitude. Autocracy was woven into the fabric of life; democracy seemed alien to all but a few. Moreover, the Muslims of the sub-continent were late in accepting Western education, so that even for the Muslim élite constitutional democracy was a novel system; the authoritarianism of Islam in politics did not make them more receptive. And though the British were the most advanced in preparing their subjects for self-government, few Muslims had adequate experience in this sphere.

The severity of the struggle for Pakistan placed a premium on 'unity, discipline, and faith'—in Jinnah's (and the Muslim League's) leadership. Indeed, for some years after independence, criticism of the League was termed treason by the Prime Minister. After independence, too, the attitude of negativism persisted in the political community, particularly among those out of power. The vacuum in leadership has already been noted. No one of stature followed Jinnah and Liaquat Ali Khan, with grave consequences: the 'national

---

[1] For a symapathetic view of the role of the officer corps in the New States, see Guy J. Pauker, 'Southeast Asia as a Problem Area in the Next Decade', *World Politics*, XI, No. 3, April 1959, pp. 325–45. See also H. Tinker, 'Climacteric in Asia', *International Journal*, XV, Winter 1959, pp. 14–24, and United States Foreign Policy, *Asia* (Conlon Report to Senate Foreign Relations Committee), 1959, pp. 31–36, 45–53, 55–62.

movement'—that is, the Muslim League—suffered irreparably, its decline beginning in the early fifties; the completion of a constitution was delayed, and friction between East and West Pakistan was exacerbated.

Pakistan did not fare better with her parties. None but the Muslim League had nation-wide influence; both the Awami League and the Krishak Sramik Party were East wing in origin and scope; the Republican Party, West wing. Most serious was the rot of corruption invading the Muslim League, ultimately poisoning the political system beyond cure. Nowhere in Asia was the spectacle of political degeneracy so evident to the public—politicians crossing the floor of the House for personal gain, factionalism run amok, the Head of State manipulating men and parties, even the killing of the Deputy Speaker of the East Pakistan Assembly. No wonder that few tears were shed when Ayub Khan cast the parties into oblivion in 1958.

Pakistan was also troubled by a large minority—the twelve million Hindus of East Bengal, who were difficult to assimilate in an 'Islamic state'. Moreover, they seemed to hold a balance-of-power position—between the Muslims of the two wings; the controversy over separate and joint electorates centred on Hindu electoral influence. They were also a source of tension between Pakistan and Hindu-majority India, a continuation of the communal discord that contributed much to Partition in 1947; the great migration of Hindus to West Bengal in 1950 and the continuous trickle thereafter (a total of three million have reportedly left East Pakistan) testify to the persistent discord arising from the presence of this minority. Finally, among the elements in the general formula, Pakistan suffered from the pitifully few experienced civil servants available at the time of independence. Most Muslims in the ICS opted for Pakistan, but there were no more than 100 in the middle or senior ranks. And this shortcoming was magnified many times over by the enormity of the burdens imposed on the state at its birth. It is also worth noting that the operative principle of tolerance in democracy is not shared by Islam in its attitude to unbelievers. And like all other new states of the region, Pakistan did not have the 'classic conditions of democracy'.

There were also special problems in Pakistan. Perhaps the foremost was geographical separation, with 1,100 miles of Indian territory between the two wings; physical contact is possible only by air across India or by the lengthy sea route around the southern tip of the sub-continent. The gap is accentuated by the fact that 54 per cent of the population live in East Pakistan, while the political élite, the army, industry, and the 'national movement' are centred in the West. Closely related was the friction between the two wings, arising out of the tendency of the 'Establishment' in Karachi to treat East Pakistan as a subordinate area. This was further aggravated by still another barrier, the ethnic differentiation of the people in the two wings. There are differences in language, customs, dress, diet, in fact in everything but the two pillars of Pakistan, a common faith, Islam, and fear of Indian (Hindu) domination. Among other effects of East–West tension was the nine-year delay in completing the new constitution, itself a continuing source of discord. One reason for the delay was the deep cleavage between secular and religious groups over the appropriate political system for a Muslim Pakistan; the rift was never healed.

From the outset, Pakistan was faced with major problems and herculean tasks: the absorption of six million refugees from India, mostly peasants and unskilled workers; the flight of six million Hindus and Sikhs, including the majority of professional men and skilled workers; the creation of an administration in Karachi, with few competent civil servants and no physical plant; the outbreak of war over Kashmir and prolonged tension with India; and the forging of a meaningful link between East and West—that is, the creation of one state out of two territories and one nation out of two peoples. Throughout its history, there have been strong centrifugal pulls, as regional, tribal, and familial loyalties were asserted. Indeed, in the light of this array of handicaps and problems, the wonder is not that Pakistan failed to establish a stable democracy but that it survived at all.[1]

Indonesia. The plight of the former Dutch Indies was no less severe than that of Pakistan—in poverty and illiteracy, in the traditions of autocracy and antipathy to government, in negativism, in party factionalism and corruption, in the paucity of trained administrators, and in other residues of the colonial era. There is no need for more elaborate recapitulation of these barriers to stability. It is rather with the few special factors that we are concerned. First is the widespread habit of violence, a much greater source of disorder in Indonesia than in Pakistan. Law and order, the first requisite of a

[1] See Charles Burton Marshall, 'Reflections on a Revolution in Pakistan', *Foreign Affairs*, 37, No. 2, January 1959, pp. 247–56, and the items in note 1, p. 52 above.

stable polity, has never been firmly established. But most important has been the attitude to political change bred by the absence of law and order and the military role in the winning of independence. The democratic process cannot easily flourish in this environment.

Indonesia has been favoured with individual leaders of stature, men like Achmed Sukarno, Mohammed Hatta, and Soetan Sjahrir, the outstanding socialist intellectual. Yet, these and others have not performed the vital roles of Nehru in India or Jinnah and Liaquat Ali for a few years in Pakistan. Sjahrir's influence waned with the decline of his party. Hatta broke with Sukarno. And the President himself, for all his fiery talk and dynamic personality, has not been an unmixed blessing.

Symbol of unity and nationalism, Sukarno has alienated many in the 'outer islands' by excessive centralization. He has interfered constantly in the parliamentary process, making and breaking cabinets. He has shown himself more interested in prestige abroad than the solution of grave problems at home; indeed, more concerned with words than deeds. Certainly he undermined the democratic experiment by an authoritarian bent—and later destroyed the constitutional order. Nor has he encouraged or permitted the rise of younger men to leadership.

Perhaps the gravest cause of instability in Indonesia has been the clash between the forces of centralization (Java) and those of genuine federalism (many of the 'outer islands'). This has sparked the four major rebellions, each further weakening the respect for democracy and stability of any kind. They also caused serious economic dislocation, aggravated the friction between Sukarno and Hatta, and brought the army and its leaders to prominence, notably General Nasution. Poor communications within each island and between them has accentuated the 'natural' tendency to throw off central control and impede unification. The fissiparous tendencies have been strengthened by powerful regional loyalties, some overriding a sense of 'Indonesian' identity, and by a corresponding desire for autonomy, for a greater freedom from Javanese control. Such aspirations have not met with respect from Sukarno and his followers. The political order itself suffered from a multiplicity of parties or, more precisely, the lack of one party with a clear majority. The necessity for coalition governments and the widespread corruption of politicians led to declining prestige for the whole democratic process. One should also mention the clash between the religious and secular forces, represented by the Masjumi and the Nationalists–Communists respectively; though not as serious as in Pakistan, it was a corrosive factor. Taken together with the long-term components, these factors provide insight into the crisis which led to the abandonment of democracy.[1]

Burma. The reasons for instability in Burma are not essentially different from those applying to Pakistan and Indonesia; the basic, enduring elements are noticeable there too. Especially noteworthy is the habit of violence. Not only did it decapitate the AFPFL leadership just before independence; it was also evident in the plethora of rebellions, political and ethnic, from 1948 to 1957. The presence of substantial minorities, not easily assimilable, has made the road to stability even more arduous; the one million Karens were extraordinarily influential in this respect. The assassination of six leaders was a grievous blow. The political élite has never been large. And U Nu, gentle and devout Buddhist though he may be, lacked the forceful quality of Aung San, so necessary during widespread revolt. Nor did Burma have sufficient qualified civil servants, whose task was made more onerous by the physical destruction of the early years.

The AFPFL had a monopoly of political power for a decade. Considering the magnitude of the challenge, its record was not unimpressive. Over the years, however, corruption and factionalism reached alarming proportions, as noted earlier. With them came declining respect for parties and the democratic process, culminating in the 'fall from democratic grace', first in 1958 and more ominously in 1962. Traditional politics have fallen into disrepute.[2]

THE WAY OUT

The year 1958 was a turning point in modern Asian history, the climax to the years of political crisis in the new states. Stated in different terms, it was the year of retreat from democracy and the rise of the military to power—in Pakistan and Burma, with Indonesia and Ceylon perched at the brink. These twin developments should not occasion surprise, in the light of the foregoing analysis. Indeed, they were part of a sweeping process embracing the Middle East, Africa, Asia, and even part of Western Europe; in half a year generals took control of the governments of seven countries—Iraq and Lebanon, the Sudan, Pakistan, Burma and Thailand, and

[1] Cf. the sources in note 2, p. 54 above.   [2] Cf. the sources in note 1, p. 56 above.

France; by the end of 1958, they headed sixteen governments in the non-communist world. What is striking is the effort being made to find a way out of the crisis, the experiments with new techniques to fill the gap between Western political forms and the Asian milieu.

Various Asian leaders spoke out boldly in criticism of Western democracy—Sukarno of Indonesia, Ayub Khan of Pakistan, Bandaranaike of Ceylon, and Narayan of India. The common theme was its alien character or, to use Sukarno's mystical phrase, 'not in harmony with the soul of the Indonesian nation'. All decried the party bickering and dissension and saw the parliamentary process as the basic cause of an instability verging on disintegration. Yet all felt the need to retain the spirit of 'democracy', perhaps because this gave the sanction of respectability to their deviations from the pure model; hence the formal link—Sukarno's 'Guided Democracy', Ayub Khan's 'Basic Democracy', Bandaranaike's 'substance of democracy', and Narayan's 'partyless democracy'. No wonder that people everywhere are confused as to the meaning of this political concept.

All who sought an alternative to Anglo-American democracy would probably share Ayub Khan's direct, soldierly formulation of the way out:[1]

Pakistan must have democracy. The question then is: what type of democracy? The answer need not be sought in the theories and practices of other people alone. On the contrary, it must be found from within the book of Pakistan itself.

To my mind, there are four prerequisites for the success of any democratic system in a country like Pakistan: (1) It should be simple to understand, easy to work and cheap to sustain. (2) It should put to the voter only such questions as he can answer in the light of his own personal knowledge and understanding, without external prompting. (3) It should ensure the effective participation of all citizens in the affairs of the country up to the level of their mental horizon and intellectual calibre. (4) It should be able to produce reasonably strong and stable governments.

Such was the rationale behind 'Basic Democracy', the most impressive political innovation in the new states of Asia.[2]

[1] In *Foreign Affairs*, 38, No. 4, July 1960, as quoted in *Pakistan News Digest*, Karachi, 1 July 1960.

[2] See Harry J. Friedman, 'Pakistan's Experiment in Basic Democracies', *Pacific Affairs*, XXXIII, June 1960, pp. 107–25, and 'Notes on Pakistan's Basic Democracies', *Asian Survey*, I, No. 10, December 1961, pp. 19–24; also Khalid bin Sayeed, 'Pakistan's Basic Democracy', *Middle East Journal*, XV, Summer 1961, pp. 249–63.

In essence, 'Basic Democracy' is a system of local government with a mixture of elected and appointed representatives. There is a heavy reliance on civil servants for leadership and a marked similarity with local government forms during the last half-century of British rule. A five-tiered structure was created by the Basic Democracies Order 1959, promulgated on the first anniversary of the military seizure of power. Both East and West Pakistan would have a hierarchy of Councils, as follows:

	Percentage elected
Development Advisory Council	$16\frac{2}{3}$
Divisional Council	25
District Council	25
Tahsil or Thana Council	50
Union Council	$66\frac{2}{3}$

This sliding scale of electees, all indirectly elected at the higher levels, is in accord with Ayub's view that a political system must be so structured in highly illiterate societies as to be close to the common man, who understands local issues and knows local candidates, and is therefore qualified to elect representatives to local bodies only.

The Union Council is the most important organ in the system. There are about 8,000 in the entire country, each serving a group of villages with a combined population of approximately 10,000. Each Union Council has an average of ten elected members. In addition, a number no more than half as many as the elected members is appointed by the district officer, to ensure adequate representation of all interests. The typical Union Council, then, consists of ten elected and five appointed members; these elect the Chairman of the Council. Town and Union Committees in urban areas are constituted in the same way. The term of office is five years, but members may be removed for misconduct or excessive absence, appointees by the district officer, and electees by a majority of the next higher Council. Funds are limited but may be raised by a special tax on adult males for public works; the bulk is provided by the provincial government.

The functions of the Union Councils are theoretically wide. They may supervise village police, assist government revenue officers, and exercise responsibility for agriculture, industry, and community development; the last is the most important, to be co-ordinated with

Development Advisory Committees. Control over the Union Councils is vested in the 'Controlling Authority', i.e., the Deputy Commissioner. He may countermand any action, suspend the execution of any resolution, or require the Council to do his bidding; he may also take any action outside the Council to achieve the ends of the Order. Indeed, these powers of overseer are remarkably similar to those of the Viceroy and the Governors in the 1935 Government of India Act. The intent is to prevent demagogic control of the Councils, but the provisions give great power to the civil servants.

The next higher body, the Tahsil Council, called the Thana Council in East Pakistan, consists of all chairmen of Union Councils and Town Committees and an equal number appointed by the district officer; thus, half the members are indirect electees; the chairman, *ex officio*, is the tahsil or thana officer. This body has only two functions, neither initiating—to co-ordinate the activities of the lower organs and to implement the decisions of the District Council.

The District Council is composed of the chairmen of the Tahsil Councils, chairmen of municipal bodies, Vice-Presidents of cantonment boards, and representatives of government departments in the area, i.e., official members, and an equal number appointed by the Commissioner; half the latter must be chairmen of Union Councils; thus, one fourth of the membership are indirect electees. The functions of the District Council are both compulsory and optional. In the former category are the provision and maintenance of schools, libraries, and hospitals, and responsibility for agriculture and community development. This body is also expected to co-ordinate the activities of all Councils in the district.

Next in the hierarchy is the Divisional Council, consisting of chairmen of District Councils, representatives of government departments, cities and cantonment boards (50 per cent of the total), and appointees, of whom half must be chairmen of Union Councils; here, too, 25 per cent are indirect electees; the chairman is the Commissioner. This is primarily a co-ordinating agency, but it may also review activities and make recommendations regarding development to the capstone of the structure, the Development Advisory Councils. On this highest body are heads of government departments in the province (50 per cent of the total) and appointees of the President, of whom one third are chairmen of Union Councils; indirect electees are, then, only one sixth of the total. Its functions are purely advisory, the supreme counsel for the Governor in the developmental field.

A formal link between 'Basic Democracy' and economic development has been forged. Village AID (Agricultural and Industrial Development) has become the National Development Organization (NDO), and its chain of command now coincides with the areas covered by the various Councils. The two can now work hand-in-hand to generate enthusiasm in nation-building activities—one of the prime motives of 'Basic Democracy'.

The first elections to the Union Councils took place in December–January 1959–60. Expenditure of candidates was limited to Rs. 200 ($40). Discussion was confined to the quality of candidates, each of whom ran on an 'individual ticket'. No candidate was allowed to criticize the system of 'Basic Democracy', foreign policy, religious issues, or regional discontents. The contests were mild in tone. Many candidates withdrew, a substantial number being elected by acclamation. Perhaps 50 per cent of the electors cast their ballot; some 80,000 'Basic Democrats' were elected to 8,000 Councils. In mid-February 1960 a referendum was held among the 'Basic Democrats' on the question, 'Do you have confidence in President Ayub Khan?' The result was a foregone certainty.

A few days later a Constitution Commission was formed, with clearly defined terms of reference—a guide to Ayub's political thought: to take account of the genius of the people, the general standard of education and political judgement, the need of sustained development and the effect of recent changes; and to submit constitutional proposals to achieve a democracy adaptable to the changed circumstances and based on the Islamic principles of justice, equality, and tolerance, the consolidation of national unity, and a firm and stable system of government. The Commission reported in May 1961, and the new Constitution was promulgated in March 1962.

Suffice it to note some of the salient features.[1] The tone is highly authoritarian, with a pronounced Gaullist influence. Indeed, the most apt term to describe the new political system of Pakistan is 'Presidentialism' or 'Presidential Democracy'. All executive authority, including broad ordinance and emergency powers, is vested in the President of the Republic who is elected (indirectly) for

[1] See *The Constitution of the Republic of Pakistan*, Government of Pakistan Press, Karachi 1962.

a five-year term by an Electoral College of 80,000, equally divided
between the two wings—an extension of the principle of 'Basic
Democracy'. He has vast appointive powers—judges, army commanders, the Attorney-General, the Auditor-General, provincial
Governors, members of the Advisory Council of Islamic Ideology,
etc.; moreover, all military and civil servants hold office during his
'pleasure'. A similar, wide-ranging power vests in his provincial
counterpart and appointee, the Governor, who doubles as *de facto*
Chief Minister. The President is responsible only to the Electoral
College. He may, but need not, appoint a cabinet of advisers. Nor
is there judicial review of executive action or legislation.

To these powers of the President are added a significant role in the
legislative process. The Constitution provides for a unicameral
National Assembly (150 members divided equally between East and
West wings and six seats reserved for women) and two provincial
assemblies (155 seats each, of which five are reserved for women).
These assemblies have the authority to frame and pass Bills. The
President may withhold assent and re-submit the Bill. The Assembly
can overcome his veto by a two-thirds majority—of total members;
and he, in turn, has the authority to refer the Bill to a referendum
by the Electoral College. In short, it will be virtually impossible to
enact a Bill without the President's support. In the vital sphere of
Finance, the President's power is even more striking. All money bills
require his recommendation. The Assembly may discuss the annual
budget, submitted by the President, but may grant or deny funds
only for proposed *new* expenditures; all recurring expenditures and
those charged on the Central Consolidated Fund are beyond its
control. This is truly Ayub Khan's constitution—in form and substance. As the preamble notes, '. . . I, Field Marshal Ayub Khan . . .
do hereby enact this Constitution.'

During the first year of the new political system, politics centred
upon four controversial aspects of the Ayub Constitution: the ban
on political parties; restricted franchise for the Presidency and
Assemblies; non-justiciability of fundamental rights; and limited
financial powers of the legislatures. (All, ironically, were deviations
from the recommendations of the Constitution Commission.) The
President has yielded to pressure on almost all points. Thus the ban
on parties was removed in July 1962, and within a few months sterile
party politics had been resumed. Similarly, a Franchise Commission
was given wide-ranging authority to recommend changes in the en-

tire electoral system. And in the spring of 1963, fundamental rights were made justiciable, by a constitutional amendment. Yet 'Presidential Democracy' is still in force.

Of 'Basic Democracy' proper a few themes have become evident. The Union Council is the key body, but it is too much under the domination of civil servants and has not attracted the most talented members of the community. The District Magistrate and Commissioner possess vast powers under the scheme which tend to throttle whatever democratic tendencies exist. The scheme has potentialities for economic development, effective, grass-roots local government, and even social progress—but it is *not* democracy. There is little popular control over the Councils and none over the government; as compensation, it is more rooted in tradition and is simple to manage, two important assets for Asians seeking alternative political systems to Western democracy. Already, the King of Nepal has declared his intention to introduce a form of 'Basic Democracy' into his backward land. General Pak Chung Hi, military dictator of South Korea, also pledged a Pakistan style 'Guided Democracy'. And Jaya Prakash Narayan, former Indian Socialist leader and a possible successor to Nehru, has expressed admiration for the Pakistani experiment. Others may follow suit.

An alternative path to stability is being followed by China—a 'People's Democracy' or 'New Democracy', to use Mao Tse-tung's phrase.[1] In reality, this is a Soviet-style Communist dictatorship, with a parallel pyramid of state and party authority and a fusion of personnel and functions at the top. This is perhaps best portrayed in tabular form:

Party Apparatus	*Government Organization*	
Party Chairman	Chairman of the Chinese People's Republic	
Politbureau and its Standing Committee	Supreme State Conference	
Central Committee	State Council (Cabinet)	Standing Committee of National People's Congress
National Party Congress	National People's Congress	

[1] *On New Democracy* (1940), in *Selected Works of Mao Tse-tung*, London 1954, Vol. 3, pp. 106–56.

Until 1959 Mao held all the key positions—Chairman of the Party, the Politbureau and its Standing Committee, the Central Committee, and the National Party Congress; he was also Chairman of the Republic, the Supreme State Conference, and the National People's Congress. His state posts have been taken over by Liu Shao ch'i, but decision-making remains concentrated in the Big Five of Chinese Communism—Mao Tse-tung, Liu Shao ch'i, Chou En-lai, Chu Teh, and Ch'en Yün. All five are members of the Standing Committee of the Politbureau and the Supreme State Conference; Mao retains his party leadership, Liu the governmental posts; Chou En-lai is head of the State Council, and Chu Teh is Chairman of the Standing Committee of the People's Congress or Parliament; Ch'en Yün is in charge of economic planning.

As in the Soviet Union, parliament is a rubber-stamp body; so too is the Party Congress. Elections to both bodies are empty ritual. And the political process is an intra-party phenomenon, governed by the principle of democratic centralism. Authoritarian direction from higher bodies, ultimately the inner élite, is the manner of decision-making on all matters of public, and often private, concern. The judiciary is simply another arm of the party. Individual freedom exists, if at all, only at the whim of the party.[1] Indeed, this curtailment reached its peak in the one innovation of 'New Democracy', the 'People's Communes'.[2]

This institution may be viewed in two settings—as the final stage in the programme of total collectivization of agriculture or as an outgrowth of changes in economic and administrative organization;

[1] The most objective study of Communist China's governmental structure is S. B. Thomas, *Government and Administration in Communist China* (2nd rev. ed.), New York 1955.

See also Chao Kuo-Chun: 'The National Constitution of Communist China', *Far Eastern Survey*, XXIII, October 1954, pp. 145–51; also 'Leadership in the Chinese Communist Party' in Howard L. Boorman (ed.), 'Contemporary China and the Chinese', *The Annals*, Philadelphia, January 1959, pp. 40–50; Harold C. Hinton, 'China' in Kahin (ed), *Major Governments of Asia*, pp. 52–96; H. Arthur Steiner, 'Ideology and Politics in Communist China', in Boorman, op. cit., pp. 29–39; and Chang Yu-nan, 'The Chinese Communist State System under the Constitution of 1954', *Journal of Politics*, August 1956, pp. 520–46.

[2] See G. F. Hudson, A. V. Sherman, and A. Zauberman, *The Chinese Communes*, London 1960; Audrey Donnithorne, 'Background to the People's Communes: Changes in China's Economic Organization in 1958', *Pacific Affairs*, XXXII, December 1959, pp. 339–53; D. E. T. Luard, 'The Urban Communes', *The China Quarterly*, No. 3, July-September 1960, pp. 74–79; Roderick MacFarquhar, 'Communist China's Intra-Party Dispute', *Pacific Affairs*, XXXI, December 1958, pp. 323–35.

either analysis would be accurate; both elements were involved. Commune-ization began in the summer of 1958, and by the end of that year it embraced all of rural China, some 26,000 communes for 500 million peasants. At the outset, the degree of 'deprivatization' was oppressive—even to observers from other communist lands; from dawn to dusk, and even beyond, life was rigidly regulated; nurseries for children, community mess halls and barracks only accentuated the loss of individuality. Later, this process was reversed and the powers of the commune were considerably reduced. By 1961 the commune fervour appeared to have vanished, as did the commune itself in its original monastic form.

The commune was a multi-purpose unit, really a fourfold entity—economic, political, military, and social. In area, it was equated with the traditional *hsiang* or district, with an average of 20,000 persons, though some had as many as 50,000. Each commune comprised about twelve former 'higher agricultural co-operatives', i.e., collectives; these were now Production Brigades; they, in turn, were divided into Production Teams of a dozen families each.

The commune was a complete, self-sufficient economic unit, with trade and credit organs, tax powers and production quotas. It was also a military category, a division in the nation's militia, with compulsory military training for all adults. The governing body was an 'elected' Administrative Council, dominated unobtrusively by Communist Party members. Its functions were all-pervasive, to control economic, educational, and military aspects of life within the commune. At first control was highly centralized, but experience led to gradual devolution of authority. By comparison with the traditional collective, the commune was much larger in area and population, broader in scope and more rigid in control. The attempt was to create a self-sufficient rural city, somewhat like the Soviet experimental Agrotown. The result was hailed by the Chinese as a 'leap forward' to the ideal society, condemned by anti-communists as an 'ant-heap', and criticized by other communists, notably Soviet leaders, as impractical. In the context of the quest for stability, the commune offered an alternative road to the ideologically uncommitted states of South and South-East Asia, especially in 1959 when Peking made grandiose claims of economic progress during the first year of the commune. When these figures were drastically downgraded, the attraction of the commune—and the political system of which it is a dramatic symbol—declined among the onlookers in the region.[1]

Amidst the experiments with 'Basic Democracy', 'Guided Democracy', and 'New Democracy', a few Asian states persisted in the effort to apply and adapt the original, Western form of democracy. India is the outstanding example, a model of this system, as Pakistan and China are of the competing types. An analysis of the system as it works in India is therefore appropriate here.

There are stable states in Asia that are not democratic, such as Communist China. Others are constitutional but not democratic, such as Pakistan. Still others are democratic but not stable, such as Ceylon. India is stable, democratic, and constitutional—a rare combination among the new Asian states. Stability is evident in the high level of law and order, despite frequent police firings and the one notable deviation, the Telengana (Hyderabad) rebellion, of 1948–50, led by the Communist Party of India. The State governments are well established; with the exception of Kerala in 1959, they have not been subject to over-turn by violence or *coup d' état*. Certainly there has not been anything comparable to the Pakistan and Burma military *coups* of 1958 and 1962 or the Sinhalese-Tamil riots of 1956, 1958, and 1960 which almost shattered the constitutional system in Ceylon. On the whole, the Union and State governments of India have been treated with respect. The civil service has been relatively efficient and has been recruited through a public service commission and merit system. The evidence of the last fifteen years suggests that, despite considerable corruption, now under impartial scrutiny, the Services have succeeded very well in the new tasks that have been imposed upon them.

The election experience reveals the nature and magnitude of the constitutional experiment in India. There were, respectively, 173 million voters, 193 million and 210 million in the three general elections of 1951–2, 1957 and 1962. No less than 3,800 seats were contested by 17,000 candidates in the first general election. Eighty per cent of the voters were illiterate in 1952, and only a slightly lower

[1] See Cheng Chu-yuan, 'The Changing Pattern of Rural Communes in Communist China', *Asian Survey*, I, No. 9, November 1961, pp. 3–9; Harold C. Hinton, 'Intra-Party Politics and Economic Policy in Communist China', *World Politics*, XII, No. 4, July 1960, pp. 509–24; Theodore Shabad, 'China's Year of the "Great Leap Forward" ', *Far Eastern Survey*, XXVIII, June 1959, pp. 89–96, and July 1959, pp. 105–9, and 'China's "Leap Forward" Reconsidered', ibid., October 1959, pp. 156–8.

percentage a decade later. Elections were conducted by an independent Election Commission. There were few electoral offences. The opposition was fairly treated. Over 50 per cent of the electorate voted in all three general elections, over 80 per cent in the Kerala state elections. An active interest was evident in rural as well as urban areas.

The results strongly support the thesis that India is a functioning constitutional democracy. The Congress won an overwhelming majority of seats in all three general elections and in almost all the state contests. But the opposition parties won more than half of the total votes cast in the three general elections. The Communist Party increased its seats in the Union Parliament from 16 to 29 in a decade, the Jan Sangh from 3 to 14. There was also a fluctuation in Congress seats, for example, sharp losses in 1957 following States Reorganization, and gains in 1962. A new Right-wing party, *Swatantra* (Freedom), was able to break into the electoral arena in 1962 and become the third largest in parliament. All this is evidence of fair elections and discriminating voters.

Parliament, too, has shown a capacity to sustain itself in conditions which were by no means ideal and to perform the functions of a western-type legislature. It has provided channels for the ventilation of grievances by opposition groups and for the expression of aspirations on the part of diverse segments of Indian society. It has served as a continuous forum for great debates on public policy. It has sustained and controlled the executive to a large extent and it has performed a vital role in educating public opinion to look favourably on the parliamentary process. There have been serious weaknesses, such as relatively small opposition contingents in the House, the lack of sufficient training among most parliamentarians, and an uncertain role for the Upper House. Judged over a period of fifteen years, however, parliament has gradually come to be accepted as an essential, though not yet the central, institution in the political system of India.

Civil liberties are amply provided for in Part III of the Constitution. There is reference to equality before the law; the prohibition of discrimination on grounds of religion, race, sex, or caste; an historic provision for the abolition of untouchability; equal opportunity in the public service; freedom of speech and expression; freedom of association; the right to hold property; the right to form unions; freedom of religion; protection of the interests of minorities, etc.

G

Practice reveals, on the whole, a positive record, certainly with respect to free assembly, freedom of religion, and a free press. There have been genuine and persistent efforts to protect minorities, not always successful. Untouchability remains, though not for want of official attempts to eradicate the evil. In the realm of civil liberties proper, there are perhaps two weaknesses. One relates to private property, as enshrined in Article 31 of the Constitution; the other, preventive detention. Two laws providing for the abolition of Zamindari land holdings in Uttar Pradesh and Bihar were challenged in the courts and were declared *ultra vires*. This led to the First Amendment Act of 1951 which clarified Article 31 to the effect that no law regarding the acquisition of property by the State could be declared null and void on the ground of inconsistency with Article 31. Those who were adversely affected then challenged the amount of compensation that had been fixed and were sustained once more by the courts. That led to the Fourth Amendment Act in 1955 which declared that the question of reasonableness of compensation was not justiciable. In other words, it was to be determined by parliament. To some this seemed a dangerous attack on the right of private property. To those who were imbued with the idea of a 'socialist pattern of society' it seemed a necessary and progressive act.

The real blemish in the realm of civil liberties is preventive detention. Article 22 of the Indian Constitution of 1950 authorized the Union and State Governments to detain persons who were suspected of being a threat to the peace, stability, or security of India. The first Preventive Detention Act was passed under the impact of the Telengana Rebellion in central India. It was renewed in 1951 for one year, in 1952 for two years, and then, in succession, from 1954 onwards, for three-year periods. It has now become a seemingly permanent part of the fabric of law and order in India. In essence, a person may be detained up to one year if the government 'is satisfied' that he is likely to engage in behaviour prejudicial to 'the defence of India, the relations of India with foreign powers, the security of India, the security of the State, the maintenance of public order, or the maintenance of essential services and supplies to the community'. Thus, a person may be detained for almost any reason if the government deems it necessary and proper. There are, of course, safeguards. The detainee must be informed of the grounds of detention within five days, the Union and State Governments must also be informed, and the case come before an Advisory Board of three persons of High

Court qualifications appointed by the Union Government. If this Board rules in favour of the detainee, he is released. It is also true that the record of preventive detention does not suggest vindictiveness. In 1950 there were almost 11,000 detainees because of the rebellion in Hyderabad. This was reduced to 2,300 by 1951, and to 325 three years later. In the late 1950s it hovered around 175, and on the eve of the emergency with China fewer than 100. Nevertheless, persons are being detained without recourse to normal legal process. For this reason it must be regarded as a blemish on an otherwise enviable record.

A critical experiment, now in process, is the decentralization of government and administration, or *Panchayati Raj*, 'rule by the [local] Councils'. This attempt to bring democracy to the village, noted in Article 40 of the Constitution as one of the Directive Principles of State Policy, was a dead letter until 1959. During the past few years, however, various States have enacted legislation, providing for the devolution of administrative authority in a wide range of subjects to local councils on three levels, the Village (*Gram*) *Panchayat*, the *Panchayat Samiti* at the sub-district or development block level, and finally, as the capstone of the structure, the *Zilla Parishad* at the district level. These have tended to take over the responsibilities which were borne by the District Boards from the 1880s onwards. It is too early to say whether this process of democratic decentralization will be effective but it represents a major effort to induce mass participation in public affairs, India's counterpart to 'Basic Democracy' in the countryside. The real intent is to galvanize the rural masses into active involvement in economic planning and community development and thereby to forge a closer link between Village and Town. The goal is to bring *Panchayati Raj* to all of rural India within five years, though the conflict with China will probably delay its realization.

There have been shortcomings in the political realm. Preventive detention has already been noted. The most striking weakness of the Indian political system, however, is the absence of a strong democratic opposition party. The gap is very large indeed. As a result of the 1962 general elections, the Congress has 353 seats in the *Lok Sabha* (House of the People). The next largest group—the Communist Party—has 29, the Swatantra 18, the Jan Sangh 14, and the Praja Socialists 12. Even in the States there is no prospect of an opposition party forming an alternative government in the near future, with one exception, the Communist Party in Kerala. The Praja Socialists have declined steadily for a variety of reasons—the lack of united leadership, particularly since the departure of Jaya Prakash Narayan to the *Bhoodan* (land gift) Movement of Vinoba Bhave, a shortage of funds, lack of organizational talent, and the lack of a distinctive programme. The Swatantra has some strength in three states: Rajasthan, Bihar, and Gujarat—but nowhere did they poll more than 25 per cent of the vote. The alternatives to the Congress, then, are the Communist Party of India on the extreme Left and Hindu Communalism. In that sense the durability of the Indian constitutional experiment has not really been tested.

The second major shortcoming is the resort to non-constitutional methods of political action. There was massive civil disobedience in Kerala in 1959. Non-coöperation and fasting in Andhra in 1952 was another illustration. The agitation of the Sikhs in the Punjab since 1959 is a third. The 1960 language riots in Assam between Bengali- and Assamese-speaking people was still another. And the Bhoodan movement challenges the system of constitutional democracy because it postulates a mass, direct-action approach to political decision which, while within the Indian political tradition, undermines a Western-type constitutional order.

Another weakness is persistence of provincialism and linguism, that is to say, the tendency of persons to identify themselves with a linguistic-cultural region at the expense of the nation. The drama of States Reorganization provided many illustrations of this danger to national unity. There was the struggle between Bengal and Bihar in 1956 over a Bengali-speaking economically-important area which hitherto had been part of Bihar. The squabble between Maharashtrian and Gujarati in former Bombay State, especially the riots in Bombay City, revealed the intensity of provincialism. Most important, perhaps, has been the continuous clash between Hindi-speaking and non-Hindi-speaking peoples in India. The Indian Constitution provided that after fifteen years (1965) English would be replaced by Hindi as the official language of the Union. But with the passage of time it became apparent that Hindi was not yet equipped to serve this purpose. It became even more apparent that the 60 per cent of the population that does not speak Hindi and does not want to speak Hindi was not prepared to accept an abrupt transfer from English to Hindi as the official language with all that this would entail in terms of disruptive administration, discrimination in the public

services, etc. A compromise was finally reached, with English remaining as the associate official language of India for at least another
decade. But this continues to be a source of major discord between
North and South India.

The widespread collapse of democracy in the new states is not
surprising. In fact, the only surprise is that it has succeeded at all.
The quest for stability remains unfulfilled, with the three competing
systems now showing their wares throughout South and South-East
Asia—Democracy, 'Basic (or Guided) Democracy', and 'New
Democracy'. The outcome of this competition will have consequences far beyond that region and its peoples.

3

A NEW SUBORDINATE
STATE SYSTEM

'ASIAN STUDIES' have long since ventured beyond the traditional limits of Orientalia to embrace History and the Social Sciences; they have not as yet, however, applied the insights of International Relations to an area framework. Similarly, International Relations specialists have all but ignored the relevance of their discipline to Asia.[1] The purpose of this chapter is to help bridge the serious gap between these two fields.

Until a few years ago the sole level of analysis in the sphere of international relations was the nation-state. Almost all texts adopted this approach,[2] and many included surveys of the foreign policy of selected states.[3] One reason was the relative abundance of data on the state actors. Another was the lack of effective supra-state authority to ensure orderly relations among them, thereby accentuating their individual role.

The unit or actor focus is not without great merit. It can provide studies in depth of state behaviour that are essential to a comparative analysis of foreign policy.[4] It encourages the gathering of data useful for the study of decision-making, motives, and élite images of the external world. And it permits an inquiry into the

[1] Whether or not International Relations is an autonomous discipline, an emerging discipline, or simply a branch of Political Science, is still subject to sharp controversy. See C. A. W. Manning, *The University Teaching of Social Sciences—International Relations* (Paris 1954); P. D. Marchant, 'Theory and Practice in the Study of International Relations', *International Relations*, I (April 1955), pp. 95–102, and Charles A. McLelland, 'Systems and History in International Relations; Some Perspectives for Empirical Research and Theory', *General Systems: Yearbook of the Society for General Systems Research*, 3 (1958), pp. 221–47 (these two articles are reprinted in whole or in part in James N. Rosenau (ed.), *International Politics and Foreign Policy* (New York 1961), pp. 18–23 and 24–35 respectively); and Morton A. Kaplan, 'Is International Relations A Discipline?', *Journal of Politics*, 23 (August 1961), pp. 462–76.

[2] A notable partial exception is Hans J. Morgenthau, *Politics among Nations; the Struggle for Power and Peace,* 3rd ed. (New York 1960).

[3] See, for example, Frederick L. Schuman, *International Politics: the Western State System and the World Community,* 6th ed. (New York 1958).

[4] A preliminary effort in this direction, not entirely satisfactory, is Roy C. Macridis (ed.), *Foreign Policy in World Politics,* 2nd ed. (Englewood Cliffs, N. J. 1962).

content of 'national interest'.[1] This focus micro-analysis, will probably continue to be the most widely used because 'as things stand today—and are likely to remain for an indefinite period—there can be no serious doubt about the paramount position of the nation-state or about the superiority of its influence and power'.[2] Yet new macro-perspectives have emerged.

Some of the ablest minds in the field of international relations have set out on 'the long road to theory', as part of the general search for a science of politics.[3] Their most suggestive innovation, creating a new level of analysis, is the concept of 'International System'. As so often in the past, the more rigorous models of economic theory have provided both a challenge and an assumed analogy. Since an international economic system exists apart from the national economic systems within it, there must also be an international political system related to, but distinct from, the political systems of nation-states; such is a rationale of the new approach.[4]

The body of literature is already impressive and the range of method striking. At one extreme is the pure theory of Morton Kaplan who postulates six types of system—'balance of power', loose bipolar, tight bipolar, universal, hierarchical, and unit veto; only the first two have historical counterparts and 'essential rules', but all are

---

[1] This has long been concealed by the exponents of metaphysical realism. See Hans J. Morgenthau, *In Defense of the National Interest* (New York 1951).

[2] Arnold Wolfers, 'The Actors in International Politics' in William T. R. Fox (ed.), *Theoretical Aspects of International Relations* (Notre Dame 1959), p. 101. For dissenting views on this point, see Edward Hallett Carr, *Nationalism and After* (London 1945), esp. pp. 53 ff., and John H. Herz, *International Politics in the Atomic Age* (New York 1959), Part 1, esp. pp. 96 ff.

[3] The rapidly-growing interest in theory and method is well reflected in five recent collections of papers and one volume: Fox, op. cit.; Stanley H. Hoffmann (ed.), *Contemporary Theory in International Relations* (Englewood Cliffs, N.J. 1960); 'The Place of Theory in the Conduct and Study of International Relations', special issue of *The Journal of Conflict Resolution*, IV (September 1960); Rosenau, op. cit.; Klaus Knorr and Sydney Verba (eds.), 'The International System', special issue of *World Politics*, XIV (October 1961); and Quincy Wright, *The Study of International Relations* (New York 1955).

Among the notable illustrations of model-building in International Relations are Morton A. Kaplan, *System and Process in International Politics* (New York 1957) and George Liska, *International Equilibrium* (Cambridge, Mass. 1957). For a critique of 'scientism' in American political science, see Bernard Crick, *The American Science of Politics: its Origins and Conditions* (London 1959).

[4] See Fred A. Sondermann, 'The Linkage between Foreign Policy and International Politics', in Rosenau, op. cit., p. 10. A notable earlier example of the use of economics concepts for the analysis of international politics is the 'developmental' and 'equilibrium' concepts in Harold D. Lasswell, *World Politics and Personal Insecurity* (New York 1935), ch. 1.

logically plausible.[1] At the other extreme is the inductive method of Stanley Hoffmann based on 'systematic historical research' or a comparative historical sociology.[2] Others concentrate on the contemporary international system, the most stimulating model being that of John Herz in *International Politics in the Atomic Age*.[3]

The basic features of this contemporary system, as viewed by Herz and others, may be noted briefly. First is its universality, its geographic expansion to global terms with the coming of independence to Asia and Africa; the state membership has more than doubled in fifteen years. Second is the continued absence of law and order within the system and a fragmentation of power; this is in sharp contrast with the authority pattern in the state units of the system where a monopoly of the means of violence usually obtains. Third is a unique pyramid of power which takes the form of bipolarity, with two super-powers acting as centres of decision, military organization, economic co-ordination, and diplomatic co-operation, involving a large segment of the system—though not all its members. Fourth is the presence of new types of actors; states still predominate in number and influence, but there are also bloc actors, a universal actor (the United Nations), and various regional actor organizations. Fifth is the decline of Europe, a shift in the power centre from the continental core of the Western State System to the periphery (Soviet Union) and beyond the seas (United States); this was due partly to the end of empire, partly to the division of Europe by power and ideology into two blocs, and partly to a technological revolution, the sixth and most vital feature of the contemporary system.

Massive technological change, especially the development of nuclear weapons and missiles, has tended to undermine (Herz says has ended) the physical defensibility or impermeability of states, the material basis of the preceding system; even if exaggerated as far as the super-powers are concerned, the 'decline of the territorial state' and the technology responsible for it have had a tremendous impact on the system. They have created both the possibility of and the necessity for the creation of blocs—in order to provide greater security for related units; they have produced the new type of actor, the super-power, which raises the level of fear for all other units

---

[1] Kaplan, *System and Process*, ch. 2. See also his 'Problems of Theory Building and Theory Confirmation in International Politics', *World Politics*, XIV (October 1961), pp. 6–24.

[2] Hoffmann, 'International Relations: The Long Road to Theory', *World Politics*, XI (April 1959), esp. 366 ff.   [3] (New York 1959).

and thereby induces bloc formation; and they have destroyed the classical balance of power. The very presence of super-powers eliminates the role of balancer—in global terms—and the traditional balancing process; what exists today is a balance of terror, which performs only the negative function of the classical balance, namely, to deny preponderance of power to states seeking to change the *status quo* by violence, not the positive function of facilitating preponderance on the side of the *status quo*.[1]

A seventh characteristic of the contemporary system is the rise of ideology to prominence, another component of the multiple revolution still in progress. In the Europe-centred nineteenth-century system, inter-state conflict was for limited power, prestige, and profits—with exceptions, notably Napoleonic France. The coming of fascism, Nazism, and communism, however, sundered the value consensus of the international system. The last, especially, helped to accentuate intra-bloc rigidity and inter-bloc rivalry; ideology and power became intertwined, each strengthening the intensity of the other; the result was to aggravate the tendency of actors to seek unlimited power, now possible because of the technological revolution.

This, in turn, points up another critical feature—the total character of the political process in the contemporary system, in every sense. The goals have become total, whether defined in terms of Morgenthau's 'nationalistic universalism' or 'liberation' or world communism; the instruments have become total, with weapons of unparalleled destructive capacity; and the consequences have become total, for people everywhere on the planet.[2] The globalization of politics, referred to earlier, has also marked the disappearance of the colonial frontier, at least in the traditional meaning of that term.[3] Finally, there is an ever-widening gap between the rate of progress in means of destruction and the rate of progress towards international order, incomparably greater than at any other time in history.

Much of the literature on international relations in the past decade or more reveals an almost pathological concern with Soviet–American relations, most of it policy-oriented and transitory. Even among the few, like Herz, who have constructed a sophisticated model,

[1] Ernst B. Has, 'The Balance of Power: Prescription, Concept or Propaganda?' *World Politics*, V (July 1953), pp. 442–77.

[2] Morgenthau, *Politics Among Nations,* ch. 22.

[3] For a stimulating general analysis of the Western colonial epoch in Asia and Africa, see Rupert Emerson, *From Empire to Nation; the rise to self-assertion of Asian and African peoples* (Cambridge, Mass. 1960), esp. Part I.

there is evident a preoccupation with the dominant system of inter-state politics, i.e., the bipolar bloc system. This is natural and appropriate, for as William Fox observed many years ago, '. . . we will never reach [a well-ordered world] by ignoring the differences between the elephants and the squirrels of international politics'.[1] Apart from assisting a rational process of framing policy, the primary stress on the Dominant (bipolar bloc) System provides data to test and refine models of international systems—notably Kaplan's loose and tight bipolar types.

By the same token, it is dangerous to assume that the elephants are the only members of the system or to ignore the squirrels by virtue of a specious claim that the elephants determine all or most of their actions. Yet this is often done. The focus on the super-powers rests on the premise, rarely stated, that the Dominant System is synonymous with the International System. This assumption is then elevated to the status of truth and is invoked to justify the exclusion or neglect of all other inter-state patterns. For certain features of contemporary international politics the assumption is valid. But there is an array of inter-state problems, conflicts, and relationships among actors outside the blocs that have nothing or little to do with the bloc system, in the Americas, Africa, Asia, and even in Europe; and these are ignored, or distorted, by a model that identifies the bipolar bloc system with the totality of inter-state politics. More important, this assumption obscures another vital pattern of relations—the Subordinate State System.

The existence of this pattern would seem to be obvious. A few writers pay lip service to it.[2] Kaplan's type-models and Hoffmann's historical systems can theoretically be applied with this focus. Yet thus far there have been few efforts to explore a specific subordinate system of inter-state politics.[3] This gap in both International Relations and Asian Studies suggests a need to apply the combined skills of a discipline and area knowledge.[4]

[1] Fox, *The Super-Powers: the United States, Britain and the Soviet Union—their responsibility for peace* (New York 1944), p. 3.

[2] See, for example, Rosenau, op. cit., pp. 77–78.

[3] Leonard Binder, 'The Middle East as a Subordinate International System', *World Politics*, X (April 1958), pp. 408–29; George Modelski, 'International Relations and Area Studies: The Case of South-East Asia', *International Relations*, II (April 1961), pp. 143–55; and Thomas Hodgkin, 'The New West Africa State System', *The University of Toronto Quarterly*, XXXI (October 1961), pp. 74–82.

[4] A thoughtful policy-oriented paper is Guy J. Pauker, 'Southeast Asia as a Problem Area in the Next Decade', *World Politics*, XI (April 1959), pp. 325–45.

The foregoing discussion gives rise to the following propositions:

(a) there are two broad levels of analysis, the unit (nation-state) level and the systems level; the latter, however, reveals three distinct foci of attention—in ascending order, Subordinate Systems, the Dominant System, and the World or Global Political System; in theory, the Dominant System may be geographically and organizationally coterminous with the Global System, but this threefold classification is valid for the contemporary world;[1]

(b) there are at least five definable subordinate systems at present—Middle Eastern, American, Southern Asian, West European, and West African; and

(c) the World System is not merely the sum of relations within the Dominant (bipolar bloc) System and in all subordinate systems; rather, there is a need to link a model of the Dominant System with those of the subordinate systems in order to devise a comprehensive model of the World System. This task has not even been started.

The focus of this chapter is the Subordinate State System of Southern Asia. Some of its features will be sketched and, where appropriate, comparisons with other systems will be drawn. The strokes will be sweeping, as befits a preliminary inquiry. The operative terms are 'structure' and 'texture'. Structure will be used here to denote the basic features of the pattern of relations among and between the units of the system.[2] Texture connotes the broad characteristics of the environment—material, political, ideological—in which those relationships function.

What is the rationale for exploring the Southern Asian System or any Subordinate System? In the broadest sense, it will enrich both Area Study and International Relations. The concept of system gives the one-country Asian specialist a region-wide perspective that can deepen his insight into the foreign relations of his particular state. Moreover, this approach can contribute a common analytical framework and hence comparable data to all students of Asia with an International Relations interest, and thereby enrich the study of inter-state relations in the region as a whole; the area has too long been characterized by isolated, one-country, compartmentalized

---

[1] For a discussion of levels of analysis, see David J. Singer, 'The Level-of-Analysis Problem in International Relations', *World Politics*, XIV (October 1961), pp. 77–92.

[2] Used in this way, 'structure' is very similar to Herz's 'system'. Herz, op. cit., p. 7.

study. Stated in different terms, this focus will permit a study of the *interaction* among states in Southern Asia rather than *action* alone, i.e., the foreign policy of one state. To the International Relations specialist the application of systems concepts to a region will increase greatly the data for case studies of state systems. There have been relatively few Dominant Systems in history; the Subordinate System focus will permit tentative hypotheses about unit behaviour in comparable milieux. It will, therefore, be a step towards an empirically-oriented theory of comparative systems.

Various specific reasons strengthen the case for this approach. First, a system sets limits to the foreign policy choices of all actors within it, i.e., it creates external conditions that impinge on both the contents (goals) and conduct (techniques) of all actors' foreign policy. Some writers attach great importance to the notion of 'system determinism', i.e., that policy is determined by the character and distribution of power within the system of which it is a member.[1] Although this may be exaggerated, it points up the vital fact that a state's foreign policy is the product of external, as well as internal, conditions. A second factor is that states operate at different levels and usually have various associations. Apart from being part of the Global System, they may be members of the Dominant System and one or more subordinate systems. Different actions and decisions derive from different associations; it is useful to separate and correlate policy acts with specific membership roles. Thus, for example, Pakistan belongs to two subordinate systems (Southern Asian and, marginally at least, Middle Eastern), the Dominant (bipolar bloc) System, and the Global System. Its policy on Kashmir, Israel, Germany, and nuclear tests may be viewed in terms of these four associations respectively.

A third justification, noted earlier, is that an exclusive Dominant System focus distorts all inter-state relations except those within the bipolar bloc system—and most exist outside that framework. The constant intrusion of that focus leads to errors of judgement and, frequently, of policy as well. Finally, the study of subordinate systems would help to resolve a sterile debate on the merits of deductive and inductive approaches to a more rigorous discipline of International Relations.[2] Both methods have a legitimate place in

[1] See, for example, Herz, op. cit., p. 115, and Sondermann, in Rosenau, op. cit., p. 13.

[2] For extreme formulations see Singer, op. cit., p. 92, and Hoffmann, 'International Relations', pp. 356–8.

this quest. An application of existing models will test their validity and lead to refined theory. The accumulation of data about subordinate inter-state politics will facilitate inductive hypotheses, to be tested frequently in the light of steadily increasing data. In the cross-fertilization of International Relations and Asian Studies, both will benefit.

DEFINITION OF THE SOUTHERN ASIAN SYSTEM

Any concept must be defined precisely if it is to serve a useful analytical purpose. Yet as James Rosenau observed, since all bilateral interaction may be viewed in a systems framework, the one hundred contemporary states can theoretically form almost five thousand dyadic systems.[1] The concept of Subordinate State System is more rigorous and requires six conditions :

(i) its scope is delimited, with primary stress on a geographic region;

(ii) there are at least three actors;

(iii) taken together, they are objectively recognized by other actors as constituting a distinctive community, region, or segment of the Global System;

(iv) the members identify themselves as such;

(v) the units of power are relatively inferior to units in the Dominant System, using a sliding scale of power in both; and,

(vi) changes in the Dominant System have greater effect on the Subordinate System than the reverse.

In the present Global System, as we have said, there are five subordinate systems—Middle Eastern, American, Southern Asian, West European, and West African; others may emerge.

Using conventional geographic terminology, Southern Asia extends from Pakistan to Indonesia; the state members are Pakistan, India, Nepal, Ceylon, Burma, Thailand, Cambodia, Laos, North Vietnam, South Vietnam, Malaya, the Philippines, and Indonesia. China is not formally within the region and is usually excluded from the designation 'South and South-East Asia' or the more recent category, 'Southern Asia'. However, the Subordinate System is a political as well as a geographic concept; the region is a necessary but not a sufficient basis for definition.

China is a vital peripheral state, analogous to Russia in the eighteenth-century European system, Macedon in the Greek city-

[1] Rosenau, op. cit., p. 77.

state system, and Ch'in in the Chou system of China before the seventh century B.C. Moreover, the subsequent roles of Macedon and Ch'in are not wholly irrelevant to China and the present Southern Asian System.[1]

There are other persuasive reasons for China's inclusion in this system. The presence of 12 million Chinese in the states of South-East Asia gives China great influence within that region, comparable to that of the scattered German communities in Eastern Europe in the past half-century; more pointed is the analogy of the Chinese in Singapore–Malaya and the Germans in Sudetenland. Closely related is the unstabilizing effect of China's minorities in the internal politics of various states; this accentuates her influence in the system. Another reason derives from China's territorial contiguity with many states of the region; this permits continuous Chinese interaction with these weaker units, a vital test of membership in any international political system. This pattern assumes special significance in the light of China's historic hegemony in South-East Asia and its goal of renewed domination of that area.[2] Thus, this chapter treats China as a member of the Southern Asian system.[3] She is, of course, a member of the other systems too.

China's inclusion suggests a system comprising three overlapping fields—South Asia, South-East Asia, and China.[4] Only two actors, India and China, have a high intensity relationship to and influence on most actors in all three fields, both through bilateral links.

The selection of a date for the origin of the system is somewhat arbitrary. The year 1949 would seem to be valid, for it marks the rounding out of the system—with the coming of independence to Indonesia and the emergence of a united mainland China, following on the transfer of power to the Philippines, Ceylon, Pakistan, India, and Burma. The remaining two phases, the creation of four weak units in Indo-China in 1954 and the end of British rule in Malaya in

[1] A brief description of inter-state politics in antiquity is to be found in Schuman, op. cit., ch. 1.

[2] See Victor Purcell, *The Chinese in Southeast Asia* (London 1951).

[3] For a different view, excluding 'great powers' from subordinate systems in this case India and China, see Modelski, op. cit., pp. 148–50.

[4] Neither Japan nor either of the Koreas is included in the Southern Asian Subordinate System. Unlike China, they do not meet conditions (iii) or (iv) as noted earlier, i.e. they are not (usually) treated as part of that system by outside actors and do not so identify themselves. They do, of course, have relations with some states in Southern Asia and, in theory, could become full members of the system. Apart from periods of disunity, by contrast, China has regarded itself as part of the Southern Asian system and has, throughout history, played a major role therein.

1957, were marginal to the system. Prior to the end of the Second World War, the entire area, except Thailand and a weakened China, was totally dependent on European actors; Southern Asia was a geographic, economic, and political appendage of the Dominant (European) System. The countries of the region were objects not subjects of politics; they lacked autonomy of power and freedom of decision-making in external affairs.

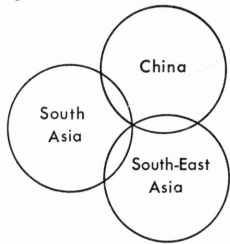

Having delineated the State System of Southern Asia in space and time, we may now turn to its salient structural and textural characteristics.

STRUCTURAL FEATURES

A key structural feature of any system is the configuration (distribution and level) of power. The general level in Southern Asia is low, in both absolute and relative terms. No member of the system appears to be capable of producing nuclear weapons or missiles; the armed forces of all states, except China, are small in number and severely limited as to skills and weapons. All units are characterized by an arrested economy, a low standard of living, a stagnant agriculture, a shortage of capital and skills, little heavy industry, and (most states) a disturbing rate of population growth.[1] Only India

[1] Strictly speaking, the level of technology and economy is an environmental or textural feature. However, the level of power is a direct function of technological and economic characteristics in the area covered by this system. In short, this is an overlapping feature, falling into both Structure and Texture categories.

and China are potential 'Great Powers'; Pakistan, Indonesia, and the Philippines are 'Middle Powers'; all the rest are squirrels.

In systems of advanced technology—for example, where two actors possess thousands of H-bombs and adequate delivery systems—the power margin is inconsequential. In Southern Asia the differences *tend* to be accentuated by the low general level. Yet this tendency is offset by other factors. Vast geographic distances, along with an underdeveloped economy, confine the effectiveness of India's and China's power to their respective fields; India's superior military strength may be effective *vis-à-vis* Nepal, Pakistan, and Ceylon, but it diminishes rapidly and steadily farther east. For China's influence, the barriers of distance and technology are especially noticeable in the offshore island areas of South-East Asia; there, the lack of naval and air power is crucial. For all other actors in the system, their low level of power and technology restricts the exercise of influence, at best, to neighbouring states.

This general weakness also invites intervention by super-powers and blocs to fill the 'power vacuum', a penetration that is resented and feared by many states in the Subordinate System.[1] Indeed, it is the low level of power in Southern Asia that gives China, an extra-area actor, virtual *carte blanche* access to the system, as well as *de facto* membership in it. Moreover, the presence of a relatively power-ful peripheral state, China, further diminishes the application of India's power, not only in South-East Asia but also with respect to immediate neighbours, such as Nepal and Pakistan. There is, then, diffusion of power in Southern Asia, with neither of two potential 'Great Powers' able to dominate the system because of technological under-development.

How does this power configuration compare with other systems? The pattern in Southern Asia is much more pyramidal than in nine-teenth-century Europe where there were five relatively equal Great Powers—England, France, Prussia (Germany), Austria, and Russia. Another striking difference was the absence of a major peri-pheral state upsetting all power calculations within the system proper; Russia had by then become a formal member, and the United States, the only possible analogy to China *vis-à-vis* Southern Asia today, remained a passive onlooker until the last years of the

---

[1] An extreme illustration of resentment was Krishna Menon's comment on SEATO: '. . . this is not a regional organization. . . . It is a modern version of a protectorate. . . .' *Daily Indiagram* (Ottawa), 30 August 1954.

European system's 'century of peace'. Like China in Southern Asia, when the United States became an active participant in 1917, it, too, acquired *de facto* membership in the system.

The distribution of power also differed in the state system of ancient China. Among the multiplicity of states were seven major units—notably leagues of states under the leadership of Ch'u, Chin, Ch'in, and Wu. Gradually, over the course of centuries, a bipolar pattern emerged, with Chin and Ch'u as the super-powers—until the peripheral state, Ch'in, established its hegemony.[1] A similar pattern is observable in ancient Greece, with most city-states ultimately being linked to Athens or Sparta—and Macedon destroying the system. Southern Asia today does not reveal a bipolar pattern. Moreover, neither China nor Greece was a subordinate system; both were autonomous during most of their existence.

The hierarchy of power in Southern Asia is superficially akin to the contemporary Dominant System, with its two super-powers, its four 'middle powers'—England, France, Germany, and China— and the host of squirrels. There are, however, striking differences. The general level of power in the Dominant System is infinitely higher. And the power margin of the super-powers in the Dominant System is greater both quantitatively and qualitatively. This, in turn, has two vital consequences: it makes each a hegemonial state within each bloc, to a much greater degree than India in South Asia; and it enables both to exert a life-and-death influence on all actors in the Dominant System, which neither India's nor China's power margin permits in the Subordinate System. The substantive differences, then, are very great indeed.

The level of power in Southern Asia is comparable to that of the Middle East system, but the distribution is markedly different. There is no 'Great Power' in the Middle East, real or potential. Most units in the Arab core are of the same order of power; Egypt and Iraq are the strongest, but neither has the power status of India or China in Southern Asia. In fact, two of the peripheral states, Turkey and Israel, are at present stronger than any single Arab actor—though the margin is not decisive. The distribution of power in the American System reveals still another pattern, that of a super-power whose superior technology and military and economic strength give it hegemonial status. Not even the Soviet Union can claim such

[1] On this and other aspects of inter-state politics in that autonomous system, see Richard L. Walker, *The Multi-State System of Ancient China* (Hamden, Conn. 1953).

H

unqualified domination within its bloc in the Dominant System. Another structural feature concerns organizational integration (as distinct from social integration). Southern Asia is acutely under-developed in this respect. There is no system-wide political institu-tion, judicial body, or security machinery. And neither of the two economic organizations embracing almost all units plays a vital role. Indeed, the process of integration has barely begun.

The political sphere is characterized by infrequent conferences among the actors of the system. Noteworthy events were the Asian Relations Conference in 1947, the Delhi Conference on Indonesia in 1949, and the Bandung Conference of 1955. No permanent machinery for regional co-operation emerged, despite serious efforts at the first and third of these conclaves. One reason was the rivalry of India and China, neither willing to concede Asian leadership to the other. A second was fear among the smaller states that one or both giants would dominate the system. As for the 'Colombo Powers', formed in 1954, or the Asian Group within the Afro–Asian bloc at the United Nations, they lacked organic unity or even a common attitude to the Dominant System and its conflicts. Yet Bandung was a turning point in the evolution of the Southern Asian System, for it symbolized rejection of the Western view that everything was secondary to the Cold War. By asserting the primacy of anti-colonialism, the Conference proclaimed the regional autonomy of this Subordinate System and its non-involvement, where possible, in the bipolar struggle for power.[1]

The lack of integration in the security field is even more striking. The only formal organization, SEATO, includes but three units of the system, Pakistan, Thailand, and the Philippines, and is domi-nated by extra-area Powers; it is also opposed by various states within Southern Asia. Nor are the members' obligations impressive—'to meet the common danger in accordance with [their] constitutional processes' in case of aggression, and to consult immediately on appropriate measures in case of subversion (Article 4); and even this is aimed at only one kind of danger, the threat from Communist

---

[1] For accounts of Bandung, see George McTurnan Kahin, *The Asian–African Con-ference* (Ithaca 1956) and A. Appadorai, *The Bandung Conference* (New Delhi 1955). On the steps taken in the direction of political integration, see Russell H. Fifield, *The Diplomacy of Southeast Asia, 1945–1958* (New York 1958), ch. 10; Guy Wint, *South Asia: Unity and Disunity*, International Conciliation No. 500 (New York, November 1954), pp. 162–73; and William Henderson, 'The Development of Region-alism in Southeast Asia', *International Organization*, IX (November 1955), pp. 463–76.

China. Finally, the organizational links are minimal and the military power of the Southern Asian members grossly inadequate; it is extra-area power, that of the United States, which gives SEATO meaning.[1]

The efforts to forge economic unity are more impressive and more successful. The United Nations Economic Commission for Asia and the Far East (ECAFE) has functioned since 1947, and the Colombo Plan since 1950. Both include most states in Southern Asia, as well as extra-area units. Both were designed to assist the process of economic development, but both are advisory in character. ECAFE possesses a permanent secretariat which conducts valuable research and recommends policies to members who meet annually in formal conference and more frequently in sundry committees; the Commission proposes, but the states dispose. As for the Colombo Plan (really a collection of individual state plans), the organizational links are even less developed. A Consultative Committee meets annually to hear reports and to facilitate an exchange of views. The Bureau in Colombo acts as a clearing house for information, technical assistance, and the like. Both institutions have achieved much in promoting international co-operation and in creating a climate of opinion conducive to the granting of aid by wealthier actors outside the area.[2]

The level of organizational integration in Southern Asia is much lower than in other systems. Although not highly institutionalized, the Concert of Europe performed security and political functions from 1815 to 1848, and in a modified form throughout the nineteenth century. The Permanent Court of Arbitration provided quasi-judicial services towards the close of the European System, and a series of technical inter-state organizations emerged to serve members' needs.[3] Each bloc in the current Dominant System has a high degree of integration. Thus, in the United States-led bloc there is a sophisticated security institution (NATO), a judicial body (European Court),

---

[1] See Ralph Braibanti, 'The Sountheast Asia Collective Treaty', *Pacific Affairs*, XXX (December 1957), pp. 321–41, and Royal Institute of International Affairs, *Collective Defence in South East Asia: the Manila Treaty and its Implications* (London 1956).

[2] For the work of ECAFE and the Colombo Plan, see, respectively, United Nations: *Economic Survey of Asia and the Far East for* . . . (annually since 1947, New York), and Colombo Plan: Consultative Committee. *Annual Report*, Colombo Plan for Co-operative Economic Development in South and South-east Asia (London, Wellington, Singapore, *et al.*).

[3] See Gerard J. Mangone, *A Short History of International Organization* (New York 1954), ch. 2 and 3.

a host of economic organizations (OECD, Schuman Plan, Common Market, etc.), and a legislative–executive organ (Council of Europe).[1] The Soviet bloc also possesses a security machine (Warsaw Pact), an economic organization (Council for Economic Mutual Assistance), specialized organs (Danube Commission and the Institute for Nuclear Research), and a multitude of bilateral agreements covering a wide range of inter-state co-operation. Underpinning these institutional aspects is the Communist Party; frequent meetings of Politbureau (Presidium) members and gatherings at Congresses enhance the integration process.[2]

An extreme contrast to Southern Asia in this respect is the American System. Indeed, the Organization of American States (OAS) provides the most comprehensive, formal machinery in the history of state systems. There is a legislative organ (Inter-American Conference), a permanent executive body (the Council), a secretariat (Pan American Union), a multi-faceted security machinery (Foreign Ministers' meetings, Inter-American Peace Committees, Defense Board and Advisory Defense Committee), specialized organs (Economic and Social Council, Cultural Council and Council of Jurists) and specialized agencies (Commission of Women, Statistical Institute, Sanitary Bureau, etc.), and, finally, an abundance of conferences and congresses on functional matters. The structure is impressive on paper, but its effectiveness as an instrument of co-operation among the twenty-one republics is often wanting.[3] A similar duality obtains in the Middle East System. The counterpart of the OAS is the Arab League which has an organ of consultation (Majlis or Council), seven permanent committees to deal with political, economic, social, cultural, and health matters, a secretariat, a security machine (Joint Defence Council, Military Organization, Chiefs of Staff Committee,

---

[1] See Ernst B. Haas, *The Uniting of Europe: Political, Social and Economic Forces, 1950–1957* (London 1958) and *Consensus Formation in the Council of Europe* (London 1960).

[2] See Zbigniew Brzezinski, 'The Organization of the Communist Camp', *World Politics*, XIII (January 1961), pp. 175–209, and George Modelski, *The Communist International System* (Princeton 1960).

[3] See Manuel S. Canyes (ed.), *The Organization of American States and the United Nations*, 4th ed. (Washington 1958); C. G. Fenwick, 'The Inter-American Regional System: 50 Years of Progress', *American Journal of International Law*, 50 (January 1956), pp. 18–31; Martin B. Travis Jr., 'The Organization of American States: A Guide to the Future', *Western Political Quarterly*, X (September 1957), pp. 491–511; Arthur P. Whitaker, *The Western Hemisphere Ideal: its rise and decline* (Ithaca 1954); and C. Neale Ronning, *Law and Politics in Inter-American Diplomacy* (New York 1953).

etc.), and a growing number of specialized agencies. The League is even less effective than the OAS in security and other spheres, but it has the organizational foundations which are still lacking in Southern Asia.[1]

The degree of integration is closely related to a third structural feature—character and frequency of integration among the members. Of all the states in the system, only India has active relations with almost all other units. Apart from formal diplomatic ties, other actors have limited inter-state relations: for example, Pakistan with India and, through SEATO, with Thailand and the Philippines; Ceylon with India; Burma with India and China; the Philippines with her SEATO partners; Malaya with Indonesia and the Philippines; Thailand with Burma and Cambodia, etc. Interaction among the members is, then, incomplete or spatially discontinuous within the system. Moreover, it is almost entirely bilateral in form, the only example of multilateralism being ECAFE and the Colombo Plan, SEATO, and the United Nations, which do not bind the actors. Most inter-state relations are of low intensity, though there are variations, the extremes being the near-continuous tension between India and Pakistan and the rarely disturbed tranquillity between India and Indonesia. Mainland China has resumed active relations with many states in Southern Asia since Bandung, but these remain less stable than those of India.[2]

In this sphere, too, Southern Asia is less developed than other systems. In the Middle East, for example, relations among the core Arab members are spatially continuous and complete, intense and acutely multilateral. The half-dozen actors are in constant contact at every level, and use every form of interaction—diplomatic, political, social, economic, cultural, personal; the process of interaction even includes close links between domestic politics in any one state and the internal and external affairs of all others. At the same time, there are no relations with one peripheral unit, Israel, and limited ties with two others, Turkey and Iran.[3]

[1] See T. R. Little, 'The Arab League: A Reassessment', *Middle East Journal*, X (Spring 1956), pp. 138–50, and Paul Seabury, 'The League of Arab States: Debacle of a Regional Arrangement', *International Organization*, III (November 1949), pp. 633–42.

[2] On China's role in international politics, see H. Arthur Steiner, *Communist China in the World Community*, International Conciliation No. 533 (New York, May 1961), and Howard L. Boorman, 'Peking in World Politics', *Pacific Affairs*, XXXIV (Fall 1961), 227–41.

[3] Binder, op. cit., pp. 423–6.

The pattern differs somewhat in America. All actors have continuous bilateral ties with the hegemonial power. Multilateral ties in the system as a whole are channelled through the OAS. And contact among the 20 Latin units varies in intensity. It is at a high level in Central America, which resembles the Arab core in this respect, fairly high in the deep south of the hemisphere, and declines sharply among the others.

Apart from these three basic structural features, which apply to all systems of inter-state politics, there is the question of the linkage between the Subordinate and Dominant Systems of the time. An inquiry into the nature and extent of penetration (or inter-penetration) of the two systems will shed light on the degree of autonomy of the Subordinate System and its units. It will also represent a first step towards achieving the goal noted earlier—an all-inclusive model of the World Political System.

All states in Southern Asia are members of the Global System, and almost all belong to the universal international organization, the United Nations. Some also participate in the Dominant System—Pakistan, Thailand, the Philippines (and South Vietnam) via SEATO; China and North Vietnam via the Soviet bloc. Others are relatively free actors—India, Indonesia, Burma, Ceylon, and Malaya.[1] All, of course, are also units of a subordinate system.

Perhaps the most important feature of the Southern Asian Subordinate System is the constant penetration by the Dominant System. The Western bloc penetrates through a security instrument (SEATO), an economic organization (Colombo Plan), a multipurpose association (Commonwealth), bilateral aid, and propaganda. The Soviet bloc penetrates through a security instrument (Communist military bloc), bilateral aid from Moscow and Peking, subversion (Chinese minority), a political organization (Communist Party), and propaganda. Both blocs court the uncommitted states in Southern Asia, notably India and Indonesia. Both blocs also intrude in the problems of the area—directly in Laos and Vietnam, indirectly in Kashmir and West New Guinea (West Irian).[2] This intervention is facilitated by three conditions: the dire need of Southern Asian states for economic aid, which can be provided only by extra-area

---

[1] Nepal, Cambodia, and Laos are too exposed to be termed 'free actors'. At the same time, they do not participate formally in bloc military alliances.

[2] As reflected in various Anglo-American-sponsored resolutions on Kashmir in the Security Council and the Soviet vetoes, and the U.S. (Bunker) mediation between the Netherlands and Indonesia.

Powers; ideological disunity; and the lack of integration and the political instability of most units within the system.

Among all members of the Subordinate System only India reciprocates actively. Indeed, it penetrates the Dominant System effectively and continuously, through a conscious mediatory role at the United Nations and elsewhere, in regard to the Middle East, the Congo, Laos, disarmament, and Berlin. For all states but India and China, the Subordinate System is the primary, if not exclusive, framework for their foreign policy. Even those units that are militarily linked to a bloc are motivated essentially by regional considerations—Pakistan fears India and desires aid in the struggle for Kashmir, Thailand and the Philippines fear Chinese expansion.

India's policy towards some issues reflects a local ('national interest') or subordinate-system outlook, for example, on Goa, Kashmir, and the treatment of Indians in Ceylon, Burma, or Malaya. On other vital questions, however, there is a primary stress on implications for the Global System or the Dominant System—Tibet in 1950, Laos since 1954, South Vietnam today.

China's motivations are more difficult to unravel. In some cases, her role in the Dominant (bipolar bloc) System is primary, as with her aid to Castro and the F.L.N. in Algeria, and her attitude in the Congo, and in Hungary in 1956. In others, her membership in the Subordinate System is decisive: for example, the border disputes and settlements with Burma and Nepal, her performance at Bandung, and the placatory offer to Asian states on the double-nationality problem. But in another category the lines are blurred, with both systems appearing to fuse; the outstanding examples are Formosa and the border conflict with India. China's aim of hegemony in Southern Asia is clearly involved, but so is the larger struggle in the Dominant System—between the blocs in the Formosa case, within the communist bloc in the Indian border case. For the two giants of Southern Asia, then, interpenetration is frequent and vital.

The Middle East Subordinate System is similar to Southern Asia in this respect, but not altogether. The blocs penetrate through security or military ties (CENTO and Soviet arms in Egypt), economic assistance and propaganda. They also intervene in regional problems—the Arab–Israel conflict continuously, Jordan and Lebanon in 1958, Kuwait in 1961, etc. The basic difference is the absence of a reverse penetration, except by Egypt on a rare occasion, as a prominent Afro-Asian neutralist. The American System was strikingly different until 1959. Apart from limited diplomatic contacts and the presence of some weak communist parties, effective Soviet bloc penetration was prevented by United States hegemony; this is simply another way of saying that Southern Asia was a power vacuum, open to extra-area pressure, and that America was not. This has changed somewhat with the rise of Castro, facilitating Soviet bloc entry into the American Subordinate System on an unparalleled scale. Like the Middle East, and unlike Southern Asia, reverse penetration is non-existent, except at the United Nations, for no Latin American state is powerful enough or sufficiently uncommitted to play India's role.

TEXTURAL FEATURES

Various textural features of Southern Asia merit attention, however brief. One is the low intensity of communications and transport within the system. Another is the complex of common and conflicting ideologies and values. A third is the diversity of political systems. And a fourth is internal instability within the member-units. Contrasts and similarities with other systems are striking.

Distances are vast in Southern Asia, topographic barriers are great, means of transport are limited, and extreme poverty restricts travel to a few. Inter-state radio contact is minimal, except for India–Pakistan, India–Ceylon, India–Burma, and bilateral links in parts of South-East Asia. Press communications are also minimal, though some leading Indian, Pakistani, and Ceylonese newspapers may be available in the other countries, Television is practically non-existent. And the language barrier is formidable, not only within the system but often within individual states as well. There are, for example, fourteen languages in India, two or more in Pakistan and Ceylon, and no less diversity in other lands. Indeed, inter-state communication is confined to the élite—at the United Nations, diplomatic conclaves, regional conferences and the like. Each unit is virtually a closed communications network to the others, hardly an inducement to integration and co-operation.

The Middle East System lies at the other extreme of communications interaction. Distances are much less, states are territorially contiguous, and topography, though a barrier, is not insurmountable. The great contrast, however, is the common language of the Arab core which eases communication via press, radio, visiting leaders, and the spoken and written word generally. Face-to-face contact is much greater. Arabic is also widely understood in the peripheral states—Israel, Turkey, and Iran. There is, in short, an open communications system, which strengthens the interaction process. The American System is similarly endowed with an integrated communications network. A common language is an asset, though the hegemonial power and Brazil stand apart. A developed air transport service assists the process. And radio, press, and TV knit the actors together.

All states in Southern Asia share the goals of economic development, social progress, and a viable political order; this permits widespread co-operation in such associations as ECAFE and/or the Colombo Plan. Most have a common experience of foreign, white, rule, inducing a common reaction to international issues involving the ills of colonialism and racialism. They are also deeply attached to nationalism and fear renewed domination. In all these important intangibles they are psychologically knit together in a community, fulfilling the fourth condition of a Subordinate System; this is also a temporary substitute for organizational integration.

Beyond these, however, is a wide gulf over values. There is a clash between the secular and religious orientation to public policy, as illustrated in Indian and Pakistani constitution-making.[1] A variant is the conflict between modernist and traditionalist approaches to the achievement of common goals. Some follow the liberal path in politics and economics, others the communist way, and still others various types of 'middle way'. There are sharp cleavages within the system on the proper attitude to the bloc struggle within the Dominant System. Unlike Western Europe or America, there are several distinct civilizations, Buddhist, Muslim, and Hindu. Their economies are competitive. Enormous distance is a barrier to close contact. Racial, linguistic, and cultural differences are numerous and deep. Historic antagonisms persist, especially fear and resentment by the weaker peoples and states in Southern Asia. And, as in Africa, there are zones of English, French, and Dutch influence, with different traditions of education, law, and administration. No wonder, then, that the initiative for inter-state organizations in Southern Asia has usually come from outside the system, as with SEATO, ECAFE, and the Colombo Plan.[2] Yet their existence testifies to the

[1] See, for example, Leonard Binder, *Religion and Politics in Pakistan* (Berkeley and Los Angeles 1961).

[2] Exceptions are the quiescent Asian Relations Organization and the Association of South-East Asian States.

presence of the third condition of a Subordinate System—objective treatment by outside actors as a distinct system or community.

In nineteenth-century Europe, too, there were differing values and ideologies—liberalism versus conservatism, revolution versus legitimacy, democracy versus absolutism. It is true that Christian civilization provided a unifying thread and common standards of behaviour —until 1917. And yet, the great gulf in values between the blocs today does not detract from their membership in a system—indeed, the Dominant System. Nor does ideological diversity, *per se*, deny the existence of a Southern Asian System. The Middle East Arab core is far more united in values and ideology: it has a common religion for the most part, a common way of life, thought, and action, and the common experience, problems, and aspirations of Southern Asian states. Yet there is a basic clash in values with other members of the system. Apart from the United States, the American System is immeasurably more homogeneous in terms of cultural and ideological foundations—a common history, religion, way of life, and basic values.

There are three general types of political system in Southern Asia. As noted earlier, democracy, based on the Anglo-American models, may be found with deviations in India, the Philippines, Malaya, and Ceylon. The Soviet or communist model is evident in China and North Vietnam. All other states reveal some form of authoritarianism. It may be mild as in Pakistan since 1958, or severe, as in South Vietnam since 1955. It may be military rule, as in Thailand and Burma, or civilian dictatorship, as in South Vietnam, or an uneasy blend of civil-military control, as in Indonesia, or absolute monarchy, as in Nepal. In all these cases the essential components of democracy are absent, in whole or in part. In some, the disregard for civil liberties is as great as in communist lands, and the instruments of control are no less oppressive. In most, the army has become a major political force, either exercising power directly or standing in the wings ready to seize control from a faltering civil authority and acting as guardian of the political order. But in none of these states is authoritarianism total; this is one vital distinction between communist governments and those of the middle zones. Another is the commitment in principle to democracy, though this has lessened in recent years. For the present, however, they remain almost as far removed from democracy as is communism; and many are less welfare-oriented than either of the polar models. All three types of political system in

Southern Asia are 'Western' in the sense that they are legacies of the Western epoch in Asian history.

Diversity in political forms and substance is not unique to Southern Asia. Nor is it a necessary source of conflict within the system. Nineteenth-century Europe had constitutional democracy (England) coexisting with autocracy, constitutional and other (Prussia, Austria, Russia, etc.). In the Middle East today there is democracy (Israel and, with qualifications, Lebanon) and non-communist authoritarianism of different forms—military (Egypt, Iraq, Turkey, Yemen), absolute monarchy (Saudi Arabia), and constitutional autocracy (Iran and Jordan). As for America, all three types are represented—democratic (United States, Uruguay and, occasionally, others), communist (Cuba), and authoritarian (the majority most of the time).

The dominant feature of internal politics in Southern Asia is instability. The record is emphatic on this theme.[1] The pattern of instability in the Middle East System is similar; if anything, more acute. There, it has led to sharp change in foreign policy, as with Nasser in Egypt and Kassem in Iraq. In the American System, only when the entire political order is transformed, as in Cuba, does instability lead to a new path in external affairs. Thus far, the ubiquitous flux of Southern Asian politics has not seriously undermined the continuity of foreign policy—in Burma, Pakistan, or Indonesia for example. However, this is a potential effect on the actors. Moreover, political change within the states makes a prediction of probable actor behaviour more difficult. It also accentuates the image of power weakness in the system as a whole.

CONCLUSION

The foregoing analysis suggests certain observations. The state system of Southern Asia consists of fourteen units, most of which are weak and under grave internal stress. Each jealously guards its newly-won status and asserts the primacy of 'national interests' over group interests that could induce organizational integration. The process is rudimentary and is likely to remain so in the foreseeable future. Indeed, Southern Asia is clearly the most underdeveloped of all contemporary Subordinate State Systems.

[1] The record and the causes are examined in 'The Search for Political Stability', (ch. 2, pp. 49–73 above).

The vast majority of states lack sufficient power to ensure their independence. Apart from India and China, it is certain that no actor will have the surplus power to play a major role outside the system in the coming decades. The region of Southern Asia is a power vacuum buffetted by both blocs in the Dominant System. The presence of American and Soviet–Chinese power, real and potential, creates a precarious equilibrium and a dangerously rigid link between Dominant and Subordinate Systems.

Viewed in these terms, Southern Asia bears a striking resemblance to the Balkans before 1914. It lies between two centres of power and ideology. Its units are very weak compared to extra-area powers, three of which have actively intervened—like Germany and Russia in the Balkans; indeed, one of them is a member of the system. And conflicts within Southern Asia—for example, in Laos and Vietnam—attract intervention by the super-powers.

The real danger in such an unstable system of power is that one or more of the units will disintegrate or even come under the control of outside states. If this were to occur in a unit like India or Indonesia, the consequences would be far-reaching. The whole system would be unsettled and pressure from without would increase for all Southern Asian states. The line dividing Dominant from Subordinate System would disappear, and bloc rigidity would be further accentuated. In case of Indian disintegration, probably nothing could prevent the rapid assertion of Sino–Soviet domination over the whole system. In brief, the domestic stability of most units in Southern Asia is necessary for the maintenance of a system at all. And the maintenance of an autonomous system in Southern Asia is conducive to stability in the World Political System.

There are two logical next stages of the analysis. The first is a demonstration of how the Subordinate System of Southern Asia *qua* system helps to shape the broad outlines and specific acts of the foreign policy of member-states. The other is a projection of the likely evolution of the system as a whole. This chapter has attempted only to provide an analytical framework within which these tasks can be performed fruitfully. It is now up to those with special knowledge of individual states in Southern Asia to link the system and the foreign policy of a particular unit. Only then can the broader task of charting the future of the system be undertaken.

4

NEUTRALISM: AN ANALYSIS

I

THE term 'neutralism' has evoked strong emotions in recent years. Various words are used interchangeably: neutrality, neutralization, non-alignment, and neutralism. The result is widespread obscurity about its meaning and implications for world politics. A brief semantic exercise may set the stage for a more rigorous analysis.

Neutrality is simply a legal status of states that demand certain rights of the belligerents in time of war and accept certain obligations towards those belligerents. It is a status that comes into existence only *after* a war has begun. It is, therefore, a term to designate a particular status in a period of overt conflict; and a neutral state is one that practises neutrality—for example, the United States between 1914 and 1917 and between 1939 and 1941.

There are situations in which states proclaim themselves in advance desirous of avoiding participation in any war at any time. These states, if they are favoured with special geographical positions, if they happen to be small enough and not especially attractive to the more rapacious Great Powers, may then be given a status of *permanent neutrality* or *neutralization*; that is to say, in terms of power politics, they are removed from the arena of conflict. In time of war these states accept the obligations and demand the rights of all other neutral states. In time of peace they accept the fundamental obligation never to join an alliance which could conceivably involve them in war. In modern history there are five outstanding examples of this type, namely, Switzerland, neutralized in 1815, Belgium in 1831, Luxembourg in 1867, Austria in 1955, and, most recently, Laos, in 1962. Only Austria and Laos remain as permanently neutralized states, which in effect have abandoned any pretensions to an active role in world politics, though they claim to be sovereign states and may even, as in the case of Austria, join the United Nations.

Non-alignment, by contrast, is a political status. It refers to a state that declares itself aloof from bloc conflicts; nothing more. It proclaims itself free from *a priori* alliances, notably military entanglements with any bloc or Great Power anywhere in the world. It also asserts that it will judge all policy issues 'on their merits'. This is not neutralism, however. It is, rather, the passive, first stage of neutralism.

Neutralism has in common with non-alignment an expressed desire to remain aloof from bloc conflict. But neutralism goes much further, for it involves a positive attitude towards bloc conflicts. A neutralist state assumes an obligation to help reduce tensions between blocs with a view to maintaining peace or bringing about peace, and more particularly to prevent the outbreak of war. In other words, non-alignment is the policy guide of the neutralist state, but neutralism represents an attitude and a policy which are much more activist than non-alignment as such. India is the outstanding example of the *neutralist state*. Sweden is a good example of the *non-aligned state*. And, as I suggested, Austria and Laos are *neutralized* states. In time of war, any state, whether it be Turkey or Sweden or the United States, which manages to remain aloof from the conflict, is a *neutral state*. This semantic exercise suggests a crucial link: both neutrality and neutralism derive from the same basic aspiration, though they use fundamentally different techniques because of the changed character of the world political system in which they have to operate. In short, neutralism is a contemporary expression of the time-honoured theme of neutrality.

We may explore this proposition by glancing at the origins and evolution of neutrality. As early as Kautilya's *Arthasastra*, a text on politics and administration in ancient India, there was a recognized concept of neutrality as one of the six possible roles of actors in inter-state politics. The Greek city-state system, of course, had a rather sophisticated view of neutrality both in theory and practice. Thucydides, in his account of the Peloponnesian War, refers quite frequently to states that were neutral during that war. If there were no neutrals in the Age of Rome, it was simply because Rome was a hegemonial state that would not countenance the idea of aloofness from conflict. But as we move towards another state system in which there was a multiplicity of units with comparatively equal power, for example, the Italian city-state system, neutrality is revived in theory and practice. And from the fifteenth to the nineteenth century neutrality as a legal status emerged full blown as a result of conflicts on the sea. Indeed, it was over trading rights and duties, and the claims of states that wanted to engage in commerce while others were engaged in open hostilities, that the problem of neutrality arose.

A painful conflict developed between neutrals who claimed the right to trade and belligerents who claimed the right to contraband or to take over ships if they interfered with the conduct of hostilities. Over a few hundred years there emerged in international law, both in custom and in treaty, recognized rules of neutrality. These reached their zenith in two important Hague Conventions in 1907 and the Declaration of London in 1916. This represented the high water mark of neutrality.

It was precisely at that point that technological changes in the character of warfare occurred, making neutrality almost *passé*. In the First and, more particularly, in the Second World War, when the stakes were total and the character of the conflict was total, the belligerents were unwilling to accept the niceties and nuances of international law; the result was that they interfered with neutral rights whenever they could. The only states in the Second World War which managed to remain neutral were those that were favoured by geography, or were sufficiently armed so that invasion would be more costly than the value of conquest to the invader, or were useful as listening posts, such as Turkey, Sweden, and Switzerland. All through history, then, one finds the development of the idea and the status of neutrality. By the Second World War it was no longer respected by belligerents. Nevertheless, the aspiration to neutrality continued. And that aspiration was to remain aloof from war.

It is in this sense that neutralism emerges as a policy version of the classic status of neutrality. There are basic differences, of course. Neutrality is isolationist and neutralism is interventionist. The neutral contends that one can best stay out of war by being impartial towards all the belligerents, claiming certain rights and performing certain duties. The neutralist claims that one can best remain out of war by preventing war. This is the heart of the case for neutralism. For, argues the neutralist, in the changed character of war—the development of nuclear weapons, bi-polarity, and ideological conflict—even if one could stay out of war, as the neutral did, it wouldn't be particularly desirable, because one could not neutralize oneself against the adverse consequences of thermonuclear war. Therefore, the only way to remain out of global war is to do everything possible to prevent the outbreak of global war.

It is interesting to note in this connexion the policy evolution of the leading neutralist state. From 1947 to 1950 Delhi's posture was strikingly similar to classical neutrality, with the frequent expression of hope that India could remain outside a war, should it occur. After the Korean War, however, there was a realization that non-belligerency or neutrality were not sufficient. And so India moved to the second stage—an open rejection of the leadership of both blocs but still passive in its orientation: that is, non-alignment. In the early fifties India moved to the third stage—a positive role in world politics and attempts to alleviate tensions with the ultimate purpose of avoiding a global conflict, in the belief that this was the *sine qua non* of India remaining free from war. Mr. Nehru most recently has gone beyond neutralism because of its verbal associations and called this a 'Positive Policy for Peace'.

II

Staying out of war, the initial aim of neutrality, is one of the sources of neutralism—but it would be a grave error to assume that neutralism is merely a twentieth-century response to that age-old problem. On the contrary, there are many sources *sui generis*. The great merit for the practitioners of neutralism is that the objective sources of traditional neutrality and their subjective needs happen to coincide; indeed, to blend very well. Together they provide a powerful inducement to the policy of neutralism.

We may now look briefly at some of the specific sources of neutralism, focusing on India as the prototype. This is apart from the external setting—the character of world politics, the presence of nuclear weapons, the technological changes of the last fifteen years, and the awareness that war between the super-powers *ipso facto* means a war for all. These sources fall into two logical categories, material and non-material. The two key material mainsprings are geo-political and economic in character. The geo-political pressures on India are obvious. Indian statesmen are aware of the over-powering pressure of the Sino-Soviet axis on the Indian sub-continent. This does not mean that they are constantly conscious of hostility, but they are aware of the geo-political facts of life for an India which is essentially weak, which has rarely known unity, which is economically underdeveloped, and which finds itself strikingly inferior, both in economic and military terms, to a Moscow-Peking bloc. In other words, the geo-political condition leads to a simple policy of non-alienation of two very powerful neighbours, particularly when those neighbours are allied to each other.

That geo-political facet is strengthened by the seeming remoteness of all other countervailing centres of power. History tends to under-pin geo-politics here because of Indian awareness of frequent land invasion of the sub-continent; this is accentuated in turn by the Partition of 1947 and by a weak Pakistan. In other words, the facts of geography and resultant geo-political pressure create in the Indian decision-making élite a powerful inducement to a policy of non-alignment, though not necessarily of neutralism.

The economic factor is no less important. It arises from the objec-tive fact of economic underdevelopment and the subjective aspira-tion for material progress. That is to say, the desire to expand sources of foreign aid, whether of capital or technical assistance, whether co-operative, through international channels, private or public, creates a strong inducement to maintain the lines of communication with both Soviet and Western blocs as the two important sources of economic strength. There is, in addition, a deep conviction that war anywhere, whether in Laos or the Congo or in Cuba or anywhere else, is dangerous. It raises the level of tension between the two blocs, heightens the prospects of major war, and therefore reduces the prospects for economic growth, apart from the holocaust effects of global war itself. There is, then, an intertwining of objective and subjective pressures towards a policy of at least non-alignment or passive non-involvement in blocs.

Among the non-material factors, one may mention the legacies of history and philosophy. The legacy of history is twofold, but the two are so closely related that they constitute one driving force in the foreign policy of all neutralist (and most non-aligned) states: 'anti-colonialism' and 'anti-racialism'. These have strong policy implica-tions and overtones. Both derive from experience with the Western world. This is very significant, for both tend to offset political and economic affinities with the West and lead to greater tolerance of Soviet actions that would otherwise be the case. Whenever any great Western power is involved with a small power, whether in the Western hemisphere or, more particularly, with an Afro–Asian state—where it is accentuated by racial overtones—there is an instinc-tive response of condemnation. This is not true of Soviet actions, simply because the experience of India and other neutralist states with the Soviet bloc was different; in fact it was non-existent for a

I

long time. These twin elements, 'anti-racialism' and 'anti-colonialism', are even reflected in something like the neutralists' attitude to Cuba, remote as it is from their interests.

As for the legacy of philosophy and tradition, the notion of tolerance in Hinduism and Buddhism merits attention. This has certain implications for Indian, Burmese, Cambodian, and Ceylonese policy. The idea of tolerance is deeply embedded in Hindu–Buddhist society, and it has the political consequence of rejecting automatically all claims to the totality of truth, justice, and good in the world. The idea that many different religions have equally valid claims to contributing to the total understanding of truth reflects itself in the political realm in the rejection of the absolute perspectives of either the Marxist ideology or Western democratic beliefs. There is the reluctance to accept any claim to absolute truth, justice, or good, with the resultant blunting of the tone of their participation in conflicts that arise between East and West. Taken together, these external and internal factors create an integrated and powerful inducement to neutralism.

III

Three cases which reveal important aspects of Indian neutralism are the Korean War, and Suez and Hungary.[1]

The most striking feature of India's role in the Korean truce-making settlement from 1950 onwards is the extent to which its support alternated between one side and the other. On the four major issues that arose in the Neutral Nations Repatriation Commission (NNRC), India's chairman agreed in letter with the Polish and Czech delegates to the Commission but sided with the Swiss and Swedes in action. These four examples were on: (1) the use of force at the time of repatriation of prisoners; (2) the dismantling of prisoner-of-war organizations during that period; (3) the extension of the explanation period when prisoners were being persuaded as to whether they ought to return to their homelands; and finally, (4) the ultimate disposition of the prisoners of war.

From the very outset, in June 1950, India voted for United Nations condemnation of North Korea, but it insisted throughout that North Korea ought to be heard in the Security Council. India opposed the

---

[1] A careful and valuable study, from which the following analysis has benefited greatly, is B. S. Steinberg, *India's Neutralism in Theory and Practice* (unpublished Ph.D. thesis, McGill University, 1961).

crossing of the 38th parallel, but after all efforts to bring North and South Koreans together at the conference table seemed to be exhausted, India agreed to the crossing. India refused to condemn China as an aggressor in 1951 yet she maintained her ambulance unit in South Korea throughout the war. On the prisoner repatriation question, she drafted a resolution which favoured the Western position for the most part but with enough modifying clauses to make it palatable to the Chinese and North Koreans. As for India's role in the Neutral Nations Repatriation Commission, one finds this curious, perhaps unique, capacity to satisfy both sides on all the major issues—the positive contributions of neutralism in that case.

On the breaking-up of the prisoner-of-war organizations, India agreed that this was undesirable; on the other hand, it agreed with the Poles and Czechs that it would be desirable to segregate the leaders of these prisoner-of-war concentrations because of the trouble they were causing; then it proceeded to turn round once more and say that this would be very difficult because it would involve the use of force, and the Commission did not have enough power to do this. On the question of the right to use force, India agreed with the Polish and Czech delegates that there was nothing to prevent it in the terms of reference of the NNRC but added that the use of force was a major, substantive step and should not be taken without unanimity in the Commission. Since this was lacking, force was not used.

Another example concerns the extension of the explanation period, which was to be ninety days. The Polish and Czech members of the Commission pointed out that of the ninety days about fifty days or more were wasted because the United Nations and South Korean Commands were not acting in a way to facilitate explanations. According to the Communist delegates, 'ninety days means ninety days for explanations, and therefore, the ninety-day period ought to be extended until there were ninety full days of explanations'. The Indian chairman agreed 'because the prisoners had in reality only forty days'. 'On the other hand,' said the Swiss and Swedish delegates in effect, 'the terms of reference provide specifically for ninety days from the beginning of the explanation period; therefore, explanations must cease exactly ninety days thereafter; according to the letter of the NNRC, the ninety-day period has ended, so there must be no extension.' India agreed.

Finally, the Korean settlement provided for a return of prisoners only after a political conference took place. 'Well,' said the Polish and Czech delegates, 'the prisoners must remain in the compounds until a political conference meets [the proposed 14-power conference].' The political conference never took place. India agreed and so it could not officially transfer them to civilian status. But, unilaterally, it did restore the prisoners to the detaining sides without violating the letter of the NNRC.

Is this not a curious type of policy? Not at all. The Indian motive was clear, and I think consistent with neutralism. It was mainly to keep the Commission alive and to achieve the important objective of a Korean settlement. The phrase 'to judge every issue on its merits' does not mean to judge it, in the narrowest sense, on the merits of each tactical issue as it arises; rather, on the larger merits of reducing the level of international tension. By this unusual capacity to satisfy the four delegates to the Left and Right, India did bring off a Korean settlement. Not everybody was satisfied. But the record demonstrates that on the whole the NNRC was a major success in mediation in difficult circumstances.

The significance of the Korean episode in terms of neutralism is something else again. In so far as anyone in the Western world knew what neutralism was, and not many people did—not that many know even now—it seemed rather peculiar. To most people it was neutrality, and neutrality was isolationist. As a result of the NNRC the stigma of isolationism attaching to neutralism was terminated. People began to ask themselves the question, 'What kind of neutrality is this, when the neutral state actively intervenes in the settlement of disputes? This is not classical neutrality.' Of course it wasn't, but since neutrality and neutralism are almost indentical words it was assumed that they were the same policy or status.

In the Suez and Hungary episodes, India's response was strikingly inconsistent. Both of them were clearly invasions; without getting into the legal technicalities of aggression or non-aggression, they were both invasions of foreign territory by alien troops. Yet India invoked a peculiar double standard on these two issues. In the case of Hungary, India stressed what it called the broader implications of the problem, and in the case of Suez it adopted a narrower approach. Nor was this purely chance. To Delhi the Suez war was an attempted return of Western powers to an area from which they had recently withdrawn, an act not likely to win support in Asia.

Hungary was blurred. Certainly it is always easier for Indians to identify themselves with Egyptians than with Hungarians. To most Asian and African leaders violence between whites and other whites is bad, but violence of whites against non-whites is infinitely worse. And there are two levels of response to overt conflict involving a European and an Asian, or two Europeans. The latter is true of two Asians as well, as revealed by the incapacity to identify Japanese imperialism in the thirties and forties as of the same *genre* as Western imperialism of earlier epochs. It tended to be relegated to the category of the special case. Because it involved Asians and Asians, it did not have the same emotional impact as the British– French assault on Suez.

There are, I think, two further reasons for this inconsistency. First, criticism is expected in the Western world, Indians assume; that is part of the fabric of a constitutional democracy, they say. Westerners don't really mind it; they tend to flourish on it; and sometimes it has effect, as the criticism of British action by the British Labour Party and certain American and Commonwealth groups revealed. But criticism of the Soviet bloc meets a stone wall and is only likely to alienate without having any positive effect. Secondly, Hungary was viewed as a cold-war dispute which, if exacerbated, would lead to a higher level of tension between the Soviet and Western blocs. Suez was not. Suez involved a weak Afro-Asian state and two powerful Western states (leaving Israel apart, in this context). This was a case that did not have the likelihood of aggravating the cold war, unless the Soviets became directly involved. In short, it differed basically from Hungary, in India's view.

That glaring differences did exist in the Indian response is amply revealed by the records of the United Nations. The Indian reaction to Hungary was mild and slow, painfully slow, painful even for them in 1956. The Indian reaction to Suez was harsh and quick. Within less than twenty-four hours Mr. Nehru, on the basis of a single press report, used such highly-charged terms as aggression, invasion, dastardly actions, and so on. The demand for withdrawal was immediate and sharp in the case of Suez; it was not in the case of Hungary, at least not for a long time.

India's role in Korea reflects one aspect of neutralism—the belief that a neutralist state has a positive role to play in relaxing tensions. Suez and Hungary reveal other aspects, notably the crucial role of 'anti-colonialism' and 'anti-racialism' in the response of neutralism whenever a former colonial power of the West is involved with a non-Western colonial area.

IV

The criticism that is generally levelled at neutralism is twofold. One is that it is immoral, that it doesn't distinguish between good (the West) and evil (the Soviets). The second is that it is, in fact, a basic political error, that self-interest requires full and active participation by neutralist states in military alliances with the West.

On the question of immorality much can be said. Suffice it to note that Indian leaders, because of the legacy of tradition and tolerance, do not accept this conception of absolute morality or absolute immorality in the ideology of the two major blocs in world politics. Their perspective is much more blurred. It is grey and grey rather than black and white; the notion of Soviet immorality seems unproven to the Indian.

Regarding the alleged political error, the following general propositions may be made. First, mediation is not a monopoly of neutralism; indeed, there are cases in which the neutralist state fails when it attempts to mediate. There are even situations when an aligned state mediates much more effectively than a neutralist state. In other words, the pretensions of some neutralists to a monopoly over the mediation of international conflicts is to be seriously questioned.

The Korean, Suez–Hungary, and Laos cases reveal that India is more likely to offer mediation in a cold-war dispute involving the super-powers, that this offer is more likely to be accepted in that situation, and that it is more likely to be effective in those conditions. In Korea, India's attempts at mediation between 1950 and 1953 failed on every occasion. It succeeded only when certain conditions had been created, conditions in which there was a clear-cut military deadlock, in which the super-powers were embarrassed and wanted to extricate themselves from an awkward position, because the cost of continuing warfare beyond 1953 was too great in terms of whatever goals could be achieved. It was only in the conditions of stalemate and the desire of the super-powers to find a way out by diplomacy that a neutralist effort at mediation succeeded. In other words, it was the special conditions of Korea in 1953 that made India's effective mediation possible.

There are cases in which an aligned state mediates more effectively. These are cases when a neutralist is so emotionally involved because of anti-racial and anti-colonial issues that it ceases to have the value of a mediator, as in Suez. It was Canada, an aligned state, a participant in Western military alliances, that was capable of initiating the UNEF proposal which ultimately led to a more tranquil Middle East. India had forfeited any claim to the role of mediator because of its involvement, because of the overplay of the anti-racial and anti-colonial elements.

In the case of Hungary, Indian neutralism didn't succeed, partly because only one super-power was involved and there wasn't sufficient countervailing strength for the neutralist to intervene. Only under special conditions can India's neutralism make a positive mediatory contribution in international relations.

Nor does the neutralist state have a monopoly in its desire to preserve the peace. Other states share this goal. The difference lies in their conception of the appropriate techniques. The aligned state sees virtue in an occasional limited war, the neutralist state never, because of the conviction that limited war is likely to heighten tension. The aligned state sees the preservation of peace as best achieved by a military alliance, by 'bargaining from strength'. The neutralist sees the preservation of peace in opposition to military alliances on the grounds that they have a vicious-circle effect, one spawning another.

Thirdly, I think it is true to say that in a normal cold-war dispute like Korea, only the neutralist state has sufficient trust of the super-powers to mediate successfully. Canada couldn't do it in the case of Korea; it could sit as one of the five members of the Commission, but it was identified with South Korea. Similarly Poland couldn't; only India could.

There is a good deal of confusion about the kind of role neutralist states can and do play in international relations. Is neutralism merely a twentieth-century variation of the balancing process? I think not. The basic difference is that the United Kingdom in the nineteenth century had sufficient power to prevent the outbreak of war or, if war broke out, to throw its weight into the scales in such a way as to ensure victory for one or another of the participants. Today no state can be a balancer in the nineteenth-century sense simply because the gap between the power of the two super-powers and all others is such that the addition of the power of India or anybody else won't make any difference. In short, neutralists cannot deter global war by their possession of military power. If global war breaks out they can do nothing to determine the outcome. All they can do is to try by persuasion and other means of that kind, to prevent the resort to war by the super-powers, because of the realization that only then can they stay out of war themselves.

We come now to the final proposition, which is that neutralist states play a stabilizing role in international politics just by being neutralist. First of all, they provide an important channel for diverting the surplus energies of the super-powers from direct conflict to peaceful competition for the support of the neutralists. An analogy may be drawn here with the nineteenth century—the 'Hundred Years Peace' between 1815 and 1914, when there was no global war. One of the major reasons was that the great imperialist powers of Europe at the time were able to divert their energies from direct conflict to the division of much of Africa and Asia into colonial empires. They could avoid direct military conflict because they had enough to keep them happy and busy elsewhere! In the middle of the twentieth century, neutralist states in Asia and Africa can perform a similar, though not invidious, role. That is to say, instead of carving them up, the two blocs can reduce the likelihood of direct conflict by diverting their energies into a very time-consuming and very beneficial competition in the form of economic development and aid among the states of Asia and Africa. It is in the interests of the neutralist states to be non-aligned because, *inter alia*, they derive economic aid from many states, and war is thereby made less likely. It is in the interests of the super-powers, I think, to have a zone of competition and ultimately co-operation, for this zone, the neutralist zone, offers a tolerable alternative to military warfare.

The second facet of this proposition is that a totally 'bloc'-world, in other words, a totally bi-polarized world, in which all states are aligned with one or another of the super-powers, is rigid and therefore dangerous, with the temptation to play for the big stakes since there is only one rival to total domination. The neutralists perform the valuable function of a cushioning effect, increasing the flexibility of the system. They may also provide, as India does, a link between the hostile blocs and sometimes mediation, a necessary role in bi-polarized politics.

5

ISRAEL AND AFRO-ASIA

IMAGES AND REALITY

'AFRO-ASIA' brings to mind many images. To some, it is merely a geographical expression. To others, it is the home of the great religions, whose teachings have withstood the ravages of time and men. A third symbol is colonial rule and under-developed economies. A fourth is race or colour. Finally, the term 'Afro-Asia' suggests political and economic change, of such dimensions as to transform the classical system of international relations.

Whatever image is selected, Israel clearly falls within the meaning of 'Afro-Asia'. The Jewish state is part of the Asian continent; in fact, it is located close to the point at which Asia and Africa converge. Moreover, Judaism took root in Asian soil, flourished there, and exerted a profound influence on West Asia through the absorption of many of its ideas by Islam.

Israelis share with other Asians and Africans the fruits of a lengthy, and at times bitter, struggle for national self-determination. Like Indians and Indonesians, Ghanaians and Nigerians, they have known the meaning of foreign rule. Nor was it mere chance that Israel achieved its independence in 1948, for this was part of a sweeping historical process and the ferment of national consciousness throughout Asia and Africa. To deny that there is a Jewish nation is to engage in semantic trivia; the overriding fact is that in their millennia of dispersion Jews everywhere felt and thought as members of an integrated community. And during the past seventy-five years an Israeli nation has been forged in the fires of struggle no different from that of nations all over Afro-Asia.

Israel is not economically under-developed in the same sense as are most Asian and African states; using the indices of per capita income, per acre productivity, capital (or labour-intensive industry), employment skills, and public health, Israel qualifies more as a

European state.[1] However, its paucity of resources, the large number of unskilled immigrants, and the desert character of much of its land compel the same kind of massive economic effort imposed by the shortage of capital and skills elsewhere in Asia and Africa. Nor does the flow of economic aid from the West *ipso facto* make Israel a Western state.[2]

In its racial composition, too, Israel is 'Afro-Asian' almost as much as it is Western. Originally an overwhelmingly 'white', European community, about 40 per cent of its two million people are of Asian and African extraction; like everything else in Israel, the demographic picture was basically altered by the great 'ingathering of the exiles' during the 1950s.[3] As for the awakening of Asian and African peoples, few compare in pace and depth with the change wrought by a segment of Jewry returned to its ancient homeland.

The impact of the anti-colonial revolution on the structure of

[1] For a comparison of indices of economic development among Asian and African states, see Gabriel A. Almond and James S. Coleman (eds.), *The Politics of the Developing Areas* (Princeton 1960), Appendix. Thus, per capita gross national product in Israel is $540. The next highest in Afro-Asia is Malaya with $298. The lowest is $52 in Burma, with Afghanistan and Ethiopia a mere $54. Similarly, Israel's literacy rate is 93 per cent. The next highest is the Philippines, with 62 per cent. For India, the rate is 28 per cent, while the lowest, 5 per cent, is shared by Somalia, African states of the French Community, Saudi Arabia, Afghanistan, and Ethiopia.

[2] German reparations for crimes against Jewry (Is. £72 million) and foreign grants and loans (Is. £226 million) provided 67 per cent of the funds for Israel's development expenditure in 1961–2 (Is. £445 million). Israel's total expenditure for that year is estimated to be Is. £1,869 million. *The Israel Digest* (Jerusalem) Vol. IV, No. 2, 20 January 1961, p. 5. In addition the central fund-raising machinery of Jewish communities has provided the Jewish Agency for Israel with $581 million during the eleven years following the establishment of the state, i.e., an annual average of $52·8 million. ('The Fateful Years' (brochure), *Keren Hayesod* United Israel Appeal, 1960.) This figure excludes specific projects for which aid is provided, such as the Hebrew University, the Weizmann Institute of Science, the Technion, etc., or the funds raised by the sale of Israel State Bonds abroad. Foreign financial aid to Israel is substantial. However, other Asian states receive larger amounts of foreign (Western) aid and are more dependent on such aid than is Israel, e.g., South Vietnam, Formosa, South Korea, Laos. Yet no one suggests that they cease to be Asian!

[3] From 1948 to 1958 immigration to Israel totalled 922,274. Of these Asia provided 29·6 per cent and Africa 24·9 per cent; i.e., Afro-Asian immigration in the first decade accounted for 54·5 per cent of the total or 492,638. On 1 January 1959 the population of Israel totalled 2,031,672 in the following categories: Jews 1,810,148; Muslims 152,568; Christians 47,612; and Druzes 21,344. The last three are of Asian extraction, i.e., 221,524 non-Jews. Classification of Jews by continent of *origin* is unfortunately not readily available, for those would include persons born in Asia and Africa as well as Israeli-born Jews whose families *originated* in Asia or Africa. However, estimates and projections suggest that about 40 per cent of the population of Israel in 1959 were of Afro-Asian *extraction*. The figures cited are taken from *Facts About Israel,* 1959, Ministry for Foreign Affairs, Jerusalem, pp. 36–38.

international politics does not merit elaborate treatment here. Suffice it to note that a European-centred multi-power system has given way to a bi-polar world political system in which the new states of Asia and Africa are now *subjects* rather than mere *objects* of political behaviour. Of Israel's importance as an Afro-Asian state on the stage of world politics, attention need be drawn merely to the events of 1956 and the aftermath of the Suez War—in the United Nations, in NATO, in Anglo-American-French relations, in United States–Arab relations, etc.[1]

Israel may fit these images, but its reception in Afro-Asia (in reality, Asia) was decidedly cool. At the time of the United Nations General Assembly's Partition Resolution in November 1947 there were eight Asian members of the world body, apart from the Arab states, and two African members, excluding the Union of South Africa. Only two, the Philippines and Liberia, supported the creation of a Jewish state; and both were former American dependencies. Five were opposed: Afghanistan, Iran, Pakistan, and Turkey, all Muslim states, and India, which has a large Muslim minority. Two abstained, Nationalist China and Ethiopia, and Thailand was absent.

Initial hostility gave way to a slow and as yet incomplete acceptance by the Asian community. In the first two years of statehood six Asian states recognized Israel: Turkey, Nationalist China, the Philippines, Ceylon, Burma, and Thailand. But only one, Turkey, took the logical and customary next step of establishing diplomatic relations at once. Indeed, until 1952 there were no full-fledged Israeli diplomatic missions east of Ankara and, as late as 1957, only two, in Tokyo and Rangoon. In part, this unusual state of affairs was due to the absence of tangible Israeli interests in Asia during the early years, and the dearth of Jewish communities there. But there were more basic reasons for what was at best Asia's indifferent tolerance of Israel; and these reasons point up countervailing images of Israel in Asia which persist in some measure to the present.

The Old Testament is an integral part of the Judaeo-Christian heritage. Thus, almost everyone in the West is aware of the ancient Jewish Commonwealths, of the Jewish faith, and of the powerful emotional ties of Jewry to the Holy Land down through the

---

[1] See, for example, Guy Wint and Peter Calvocoressi, *Middle East Crisis* (Penguin 1957), and F. L. Schuman, *International Politics* (6th ed., New York 1958), 'An Addenda on the Anatomy of Anarchy', pp. 396–431.

centuries. Some Christians may question the justice or viability of the state of Israel, but few would ask of Jewry, 'What is your claim to the Holy Land?' The Bible and the spiritual kinship of Jews and Christians maintain a continuous knowledge of the Jewish connexion with Zion.

Herzl did not succeed in his efforts to enlist diplomatic support for Zionist aspirations, but Christian leaders did not question the propriety of his actions or doubt the unique Jewish link to Palestine. This Christian predisposition to view the Jewish claim favourably is also revealed in Weizmann's account of his first meeting with Arthur Balfour in 1906. Balfour asked why Zionists insisted on Palestine as the Jewish National Home; the Uganda offer was then to the fore. Weizmann spoke at length on the meaning of Zionism and then conveyed the essence of the Jewish claim: ' "Mr. Balfour, supposing I were to offer you Paris instead of London, would you take it?" He sat up, looked at me, and answered: "But Dr. Weizmann, we have London." "That is true," I said. "But we had Jerusalem when London was a marsh".' Balfour was moved and asked: ' "Are there many Jews who think like you?".' When Weizmann answered, ' "I believe I speak the mind of millions of Jews . . ." ', Balfour commented, ' "If that is so, you will one day be a force" '. Although Balfour did not become an immediate convert, Weizmann became convinced 'that if someone had been found to present the case of Palestine [as against Uganda] to the British authorities, it would not have been difficult to enlist their sympathies and perhaps, in certain circumstances, their active support'.[1]

Such sympathy, let alone active support, was unthinkable among Asian leaders, because historic Israel, Jewry, and Judaism are little known east of the Arab world. The small Jewish communities in India and Iran were unable to provide a link with the peoples of Asia. The Bible, so rich in Jewish history and tradition, is as alien to the cultures of South and East Asia as are the Vedas to the West.

A spiritual leader like Gandhi might include the Bible among the great religious books, but he could not absorb the Zionist idea of an indissoluble link between the Jewish people and the Holy Land. A sophisticated and highly Westernized Asian leader like Nehru was aware of the tie but at the purely rational level. As a student of world history, he also knew of the ancient Jewish Kingdom. But that was long ago and, for him, paled into insignificance when set alongside

[1] Chaim Weizmann, *Trial and Error* (New York 1949), pp. 109–11.

the visible fact of an Arab community living in Palestine. Thus, Nehru commented on the Balfour Declaration of 1917: 'But there was one little drawback, one not unimportant fact seems to have been overlooked. Palestine was not a wilderness, or an empty, uninhabited place. It was already somebody else's home.'[1] Almost all Westernized Asian intellectuals of the past half century subscribed to this view. In short, the lack of knowledge about the Jewish connexion with Palestine depreciated the Jewish claim in the Asian view. More than that, it tended to create the image of Jews as interlopers, aliens to Asian soil attempting to expel the true natives of Palestine.

The lack of knowledge provided the basis of another, even more damaging image, namely the identification of Zionism with British imperialism. To the Asian intellectual, the Jewish link with Palestine began with the Balfour Declaration. And that Declaration was a symbol of British imperialism planting 'alien' Jews on Asian soil. For staunch anti-colonialists, this tarred Zionism with the hateful brush of imperialism.

In some respects this was unavoidable. Britain had been given the Mandate; hence, the creation of a Jewish National Home depended on the leading imperialist Power of the age. This, in turn, meant the need to concentrate Zionist diplomatic efforts in London and Geneva. Only one Asian delegate ever sat on the Permanent Mandates Commission of the League of Nations. World Jewry was and still is predominantly Western; the funds for resettlement came from Western Jews, as did potential immigrants at that stage. There was, then, little inducement or opportunity to explain the Zionist case to Asia and much evidence of a link with the feared imperial Power. To quote Nehru again: 'The Arabs tried to gain their [the Jews'] co-operation in the struggle for national freedom and democratic government, but they rejected these advances. They have preferred to take sides with the foreign ruling Power....'[2]

The image of Jews as alien to Asia was strengthened by the fact that the creation of a Jewish National Home required a large influx of Jews from Europe. Moreover, as a small minority in Palestine in 1917, and still a minority in 1947, the Jewish claim to *national* self-determination seemed hollow to many Asians. Indeed, Asian nationalists never viewed the Jewish struggle for statehood as part

[1] Letter to his daughter on 29 May 1933. *Glimpses of World History* (New York 1939), p. 763.
[2] ibid., pp. 764–5.

of the general Asian struggle for national self-determination. In Palestine, that place was reserved for the Arabs.

Zionist leaders are partly to blame for this image, for they always avoided, consciously or otherwise, any identification with the anti-colonial nationalist movements. No Zionist spokesman was to be found at the various anti-imperialist conferences during the twenties and thirties. There were no public pronouncements allying Zionist goals with those of Asian nationalists. There were, of course, severe limits to freedom of action imposed by the nature of the Mandate. And yet there was nothing to prevent left-wing Zionist leaders from championing the cause of anti-colonialism. In failing to do so, they showed a remarkable lack of foresight, for which the State of Israel was to pay dearly. To some extent, that isolation from the mainstream of Asian nationalism, now in the form of neutralism, continues.

The negative image of Zionist aspirations was perhaps most powerfully influenced by the race factor. The vast majority of Jewish immigrants to Palestine until 1947 were 'white'. How then could they be considered Asian? The fact that the racial composition of the people of Israel has changed sharply in the past decade has not altered the image. Israel was alien then because it was white, among other things; it is still white to most Asian intellectuals.

One other factor contributed to the hostility or at least non-support of the Jewish claim to Israel. The phenomenon of anti-semitism is not a part of Asian cultures, partly perhaps because there are few Jews in Asia. In any event, there was no concern about 'the Jewish Problem', nor any appreciation of the need for a Jewish state. Thus, the lack of knowledge about the Jewish link with Palestine led Asians to discount the Jewish claim; the lack of anti-semitism led them to discount the need; and the fact of a majority Arab community led them to depreciate the justice of the Jewish case. This was true not only of non-Arab Muslims but also of non-Muslim and secularist Asian intellectuals. It was with this powerful countervailing image that the new State of Israel had to contend.

PARTIAL FULFILMENT IN ASIA

Israel's early quest for Asian acceptance centred on New Delhi. For one thing, India was the rising star of the East, with China in the throes of civil war and Japan temporarily removed from the ranks of the Great Powers. For another, India was the emerging leader of neutralism, and Israel was then in its 'non-identification' phase.[1] There was, too, a strong affection for Gandhi and Nehru among the Jews of Palestine. Nehru, in particular, appealed to the predominantly socialist leadership, for his was the voice of rational-ism, modernity, progress, and Westernization; a measure of the attachment was a Hebrew translation of his *Autobiography* in the thirties, before Nehru had achieved world renown and when the Hebrew-reading public was very small. Subconsciously, some Israeli officials seemed to hope that the Indian leader, non-Muslim but highly-respected by the Arabs, would be willing and able to moderate Arab hostility and, perhaps, provide a bridge between Israelis and Arabs. They have ceased to hope.

From the outset Delhi was unsympathetic. It had opposed the Partition Resolution of the United Nations General Assembly. And when Israel was proclaimed in May 1948, India was not impressed. Whereas the United States and the Soviet Union granted recog-nition within a day, India waited. Even after the Rhodes Armistice Agreements (February to July 1949) strongly suggested that Israel was a fact, India waited. Finally, in September 1950, it granted *de jure* recognition. There the matter rests, for India has effectively, but at times uncomfortably, resisted all advances for an exchange of diplomatic missions.

The first and most important episode in this strange non-relation-ship took place in February and March 1952, when the Director-General of the Israel Foreign Office conducted negotiations in Delhi as a guest of the Indian Government. In his own account of the affair, Mr. Eytan noted:

Before Israel's representative left New Delhi, he was informed that the Prime Minister had approved the proposal.

He was now questioned in detail on housekeeping problems.... A draft budget for the Indian Legation was being prepared, though the formal

[1] The initial five principles of Israeli foreign policy, as approved by the *Knesset* (Parliament) on 11 March 1949, were as follows:
(1) loyalty to the fundamental principles of the United Nations Charter and friend-ship with all peace-loving states, especially the United States and the Soviet Union ('non-identification' was the term used at that time); (2) efforts to achieve an Arab–Jewish alliance based on economic, social, and cultural co-operation within the United Nations framework; (3) support for all measures strengthening peace and the rights of men; (4) insistence on the right of Jews to settle in Israel—and to leave their present state of residence; and (5) effective preservation of the independence and sovereignty of Israel. 'From the Ministry of Foreign Affairs' in the *Jerusalem Post,* 23 April 1950.

decision to establish diplomatic relations remained to be confirmed by the Cabinet. This was to be done as soon as the new Government was set up following the elections a few weeks later.

No one has ever challenged this account. Mr. Eytan added: 'Nobody, in fact, outside Nehru's most intimate circle has ever discovered why the Government of India did not establish diplomatic relations with Israel in the spring or summer of 1952, and no convincing explanation has been given for its sudden change of mind.'[1]

The following explanation may not be convincing, but it is almost certainly accurate. The 'sudden change of mind' in the spring of 1952 was due to the forceful intervention of Maulana Azad, intimate friend of Nehru, respected leader of India's forty million Muslims, and Minister of Education in the Indian Government. (So this writer was told in Delhi by senior officials and Cabinet Ministers.) Until his death in 1958, the Maulana exerted great influence on India's Middle East policy, as well as on domestic and party affairs.

As a Muslim, Azad was naturally pro-Arab. He was also fearful of the consequences of diplomatic relations with Israel on India's position in the Arab world. An unstated but bitter rivalry with Pakistan for Arab support on the Kashmir dispute was then at its height, for India's policy on that issue was under severe attack in the United Nations and elsewhere. Azad (and Nehru) was also concerned about the possible impact of a welcoming gesture to Israel on India's large and insecure Muslim minority. Pakistan would probably have fanned the flames of communal hatred in India by reference to Israel. This might have affected the loyalty of India's Muslims and would, in any event, have been a shock to their already bewildered state of mind following the Partition riots and mass migration, with the aftermath of distrust among many Hindus. Was an exchange of diplomatic missions with Israel worth all these risks? Azad firmly argued against the proposal. Nehru may have been convinced—for the case was strong in terms of India's 'national interests'. At any rate, he yielded to Azad's advice.

What made the decision awkward in 1952 was the fact that it would be a special diplomatic gesture, and this would probably infuriate the Arabs. A subsequent incident tended to confirm this expectation. In the summer of 1960, the Shah of Iran publicly mentioned the recognition of Israel by Iran—apparently intending

[1] Walter Eytan, *The First Ten Years* (New York 1958), pp. 169–70.

merely to reaffirm Iran's recognition of Israel *de facto* ten years earlier. Nasser raged and broke off diplomatic relations with Teheran, at the same time inciting the Iranian people to revolt.[1] This was unlikely in India's .case, but the exchange of diplomatic missions with Israel *two years after* recognition would suggest a conscious act of friendship. This was precisely the Indian error, not establishing diplomatic relations at the same time as recognition was accorded.

India's former Defence Minister and 'adjunct' Foreign Minister, Krishna Menon, stressed this point in a lengthy interview granted the writer in 1956. Moreover, the longer the delay, the more difficult the decision became. At various times and in various places, Israeli envoys raised the question with India's Prime Minister or Indian diplomats. Each time they were told that the time was 'not ripe'; each time it became more embarrassing; and each time Israel was rebuffed. The only (tenuous) link is an Israel Consulate in Bombay, eight hundred miles from the capital and without diplomatic status.

Israeli attitudes have run the gamut, from expectation to hope to disappointment to dismay, and, finally, to anger. Conversations with Israelis from many walks of life, including senior Foreign Office personnel, have impressed this writer with the intensity of Israeli feelings on this matter. It is as if their trust—in Nehru personally—has been betrayed. Moreover, they see his policy towards Israel as a glaring violation of his constant stress on morality, friendship for all, judging each issue on its merits and, most important, his plea to the United States, in the case of China, to accept the political facts of life.

The Israeli mood has been most forcefully expressed by ex-Prime Minister Ben-Gurion. On one occasion he remarked that Nehru claimed to be a disciple of Gandhi, but 'I cannot understand how Mr. Nehru fits his behaviour to Israel with Gandhi's philosophy of universal friendship. Mr. Nehru gave definite promises to the Director-General of our Foreign Ministry eight years ago that he would soon establish normal diplomatic relations with Israel, but so far he has not kept his word.'[2]

---

[1] Informative materials relating to this episode are found in two publications of the Information Division of the Israel Ministry for Foreign Affairs: *Arab Comment on Current Affairs*, Special Issue, 'On the Shah's Policy Statement Concerning Iranian–Israel Relations', 14 August 1960, and *The Middle East in the World Press*, No. 40 (103), 30 August 1960.

[2] *The Times* (London), 13 November 1959.

K

In a comprehensive survey of Israel's position in world politics three years after the Sinai Campaign, Mr. Ben-Gurion went further: 'India, under . . . Mr. Nehru, refuses to establish normal relations with Israel, although he has repeatedly promised our representatives to do so.'[1]

In the same highly-significant article, the Israel Prime Minister administered a blunt rebuke:

> Nehru too claims allegiance to neutrality. . . . He is not even neutral in regard to Israel and the Arabs, for he has close ties and normal relations with the Arab countries—but he has stubbornly refused to establish diplomatic relations with Israel, and in his frequent visits to the Middle East he has on every occasion—and not by accident—overlooked Israel.[2]

By 1952 India's posture was unmistakable. Thus, Israel turned elsewhere with vigour. In that same year it pierced the diplomatic barrier in Asia by establishing a legation in Tokyo. For some time this was of little practical value—because of the Suez and Akaba blockades—but the symbolic benefit was not inconsiderable. Towards the other Great Power in the East Israel adopted an ambivalent position. It recognized the Chinese People's Republic in January 1950 but did not follow through with diplomatic relations.

In the spring of 1955, an Israel Goodwill Mission toured mainland China, but nothing ensued. Apparently, senior officials in the Israel Foreign Office had favoured acceptance of an earlier Peking *démarche* for an exchange of envoys. But the Israel Ambassador to the United States, either on the basis of his own assessment of the likely repercussions, or under pressure, apparently opposed this in the strongest terms.[3] The majority of the Israel Cabinet was also opposed to the establishment of diplomatic relations. A unique opportunity was therefore wasted, partly because of the fear, real or imaginary, that the United States would be annoyed.

Soon after came Bandung; and, as the Peking régime prospered diplomatically, it no longer needed Israel. More than that: the Arab states began to court China, which saw an opportunity to penetrate the Middle East. This also coincided with Moscow's virulent pro-Arab line. Thus, when at last Israel intimated that it wished to exchange envoys, Communist China refused. It may well be that even

---

[1] 'Israel's Security and Her International Position' in *Government Year Book*, Jerusalem, 5720 (1959/60), p. 66.   [2] ibid., p. 75.

[3] Related to this writer by members of the Israel Foreign Office.

if diplomatic relations had been established before Bandung, the Chinese would have thrust the Israelis aside in order to please the Arabs. Nevertheless, the incident revealed something less than diplomatic foresight.

A more severe setback for Israel in Asia was the Bandung Conference in 1955. The five sponsors of the Afro-Asian Conference had declared that all independent states in the area would be invited. But in the end some exceptions were made. Israel was perhaps the most glaring because it had been recognized by the overwhelming majority of states, including three of the sponsors, India, Burma, and Ceylon. By contrast, the Gold Coast was invited even though it was two years away from independence as Ghana. As if to underline the inconsistency, both North and South Vietnam were invited, but the two Koreas were not.

The decision to exclude Israel was not taken without dissension. Burma's U Nu strongly favoured its inclusion. Nehru, too, supported an invitation. But Pakistan and Indonesia were opposed; Ceylon took no stand. Ultimately, U Nu and Nehru yielded to Arab pressure. The Indian Prime Minister admitted this in a rather embarrassed comment on Israel and Bandung:

When the proposal was made for Israel to be invited . . . it transpired that if that were done the Arab countries would not attend . . . We felt that logically Israel should be invited, but when we saw that the consequences of that invitation would be that many others would not be able to come, then we agreed.[1]

As might have been expected, Israel became further disenchanted with India as the result of this lack of support.

An even greater blow was to follow at the Conference itself. Arab delegates used the forum thus provided for a savage verbal assault on Israel—but the 'criminal' was not allowed to be present. Among the resolutions approved by the historic 29-nation conclave was an unqualified support of the Arab cause:

In view of the existing tension in the Middle East caused by the situation in Palestine, and of the danger of that tension to world peace, the Asian–African Conference declares its support of the rights of the Arab people of Palestine and calls for the implementation of the United

[1] To this writer in New Delhi on 13 June 1956. For the complete text on this point see the Appendix, pp. 210–11 below.

Nations' resolutions on Palestine and the achievement of the peaceful settlement of the Palestine question.[1]

Although the practical significance of this resolution was limited, the symbolic victory of the Arabs was not.

The one bright spot in an otherwise dismal Asian picture was the forging of close ties with Burma. An inconspicuous visit by a Burmese delegation in 1952 marked the beginning of Israel's first diplomatic success in Afro-Asia. The following year, Foreign Minister Moshe Sharett represented *Mapai* (the Israel Labour Party) at the first Asian Socialist Conference in Rangoon. This was a turning point, for Sharett put Israel on the map of Asia in his persuasive and charming manner. Diplomatic relations with Burma were established in 1953, and, soon after, the experimental phase of Israel's technical assistance programme got under way. Medical personnel, engineers, conservation specialists, and several technicians in various fields went to Burma.

The friendship blossomed in the spring of 1955 when U Nu visited Israel. Apparently the Burmese Prime Minister had also accepted an invitation from Egypt and proposed to visit the two countries in succession. Cairo attempted to put pressure on Rangoon by indicating that he would not be welcome if he visited Israel. U Nu responded by cancelling his trip to Egypt.[2]

The ties with Burma were further solidified by an increasingly complex technical assistance programme. This took five closely-related forms: Israeli experts to Burma; Burmese trainees to Israel, especially in the field of agricultural co-operation; joint ventures, notably in the field of construction; management schemes, whereby Israelis provided managerial services to Burma; and establishment of firms in Burma for the Burmese with Israeli help. Thus, for example, Israel and Burma established a shipping company, the Five Star Line, with Israeli management. A joint building contracting company was established in 1959—to build roads, government buildings, etc. In the same year the Israeli co-operative, *Hamashbir*, made an agreement to market Burmese rice in Asia and Africa. Most important, Burmese ex-servicemen came to Israel for agricultural training preparatory to establishing co-operative villages in Burma model-

---

[1] The full text of the Bandung Communiqué is in the *New York Times*, 25 April 1955. For further details on the conference see George McT. Kahin, *The Asian–African Conference* (Ithaca 1956), and A. Appadorai, *The Bandung Conference* (New Delhi 1955).

[2] Related to this writer by members of the Israel Foreign Office.

led on those in Israel. Apart from placing the relations between Israel and Burma on a firm material basis, these agreements provided the model for the ambitious and remarkably successful Israeli technical assistance programme in Africa and elsewhere in Asia. A further strengthening of the friendship occurred in 1959 when General Ne Win, then Prime Minister of Burma, and the late President Ben-Zvi exchanged visits. It was the first state visit by an Israel Head of State.

If the diplomatic success in Burma was one turning point, the military victory in Sinai was another. The Suez Canal remained closed to Israeli ships after 1956, but the Gulf of Akaba linked Israel with Asia and East Africa no less effectively. Economic relations with the East, long dormant because of the double blockade, now came alive. Potash to Ceylon, copper and phosphates to Japan, oil from Iran, groundnuts from East Africa, these and other commercial ties strengthened Israel's position in the Afro-Asian world. Eilat now became the gateway to the East.

The opening of the Gulf had been one of the major aims and achievements of the Sinai Campaign; and Israel is determined to prevent its closure. Indeed, among the few automatic *casus belli* for the Jewish state would be any attempt to interfere with shipping to and from Eilat.

The diplomatic pace quickened in the wake of the opening of the eastern sea route. The years 1957 to 1960 witnessed a broadening of relations with Asian states (apart from the dramatic entry into Africa). The pattern in Asia was to accredit a non-resident mission and then a full-fledged mission—with reciprocity if possible; occasionally, there was an interim stage of a chargé d'affaires. Thus, the Israel minister to Japan was also accredited to Thailand until 1958, when a separate legation was established.

The case of Ceylon was much more complex. The Israel minister (later ambassador) to Burma was also accredited to the island Dominion (as well as to Laos and the Philippines). In 1959 an Israel chargé was appointed to Colombo, but the head of Israel's mission was now its minister to Japan, who took the accreditation with him when he left his post as ambassador to Burma. To make matters more complicated, the Government of Ceylon, which had reciprocated by appointing its ambassador to Italy non-resident minister to Israel as well, announced in the summer of 1960 that he would be withdrawn, as he had been appointed by a previous government without due regard to proper procedure and to Ceylon's interests in the Arab countries.

The Israel link with the Philippines was confined to honorary consuls and consuls-general from 1950 to 1957. A visit to Manila by former Prime Minister Sharett in the autumn of 1956 led to the exchange of envoys on a non-resident basis. In 1958 a Treaty of Friendship was signed. Thereafter, an Israel chargé was appointed to Manila and, in 1960, a full-fledged mission was established. The Philippines accredited their ambassador to Rome as non-resident minister to Israel. Thailand did the same.

At the end of 1960 Israel's diplomatic status in Asia was much improved: embassies in Burma and Thailand; legations in Japan and the Philippines; a chargé d'affaires in Ceylon; and non-resident missions to Nepal, Laos, and Cambodia. A Goodwill Mission from Cambodia and Economic Missions from Japan and South Vietnam in 1959, along with a technical assistance agreement with Nepal in 1960, and the steady expansion of trade, indicate how Israel has succeeded in 'jumping over the Arab fence'.

With the Arab states the relationship is one of 'neither war nor peace'. But with two non-Arab Muslim states, Iran and Turkey, friendly ties have developed. There is, indeed, a certain intimacy in the relations with Iran. A steady supply of oil goes from the Persian Gulf ports to Eilat whence it is sent by pipeline to Haifa for refining and distributed throughout the country. The completion of a sixteen-inch pipeline across the Negev, with plans for one double the size, underline this important link. There is also trade with Iran in other commodities and the provision of technical assistance by Israel. A frequent exchange of visits by academicians and students reinforces the friendship.

Israelis can move freely in Iran, despite the lack of formal diplomatic relations. Iran granted *de facto* recognition in 1949 and had indicated its approval of an Israeli mission headed by a chargé d'affaires. At the last moment Teheran withdrew under strong Arab pressure. Nevertheless, the informal relations have grown steadily closer. The assault on the Shah by President Nasser in July 1960 for reaffirming Iran's recognition of Israel only helped to strengthen the bonds. As if to stress this, Teheran sent a distinguished delegation to the Rehovoth Conference on Science in the New States —just a fortnight after the incident with the United Arab Republic.

What are Iran's motives for incurring Arab wrath? For one thing, the U.A.R. is friendly with Moscow, the greatest menace to the Shah. Moreover, Israel is a desirable counterpoise to Arab strength. Israel can also provide technical assistance without posing a threat to Iran, and helps to reduce Iran's fear of isolation in an Arab sea. For Israel, the advantages are self-evident.

Relations with Turkey are not as intimate but formally more correct and friendly nonetheless. The first Israeli envoy to an Asian state presented his credentials in Ankara in October 1949. For three years this remained the Israeli diplomatic beach-head in Afro-Asia. When Turkey joined the Baghdad Pact in April 1955, Iraq extracted an anti-Israel declaration from her, and relations with Israel became perceptibly cooler. The Sinai Campaign led to a severe strain. Turkey withdrew its head of mission from Tel Aviv and, in time, Israel reciprocated. Such was the formal diplomatic position at the end of 1960. Soon thereafter, relations were normalized.

Like Teheran, Ankara sees Israel as a useful counterpoise in the area. Periodic tension with the U.A.R. over Alexandretta strengthened the image of Egyptian imperialism. Both Turkey and Iran are also concerned about Cairo's links with Moscow, and both reject the image of the Middle East as an Arab region. Israel weakens that image. Both have therefore refused to follow the Arab League line of encirclement of Israel; and both testify to the cardinal truth that cordial relations betwteen Muslim and Jewish states are possible.

There remain major gaps in Israel's diplomatic status in Asia. Peking continues to be hostile. Karachi and Jakarta are also hostile but for different reasons.[1] And Delhi is still unfriendly. Normal relations with China seem remote. Pakistan and Indonesia will probably follow the Arab lead. Thus, the one great nut to crack is India.

Leading organs of the Indian press openly call for an exchange of envoys with Israel.[2] So do leading politicians. And yet this seems highly unlikely as long as Mr. Nehru is at the helm. The Indian Prime Minister seems reluctant to take the plunge for three reasons: firstly, domestic pressures and assumed national interests, i.e., disquiet about the possible effects on India's forty million Muslims and

[1] In a play for Arab friendship, Indonesia excluded Israel from the Asian Games, held in Jakarta in 1962. This led to world-wide press criticism and to an incident with Delhi, following criticism of Indonesia's action by the Indian Vice-President of the Asian Games Federation.

[2] See, for example, editorials in the *Indian Express* (New Delhi), 9 April 1960, *The Times of India* (Bombay), 10 May 1960 and 22 April 1962, and *Hindustan Standard* (Calcutta), 23 April 1961.

rivalry with Pakistan for Arab support on the Kashmir problem; secondly, an unconscious or sub-conscious feeling that Israel is a part of the 'colonialist' world, a legacy of the assumed attachment between Zionism and British imperialism; and thirdly, an oft-stated belief that he can play a beneficial role in the Arab–Israel conflict by *not* having full relations with Israel.[1] A change in the first and second factors is almost impossible, the first because vital interests are involved, the second because of deep-seated prejudices exacerbated by the Sinai Campaign, as revealed by Mr. Nehru's abrupt condemnation of Israel and Krishna Menon's intemperate language at the United Nations.[2] Thus, normal diplomatic relations with Israel are improbable under Nehru's leadership.

TECHNICAL ASSISTANCE: ISRAEL'S 'PRESENCE' IN AFRICA

In contrast to Asia, Africa welcomed Israel with unembarrassed warmth. For one thing, there was no emotional predisposition to favour the Arab cause; some Africans had had no previous contact with either Jew or Arab, while those who knew the Arabs recalled the slave trade above all. Moreover, Africans accepted Israel as non-African and did not impose a burden of self-identification with their cause. Indeed, for many Africans, Israelis were Europeans, but this was not automatically a symbol of derision, as it was for so many Asians. For Africans generally, there was no problem of emotional exclusion or inclusion of the Jewish state; it was accepted on its merits. In this respect, they adhered to the views of a leading Burmese newspaper:

Perhaps there is very little sentiment in our approach to the Jewish problem. We are not concerned with what they have been doing, and

[1] See, for example, Nehru's remarks to the Lok Sabha on 20 November 1956. Jawaharlal Nehru, *Speeches in Parliament*, 16 November–7 December 1956, Information Service of India, pp. 34–35.

[2] As early as 31 October, on the basis of press reports, Nehru declared that the Government of India 'consider the Israeli invasion and the subsequent U.K.–France ultimatum a flagrant violation of the United Nations Charter. . . . This aggression is bound to have far-reaching consequences in Asia and Africa and may even lead to war on an extended scale.' *Keesings' Contemporary Archives*, 1955–56, p. 15209. On one occasion, Mr. Menon told the General Assembly: 'We desire to state without any superlatives that we regard the action of Israel as an invasion of Egyptian territory, and the introduction of the forces of the U.K. and France as an aggression without any qualification.' *General Assembly Official Records*, Eleventh Session, First Emergency Special Session, 1–10 November 1956, 567 Plenary Meeting, 7 November 1956, p. 116.

have had done to them, for two thousand years. They are there trying to settle themselves in a tiny bit of desert and are putting up a very good show. Some of them have come to help us, no doubt with pragmatic motives. We have no prejudice against Jews and have not the least desire to discriminate against them just to please the Arabs or anybody else. There is much to admire in the Israelis. . . .[1]

As Burma was the breakthrough in Asia, so Ghana was in Africa. Despite Arab pressure, Nkrumah welcomed an Israeli diplomatic mission on the morrow of independence. The Burmese experience seems to have been decisive in persuading the Ghanaian leader that Israel was the most admirable (and least dangerous) choice for technical assistance. The Burmese pattern was applied, but more quickly and more efficiently. Thus, the Black Star Line was jointly established by the Government of Ghana and *Zim*, the Israeli shipping company, on a 60–40 share ratio. Similarly, a joint construction company was established with the aid of *Solel Boneh*, Israel's premier organization in this field.

Apart from these co-operative ventures, a substantial number of Israeli technical experts have gone to Ghana, as to Burma, in the past six years: in public health, agriculture, education, engineering, economic planning, etc. A merchant marine training school is under the direction of Israeli naval officers. A Flight School was opened and operated by members of Israel's Air Force. And two lecturers from the Haifa Technion were loaned to the Kumasi College of Technology.

In magnitude, Israeli assistance to Burma and Ghana is comparable. But the attitude of the recipients is somewhat different. Ghana goes into joint ventures with greater vigour but is more interested in getting the donor out quickly. Thus, in 1960 the Israeli shares in the Black Star Line were sold to Ghana three years after the company was formed, Israelis remaining only in a managerial function. So too with the Ghanaian National Development Corporation in 1962. Similarly, the Air Force unit returned home at the end of their two-year contract. The by-product of warmth and friendship for Israel would appear to be greater from the Burmese programme.

Israeli technical assistance was simultaneously extended to neighbouring African states, and in the East a major programme was developing in Ethiopia. By 1960 there were about 100 Israeli experts in Ghana, 100 in Nigeria, 50 in Liberia, 20 in Sierra Leone, and 150

[1] *The Nation* (Rangoon), 20 October 1959.

in Ethiopia, apart from smaller numbers in another dozen states of Afro-Asia. By 1963 there were approximately 900 Israeli technicians in Africa (and Asia).

Accompanying this growth in technical assistance, indeed facilitating it, was the expansion of Israel's diplomatic representation in Africa. The embassy to Ghana in 1957 was followed by one to Liberia the same year. Guinea was added in 1959. And in 1960, the year of 'African independence', Israeli diplomats spread over the map of West and Central Africa more rapidly than those of any other state in the world comparable to Israel in size. The Mali Federation, later Senegal and Mali, the Congo and Malagasy, Nigeria and the French Congo, all followed in rapid succession. Since then, Israeli links have been extended, with 23 diplomatic or consular missions in 1963, buttressed by a series of Treaties of Friendship, notably with French-speaking African states and by an exchange of visitors. These two elements, technical assistance and diplomacy, are the pillars of Israel's dramatic and successful 'presence' in Africa today.

The origins of technical assistance are obscure but may be traced to international Socialist conferences in the early 1950s attended by *Mapai* and the *Histadrut* (Trade Union Federation). The actual initiative appears to have been taken by Afro-Asian visitors to Israel who suggested that under-developed areas had much to learn from the Jewish state. Israelis were initially dubious, on the grounds that their experience was unique.

The first experiment took place in Burma in 1955–6, in the fields of agriculture, engineering, and public medicine. Another key event was a tour of West African territories by Israel's Foreign Minister in February–March 1958; Mrs. Meir, until then unaware of its role, became deeply impressed with the value of technical assistance. A decision was made to proceed with a modest programme, but a struggle for control ensued. Mrs. Meir insisted that technical assistance had great political significance and could not be severed from the Foreign Office. The Prime Minister yielded and, at the beginning of 1959, a Section on International Co-operation was established in the Foreign Office. A year later, it became a full Division.

Another important event was a three-months' International Seminar on Co-operation which began in November 1958. More than fifty members of co-operative movements in fourteen Asian and African countries attended this unusual conference in Israel; lectures were combined with tours of the country and visits to co-operative villages. More than any other event, this produced an Afro-Asian awakening of Israel's possible role. A French Sudan spokesman declared: 'Our delegation is an echo of the desire of African countries to co-operate with Israel.' The Secretary of the Alliance of Ghana Co-operatives referred to 'this material and spiritual pilgrimage to the Holy Land', and others spoke in a similar vein.[1] Thereafter, the programme gathered speed and moved from one success to another.

Israel's technical assistance activities fall into three categories. The first and smallest is that channelled through the United Nations—some 12 to 15 Israeli experts and about 20 to 30 foreign trainees visiting Israel each year for brief periods. All costs are borne by the United Nations, the two-way flow being administered in Israel by the Prime Minister's Office. There is little, if any, direct benefit to Israel.

Another category consists of joint companies and ventures, both public and private. These take various forms: joint stock companies, usually on a 60–40 share ratio in favour of the local government, notably in public construction, in water supply and irrigation, and agricultural planning; management contracts, especially in shipping; and Israeli companies incorporated in Asian countries such as Turkey and Iran. Many Afro-Asian states are involved in these projects, notably Cyprus, Turkey, Iran, Nepal, Burma, Sierra Leone, Ghana, Nigeria, Liberia, Togo, and Ethiopia. The estimated value of the products of these companies in Africa alone in 1962 was $162 million. On the Israeli side, they are directed by *Solel Boneh*, the construction corporation of the *Histadrut*, and *Wared*, Water Resources Development International Company Ltd., along with Dizengoff West Africa and Maier Brothers. The Economic Ministries and Departments are also involved.

The third category consists of bilateral technical assistance agreements on a government-to-government basis. These are administered by the Division for International Co-operation of the Foreign Office. Two types of assistance are involved in what may be termed a cycle operation: Israeli experts go to other states and Afro-Asian trainees are sent to Israel in the same fields. The model is as follows: state X seeks Israeli assistance on a particular problem; an Israeli survey mission will be sent out, usually for one to three months; if its recommendations are accepted, Israel sends the required experts;

[1] *The Israel Digest* (Jerusalem), Vol. I, No. 16, 28 November 1958, p. 3.

and, at the same time, sometimes earlier, state X will send trainees to Israel. As a rule, all costs except those of the trainees while in Israel are borne by the recipient state; hence, the financial burden to Israel is small. For example, Liberia sought aid to establish a self-operating ophthalmological centre. Four Israeli doctors and nurses went to Monrovia and set up the project while some Liberians went to Israel for training. Gradually, the Israelis were withdrawn as qualified Liberians became available. Another case was that of the Government Hospital at Massawa which was taken over by Israeli medical personnel while six Ethiopian nurses were sent to Israel for training.

By far the most ambitious scheme of this type was the Burmese Agricultural Training Project. In the first stage, an agricultural and soil and water survey of a frontier jungle area in north-east Burma was conducted by three Israelis for fourteen months. Thereafter, a group of sixty Burmese ex-servicemen and their families were sent to Israel for intensive training. They lived in various co-operative villages for over a year. During their last four months in Israel, a hand-picked settlement team of four Israeli experts lived and worked with the Burmese trainees and then accompanied them to Burma. In the meantime, the Burmese Government prepared the first two villages for settlement. At the same time as the sixty families returned home, a second group of 103 Burmese families went to Israel. The first sixty families provided the nucleus for two villages and an experimental station. A third, and possibly fourth, village is being prepared, and the 103 Burmese will later provide the nucleus. The goal was an integrated plan based on the Lachish model in the northern Negev desert of Israel.

The execution of this project was not without difficulty. The Israeli experts urged an evolutionary type of development; the Burmese wanted a revolutionary approach, i.e., the immediate maximum mechanization of agriculture. The Israelis argued in favour of oxen on the grounds that this would be easier for the Burmese in their traditional society; the Burmese preferred machines, claiming that their people needed regimentation. The Israelis won. Machines were used to clear the jungle, and the experimental station for the area as a whole has a high scientific level. But within the village, the problem is one of improving seed, fertilizers, and oxen. The benefits of the project for Burma have been threefold: settlement of ex-servicemen; greater security on the frontier; and increased agricultural yield. For Israel it means a possible model for Afro-Asian states and stronger ties with Rangoon, the Israeli key to South-East Asia.

Typical of Israel's technical assistance agreements with Afro-Asian states is the one concluded between Prime Ministers Ben-Gurion and Koirala in August 1960. Israel agreed to send to Nepal 'at an early date a group of experts to determine and draw up concrete plans of technical and other assistance and joint enterprises with Nepal in the field of agriculture, industry and construction works. . . . Israel also agreed to provide scholarships for specialized and general training of Nepalese personnel and students in Israel.'[1] In September 1960 Agriculture Minister Moshe Dayan visited Ethiopia and announced that additional advisers would be sent for government ministries, medical services, etc., with joint enterprises in the making. A few months later a technical aid agreement was signed with the Republic of Mali, providing for the dispatch of Israeli experts in tropical agriculture, medicine, and vocational training.[2]

There are other types of Israeli aid to Afro-Asia. Nigeria was granted a credit of $8.4 million: in reality, a guarantee of Israeli–Nigerian trade transactions by the Government of Israel; the result is goodwill and a stimulus to trade, with little risk. Faculty members of the Haifa Technion, the Israel Institute of Technology, have been teaching or organizing teaching in Liberia, Ghana, and Ethiopia.

A path-breaking Afro-Asian Institute for Labour Economics and Co-operation in Israel opened its doors in late 1960. Seventy trade union leaders, heads of co-operative movements, and government officials from fifteen Afro-Asian countries were enrolled in the opening course of six months divided equally between lectures and practical training. Established under the joint auspices of the *Histadrut* and the AFL-CIO, with an annual working budget of about $300,000, the Institute has tended to become a focal point for trade unionism in Afro-Asia.[3] Altogether, 1500 Africans are scheduled to take a wide range of intensive technical courses in Israel in 1963.

What, then, accounts for the warm reception of Israel's technical assistance diplomacy in Afro-Asia, especially in Africa? The most succinct formula would be that Israel is Jewish, young, small,

---

[1] The partial text of the communiqué is in *The Israel Digest*, Vol. III, No. 18, 2 September 1960, p. 6.   [2] ibid., Vol. III, No. 25, 9 December 1960, p. 5.
[3] *New Outlook* (Tel Aviv), Vol. IV, No. 3, January 1961, pp. 60–61.

developing, pioneering, and skilled. Israelis are Caucasians, but they are not members of a master race. Indeed, Jewry can readily be portrayed as the guinea pig of colonialism in Europe; and the similarity of the ghetto and *apartheid*, both symbolic of racialism, is not difficult to perceive. Moreover, Israel is one of the new states emerging from the post-war anti-colonial revolution. The fact that it is small means that Israeli assistance can be accepted without fear. The danger of domination by Jerusalem is too fantastic to be real, despite Arab efforts to convey this image. The Soviet Union has backed the Arabs in this as in other respects. 'Peoples freed from colonialism cannot help but feel extreme distrust of Israel, playing the part of a Trojan horse of the oppressive forces of imperialism'; thus wrote *Izvestia* at the end of 1960.[1] The Voice of Israel replied: 'To put Israel into this category is simply ludicrous'; and so it is, to most Africans at any rate.[2]

As a developing economy, and a small one at that, Israel has an additional advantage. One African student in Israel remarked: 'In the United States I can study the history of development. In Israel I can see economic development in action.'[3] An official from Senegal reportedly said: 'It seems logical to us that since we are small we can learn more from a small, efficient country than from a big, efficient country.'[4] In short, the scale and method of development offer a meaningful model for the many small African states.

Unlike most Western states capable of granting technical assistance, Israel has a relatively large number of people willing to serve in the new states. For example, within forty-eight hours of the announcement that Israel would send a medical team to the Congo, there were two or three applicants for every job. To this pioneering spirit must be added a manner of living which contrasts sharply with that of the 'ugly American'. One English journal put the matter bluntly:

What the Africans like about the Israelis . . . and much prefer over what they get from, say, American aid units or even UN units, is the fact that the Israelis fit inconspicuously into the African scene. They live and make themselves at home in lodgings scattered over town and with African neighbours. They are an easy-going people in their khaki slacks or shorts and their open-necked shirts and are able to 'make do' without

[1] Quoted in the *New York Times*, 13 December 1960.   [2] ibid., 14 December 1960.
[3] Related to this writer in Israel in 1960.
[4] Quoted in the *New York Times*, 16 October 1960.

fuss. The 'aid people' from America must have air-conditioning and all sorts of contraptions and organize their lives in a manner that emphasises the difference between themselves and their black hosts, who don't like that kind of thing nowadays.[1]

The skills of Israelis, then, are in greater demand. And given the size of its population, Israel is among the most highly-skilled states in the world. Israel is itself dependent on capital, but in certain kinds of technical knowledge it is well-endowed—fields such as agricultural co-operation, construction, public health, and others which African states find vital to their growth.

Other factors have helped to make Israeli technical assistance popular and effective. One is speed—Israel provides experts within six to eight weeks of a request, compared with eighteen to twenty-four months for the United Nations. Another is economy—salaries and accommodation for the experts, transportation, etc. A third is the lack of any talk of charity or a feeling of strings attached to the aid. And a fourth is the Israeli willingness to move out of a venture as fast as they moved in, as illustrated in the Ghana shipping case. All these, added to the basic formula noted above, account for the striking success achieved in a few years.

There are, however, some handicaps under which Israelis labour. Virtually all their experts in Africa are light-skinned. Active counter-propaganda from the Arabs, abetted by the Soviet bloc, produces some doubt among Asians and Africans. And despite its relative wealth of skills, Israel has a shortage of experts in medium and heavy industry, which some of the new states wish to build rapidly. But these liabilities have not yet diminished the attraction of Israel's programme.

AIMS AND RESULTS

It is always difficult to uncover the motives of states and states-men; but in most cases elements of both self-interest and altruism are present. Certainly this is true of Israel's massive effort in technical assistance to Afro-Asia. There is, first, an awareness of the growing importance of Afro-Asia in the world political community, especially in the United Nations. Given the political arithmetic of the United Nations and its membership in the 1960s, the new states are vital to Israel; indeed, her 'national interest' is to identify with them, in so far as they will permit.

[1] *Time and Tide* (London), 3 September 1960.

The urgent, short-term goal is to win support in the passionate conflict with the Arabs; Afro-Asia in this sense is a crucial extension of the battle for survival. Israel's minimal aim is Afro-Asian non-alignment; that is to say, voting on the merits of each issue between Israel and her neighbours. A higher aim is pro-Israel neutralism: a predisposition to look favourably on Israeli deeds and aspirations. This is the most that could possibly be achieved, though some utopians dream about full Afro-Asian support in the Arab–Israel struggle. This wish to neutralize Africa and Asia with reference to the Arab–Israel dispute becomes a battle for counter-propaganda, and technical assistance is Israel's most effective weapon. The Arabs have marked psychological advantages in Asia and are cultivating African friendship, thereby making the Israeli effort more important and more difficult.

Closely related to this self-interest goal is the hope to reach the Arab mind via friendship with Afro-Asia. If the Arabs became convinced that they cannot persuade other Asians and Africans to their way of thinking about Israel, they may well adjust to others' thoughts about the Jewish state; so runs the argument. Thus, an impact on Arab thought and policy may result from Israeli political and economic successes on the periphery, namely, those countries surrounding the Arabs, such as Turkey, Iran, and Ethiopia, as well, of course, as the further peripheral circles of Afro-Asian states. In effect, this is an outflanking manoeuvre using psychological and diplomatic-economic means.

The negative aim is greater African ability to withstand the pressure of Nasserism, with a possible indirect effect on the Arab attitude to Israel. The long-term hope appears to be Afro-Asian pressure on the Arabs to relent in their hostility to Israel. In more practical terms, Israel values the commercial and economic relations with Asian and African states, particularly the latter, for these offset and thereby weaken the Arab economic boycott. Israelis view the Arab world as a fence which has to be surmounted both politically and economically if their isolation is to be ended. 'Climbing over the fence' to Afro-Asia is probably the most immediate and vital objective of technical assistance.

Former Prime Minister Ben-Gurion frequently gave expression to these interests and aims. Aid to Asia and Africa, he declared in late 1960, 'is the most reliable way to win sympathy, understanding and friendship in the world—in all the continents—and it is bound to lead to relations of peace and co-operation with our neighbours as well'. More expressively, 'only through . . . the acquisition of the friendship and sympathy of nations near and far . . . shall we in time breach the wall of hatred and boycott that surrounds us. . .'.[1]

The Israeli leader also pointed to other motives, among them the enhancement of Israel's status in the West: 'All these things redound to Israel's honour in Europe and America.'[2] Even more important is a sense of mission and a desire to share achievements and experience with less fortunate peoples. To the more mystical like Ben-Gurion, Jewry must perform anew the role of a 'light to the nations', viewed in spiritual and moral terms. But apart from this is an obligation flowing from its advanced civilization and place in Afro-Asia.

Israel has been granted the great historic privilege—which is therefore also a duty—of assisting backward and primitive peoples to improve themselves, develop and advance, thus helping to solve the gravest problem of the twentieth century . . . the problem of the dangerous gap between Asia and Africa on the one hand and Europe and America (and Australia) on the other.[3]

Most Israelis see Israel's role in more modest terms (Ben-Gurion did on occasion, too). For them, more secularist in outlook, there is a conviction that modern Israel has developed certain patterns and institutions which can benefit other small developing states in Afro-Asia. For both, mystics and secularists, there is a genuine desire to assist those who seek the benefits of science and technology. This idealistic strain derives its fervour from three sources: the Jewishness of Israel; the socialist and anti-colonialist legacy of Palestine Jewry; and a deep feeling of gratitude for Israel's own achievement of independence. In short, there is an element of messianism flowing from the diverse roots of the Jewish state.

There appear to be two other, unstated, sources of Israel's restless surge into Africa. One is the desire to serve as a bridge between the former colonial powers of the West and former dependent territories. The possession of Western skills, without the stigma of colonialism, fits Israel for a key role of channelling aid from the West which might be suspected if granted directly. The Israeli effort to secure

---

[1] Speech to the *Knesset* on 24 October 1960. *The Israel Digest*, Vol. III, No. 22, 28 October 1960, pp. 1, 4.   [2] ibid., p. 4.

[3] 'Israel's Security and her International Position' in *Government Year Book*, Jerusalem 5720 (1959/60), p. 69.

admission to the Common Market, and Ben-Gurion's visits to France, the Low Countries, and Scandinavia, were partly directed to this end. Of course, Israel would gain much from this role in its search for acceptance, stability, and security. Finally, Afro-Asia provides an admirable outlet for Iraeli energies. For a long time, these were concentrated on the struggle for statehood. With the establishment of Israel, new horizons were needed. Africa, in particular, provides them in a challenging and acceptable form, namely, an opportunity to contribute to the welfare of other peoples.

What has the programme of technical assistance achieved? Thus far, the positive impact has been mainly psychological. In the words of its able mentor, it 'is the most effective instrument to place Israel on the map of Africa in a favourable light'.[1] Moreover, it persuades Asians and Africans that Israel is a lasting entity in the area, despite Arab propaganda to the contrary. A rare expression of tribute from an official *Arab* source is noteworthy: 'Israel's economic policy . . . with Afro-Asian nations is renowned and has often been mutually beneficial.'[2]

In a broader perspective, technical assistance is a counterweight to the thirteen Arab votes in the United Nations; and yet the political rewards for Israel have been modest indeed. Israel's exclusion from the Bandung Conference has already been noted. Its continuing exclusion from the Afro-Asian bloc at the United Nations is a serious liability and reduces Israel's potential influence. The reaction of Asian and, to a lesser extent, African states to the Sinai Campaign was harsh, with Israel portrayed as a vassal of the 'colonialists'. Even if one excludes Asia, the political response to Israel has not been enthusiastic. Every year the African delegations at the United Nations invite all members to a cocktail party. Until 1960, however, Israel was excluded—on the grounds that Arab African states held a majority (5–4) and threatened to boycott the affair!

More serious were two episodes at African conferences in 1960–1. The Israel Ambassador to Guinea, already seated as an observer to the Afro-Asian Solidarity Conference in Conakry, was compelled to withdraw in the face of Arab insistence that 'Palestine' be repre-

---

[1] Related to this writer in Israel in 1960.
[2] *United Arab Republic Bulletin*, U.A.R. Embassy, Colombo, Vol. I, No. 7, October 1960, p. 2, as quoted in 'Arab Comment on Current Affairs', Ministry for Foreign Affairs, Jerusalem, No. 30, 15 January 1961.

sented by an Arab group. Israel also suffered a defeat at the first African States Conference in Addis Ababa. Only the U.A.R. among the Arab states pressed for adoption of a typical 'Palestine Resolution' expressing support for the Arabs of 'Palestine'. Nor were the non-Arab Africans outvoted. Yet they yielded to Cairo's pressure. Apparently the U.A.R. threatened to oppose an anti-South Africa Resolution, if the Africans did not support a 'Palestine Resolution'. Further, Cairo rejected an African request to close the Suez Canal to trade with South Africa—on the grounds that the Canal was an 'International Waterway'! What disappointed Israel most was the ease with which African states violated their pledge to oppose any anti-Israel resolution at the Conference.[1]

The most dramatic setback to Israel's policy in Africa occurred at the African 'Summit Conference' in Casablanca at the beginning of 1961. An unequivocal resolution on 'Palestine' contained the following indictment of Israel :

The Conference . . .
Notes with indignation that Israel has always taken the side of the imperialists each time an important position has to be taken concerning the vital problems about Africa, notably Algeria, the Congo and the nuclear tests in Africa, and the Conference, therefore, denounces Israel as an instrument in the service of imperialism and neo-colonialism not only in the Middle East but also in Africa and Asia.[2]

Among the signatories were the Presidents of Ghana and Mali, both recipients of substantial Israeli technical assistance. Israel's envoys to these ostensible friends in West Africa conveyed expressions of 'disappointment and profound surprise' but apparently to no avail.[3]

In those early years, too, Afro-Asia supported the Arab cause in most United Nations resolutions on controversial issues between Israel and its neighbours. The first straw in the African wind of neutralism towards the Arab-Israel conflict was President Nkrumah's implied offer of mediation in September 1960; in his address to the General Assembly, the Ghanaian leader called for a 'realistic and practical solution' based upon the acceptance of 'the political realities that prevail there today'.[4]

---

[1] This account of the Addis Ababa Conference was related to the author by members of the Israel Foreign Office.
[2] Taken from an unofficial copy of the communiqué issued by the Casablanca Conference.   [3] *New York Times*, 11 January 1961.
[4] *The Israel Digest*, Vol. III, No. 21, 14 October 1960, p. 5.

This new tone became increasingly apparent at African conclaves and at the United Nations in the next few years. Thus, at the UAM Heads of State conference in Tannarive, in April 1961, the leaders of French-speaking Africa agreed to support a U.N. proposal calling for direct negotiations between Israel and her neighbours; this was later formally expressed in the 16-member 'Peace Resolution' at the closing meeting of the General Assembly's Special Political Committee, in December 1961.[1] Although rejected by 44 to 34, with 20 abstentions, it was a symptom of the new African line.

The Monrovia and Lagos Conferences in 1962 made no formal reference to Israel or the Arab–Israel imbroglio. But at the end of the year African neutralism on that issue was vocally expressed once more—in a 22-member Draft Resolution (including 12 African states) to the General Assembly's Special Political Committee. As on the earlier occasion,

The General Assembly . . . Renews its appeal to the Governments concerned to undertake direct negotiations . . . with a view to finding a solution, acceptable to all the parties concerned, for all the questions in dispute between them, particularly the question of the Arab refugees.[2]

The Arabs countered with a well-worn attack on Israel. It soon became apparent that neither resolution would secure the necessary two-thirds majority, and so, for the first time in fifteen years, the Arab resolution was withdrawn (as was the 22-member proposal); the annual Arab thrust in the Assembly was thereby blunted—by the political arithmetic of the post-1960 United Nations.

This new African line reached a climax at the mammoth (32) Heads of African States Conference in Addis Ababa, in May 1963. There was no reference to Israel in any part of the final communiqué, though not for want of Arab efforts. The first gambit was a Cairo request that all Israelis be evacuated from Addis Ababa during Nasser's stay there, as a 'security precaution'; it was refused. Then came a demand that the Israel Ambassador to Ethiopia and Israeli journalists be excluded from the conference room during the sessions; the Emperor not only rejected this but also told Israel correspondents that 'relations between Ethiopia and Israel remain unchanged'. A more subtle approach occurred at the preliminary

[1] See A/SPC/L80/Rev. 1/Corr. 1, 19 December 1961, for the text of the Draft Resolution.
[2] A/SPC/L89, 9 December 1962.

Foreign Ministers' Conference, when Ali Sabry moved a resolution condemning 'Imperialism and Neo-Colonialism', including technical assistance. The Foreign Minister of Sierra Leone asked whether the proposal was made by Egypt as a Mediterranean, Asian, Arab, or African state; this triggered an Africanist response, and the resolution was opposed by all except the Arab states. As a final effort, Nasser enlisted the services of Algeria's Ben Bella, but to no avail; the Africans south of the Sahara did not want to become embroiled in the Middle East. In this sense, Addis Ababa was a victory for Black Africans who are tired of guidance by non-Africans or white (Arab) Africans. Their attitude to Israel on this occasion was not mainly due to positive sympathy; rather it would seem to stem from fear of political exploitation by the Arabs. Perhaps only Bourguiba's Tunisia, among the Arab states, is well regarded by sub-Sahara Africa.

As noted earlier, even African non-involvement is a major benefit to Israel in the persistent rivalry with its neighbours.[1] As the leading Israeli newspaper, *Ha'aretz*, remarked, Nasser's failure was 'a sign of the success of our efforts on the African continent . . . the Arab Foreign Ministers [as well as friendly governments in the West and those of the Soviet bloc will] have to take into consideration the sympathy that Israel has succeeded in arousing among the African people by her diplomatic activities and her practical assistance . . .'[2]

Not long before the Rehovoth Conference in 1960, Prime Minister Ben-Burion had declared that 'Israel is part of Europe'. The context was his desire for membership of the Common Market. But such a remark could only undermine Israel's position in Afro-Asia. It is true that Africans regard Israel as part of Europe and that Israel's interest today is directed more to Africa than to Asia. Further, as romantically and politically important as Afro-Asia may be, it cannot supplant Euro-America in the scale of Israel's values. As a realist *par excellence*, Ben-Gurion told the Knesset: 'Almost the entire Jewish people in the Diaspora, over 10 million Jews, live in these two continents [Europe and America]. . . . Moreover, we must not forget, even for a moment, that we cannot obtain the equipment for the

---

[1] Based upon *Near East Report* (Washington), Vol. VII, No. 12, 4 June 1963 and conversations at U.N. headquarters.

[2] (Tel Aviv), 26 May 1963, as translated in *Weekly New Bulletin* (Jerusalem), Vol. III, No. 9, 22–29 May 1963.

Israel Defence Forces from Asia and Africa . . . and for a long time to come we shall be unable to manufacture most of the equipment required by ourselves.'[1]

If Israel's continuing search for friends in Asia was made more difficult by Ben-Gurion's remark, her quest in Africa was not made easier by two specific policy decisions. On Algeria, Israel stood steadfastly by her principal ally, France; and on South Africa, while aligning itself with United Nations' opposition to the Union's racial policies, Israel trod a delicate path—because of the presence of 110,000 Jews in South Africa, described as 'hostages' by one Israeli statesman. Thus, on the two burning issues in that explosive continent, colonialism and racialism, Israel appeared to be allied with the devil. The French alliance is vital to survival; and the welfare of a large Jewish community cannot be ignored. But the resulting associations could not endear Israel to extremely nationalist and race-conscious Africans.

The task of Israel in Afro-Asia was to overcome these severe liabilities. Diplomatic relations and effective technical assistance combined to form a promising beginning. The solution of the Algerian problem removed one liability. A forthright stand on *apartheid* identified Israel more closely with the new African states. Thus, between 1960 and 1963 the Israeli posture was transformed. The results were evident in the Addis Ababa proceedings. Although negative, they pointed to a new phase in Israel's 'presence' in Africa.

[1] *The Israel Digest*, Vol. III, No. 22, 28 October 1960, p. 4.

6

THE NEW STATES IN
WORLD POLITICS

INTRODUCTION

THE new states of Asia may be grouped into three geographic regions: some Arab states and Israel in West Asia or the Near East, the sub-continent of India–Pakistan and its appendages in South Asia, and the lands of South-East Asia extending from Burma to Indonesia. It is with the latter two segments of the 'Rimland', or Mackinder's 'Monsoon Coastland', that this essay is primarily concerned.[1]

Viewed in terms of world politics, the central feature of Southern Asia[2] is the low general level of power and its wide dispersion among the constituent states. This fact, among others, led to the observation[3] that the area is a power vacuum subject to continuous pressures from units with superior technology which are organized into the bipolar bloc system.

Others have characterized South-East Asia in a similar vein. Cora Du Bois has used the apt phrase, 'a low pressure area'.[4] There has been demographic pressure throughout history induced by the ever-expanding Chinese. Indeed, this has long been a region of low population density. There has been cultural pressure, too: Hinduism in Cambodia, Java, and Sumatra; Sinicism in northern Vietnam; Islam in Indonesia and Malaya; and European Christian influence throughout the area. There has also been political penetration: from China around the entire periphery of the 'Middle Kingdom'; from India through Chola and other empires of the medieval age; from Japan in recent decades; and from the West everywhere in the region during the past four centuries. Finally, South-East Asia has experienced profound economic change wrought by Chinese and

---

[1] The 'Monsoon Coastland' is one of six 'natural regions' of the 'World Island', of which the 'Heartland' is the core. For an illuminating discussion of these original concepts see Halford J. Mackinder, *Democratic Ideals and Reality*, New York 1919, ch. 3–4 and Fig. 16.

[2] This term is used throughout to designate South and South-East Asia combined.

[3] See pp. 98, 110 above. [4] *Social Forces in Southeast Asia*, Minneapolis 1949, p. 68.

Indian immigrants and, especially, by the colonial rulers from the West.[1] All this has been without any counter-pressure from the polities, economies, or societies of the area.

The new states of South-East Asia are the inheritors of that tradition and are not in a position to alter it, for the present at any rate. They remain objects of attention, drawing in people, cultures, ideologies, political systems, and power rivalries from outside the region.[2] Thus Guy Pauker designates this 'a problem area' and a power vacuum because of the 'lack of unity, political instability, economic stagnation, and cultural heterogeneity'. He also comments: 'Politically and economically, South-East Asia's role in world affairs will be the result of its weakness, not of its strength. While the rest of the world will affect decisively the future of South-East Asia, the reverse is not equally true.'[3] This sombre portrait may not be entirely valid for India today and in recent years, but it certainly applies to all the other new states of South as well as South-East Asia. And in the aftermath of China's incursion in the autumn of 1962 it may not be incorrect for India too during the next decade. In any event the points of congruence would seem to justify the term 'power vacuum' for Southern Asia as a whole.

This is not to suggest an equality of power within that area. Indeed, a distinct power-pyramid is discernible among the new states. Only India is a potential Great Power in global terms, measured by the standard indices of national power—geo-political features, food and raw materials, industrial plant, transportation and communication systems, armed forces and arsenals of modern weapons, labour and managerial skills, political stability, a large population, etc.[4] It is certainly the most influential member of the group. Pakistan, Indonesia, and the Philippines may be regarded as Middle Powers in the context of Southern Asia. The rest are Small Powers.

The new states play various roles. Some participate actively in the Dominant (bipolar bloc) System and all are influenced, directly or indirectly, by the political and ideological struggle of the super-

[1] See Fred Greene, *The Far East*, New York 1957, ch. 2, for a succinct analysis.

[2] This theme is explored in Amry Vandenbosch and Richard Butwell, *Southeast Asia Among the World Powers*, Lexington, Kentucky 1958, ch. 1.

[3] 'Southeast Asia as a Problem Area in the Next Decade', *World Politics*, XI, 3, April 1959, pp. 325–6.

[4] For a lucid exposition of these indices see Hans J. Morgenthau, *Politics Among Nations* (3rd ed.), New York 1960, ch. 9.

powers. Their relations with other states in the Subordinate System of Southern Asia include intense bilateral links and/or disputes with one or more states. Almost all the new states in Southern Asia belong to the United Nations. Perhaps the most fruitful approach to the new states in world politics, then, is to explore their behaviour in these three spheres of action. The scope is theoretically so vast that the inquiry will of necessity be selective.[1]

THE DOMINANT SYSTEM AND THE BLOC STRUGGLE

Southern Asia emerged into world politics in the late 1940s just as the two great power blocs were being formed. Japan's military sweep of 1941–2 had shattered the foundations of the colonial order. In the aftermath of the Second World War a dozen states acquired independence in the region: Pakistan, India, Nepal,[2] and Ceylon; Burma, the Philippines, Malaya, and Indonesia; Cambodia, Laos, and the two Vietnams. What were the attitudes and policies of the blocs towards these new states? How did the new states respond? What links were forged and for what purposes?

Aside from the Korean War, the bloc leaders were rather indifferent to the new Asian states as possible allies or satellites until 1954. There were cases of super-power intrusion: for example, American pressure on Holland to hasten Indonesia's independence and the Cominform-sponsored uprisings of 1948 in many lands. For the most part, however, the bloc struggle was confined to Europe and Korea in the early years. The new political units in the Rimland were weak and inconsequential and could be readily ignored in the grand design of a bipolar world. In any event the Soviet Union was preoccupied with the tasks of reconstruction at home and the consolidation of power in Eastern Europe. The United States adopted an ambivalent policy—support to colonial peoples asserting the right of self-determination combined with sympathy for allies in the crystallizing Western bloc.[3]

The insulation of the new states yielded to the pressure of events. First came the triumph of Chinese Communism in 1949, causing a radical change in the strategic balance of power in Asia with the

---

[1] The theoretical framework for this type of analysis is set forth in ch. 3 above.

[2] As late as 1947 Nepal was a *de facto* protectorate of British India although nominally independent. And it was not until 1950—the revolt against the Rana oligarchy—that the Himalayan kingdom emerged from feudal isolation to become an autonomous actor in inter-state politics.

[3] On this policy of supporting both sides see Paul M. A. Linebarger, 'Leadership in the Western Pacific and Southeast Asia', *The Annals*, Vol. 318, July 1958, pp. 58–71.

revival of a united, assertive China after a century of decay. Soon after came the Korean War. This was a prolonged test of arms between the blocs although one super-power remained formally aloof. (Few took notice of China's occupation of Tibet in 1950, with grave consequences a decade later.) Then, in succession, came a new United States Administration with a forceful Secretary of State, the death of Stalin and a 'new look' in Soviet leadership and policy, and finally the climax of the France–Viet Minh war at Dien Bien Phu. The cumulative effect of all these developments was to extend the bloc struggle into South-East Asia.

One expression of the change in bloc attitudes and policies was the creation of SEATO in 1954 and, with it, the direct intrusion of American military power into the apparent vacuum. The *de facto* United States commitment to defend the regional members— Pakistan, the Philippines, and Thailand—against external aggression and internal subversion, and the extension of the American protective umbrella to the successor states of French Indo-China, meant that the bloc conflict had enveloped this area. Some of the new states, especially India and Indonesia, protested against this Western penetration, but to little avail; the dynamics of cold war were irresistible.[1] A closely-related symptom of change in American policy was the arms aid agreement with Pakistan, also in 1954, with consequent heightening of Indo-Pakistani tension.[2]

The other bloc leader also became more directly involved in the affairs of Southern Asia. The curtain was raised by the Bulganin– Khrushchev tour of India and Burma in 1955–6. Open support of India's claim to Kashmir heralded the active courting of the leading new Asian state by the Soviet bloc.[3] Frequent reiteration in the United Nations Security Council and elsewhere (including effective vetoing of resolutions calling for renewed negotiations—which

[1] A revealing source on the formation of SEATO is Sir Anthony Eden, *Full Circle,* London 1960, ch. 5, 6.

[2] For assessments of this agreement see Michael Brecher and Owen Lattimore, 'Pakistan Pact: Two Views', *The Nation,* New York, Vol. 178, No. 4, 23 January 1954, pp. 67–71. A suggestive analysis of the forces and persons responsible for the American decision and its cost is to be found in Selig S. Harrison, 'India, Pakistan and the United States', *The New Republic,* Washington, 10 and 24 August 1959.

[3] During a speech in Kashmir, Khrushchev declared, 'The question of Kashmir as one of the States of the Republic of India has already been decided by the people of Kashmir.' *Keesing's Contemporary Archives,* 1955-56 edition, pp. 14603-4. A similar view was expressed by Khrushchev in an address to the Supreme Soviet. The text is in the *New York Times,* 30 December 1955.

India bitterly opposed until late 1962) was a measure of Soviet determination to secure Delhi's diplomatic support in various aspects of the bloc conflict. The loudly-proclaimed pledges of economic aid to India, Burma, and Indonesia, as part of a larger design to secure friendship among the non-aligned states, was a further method of Soviet bloc intrusion.[1] The amount of aid was less important than the well-publicized fact of assistance to non-communist states, its continuity, the type of project—dramatic and visible symbols like steel plants and sports stadia among others. When the United States turned with vigour to the task of providing economic aid to Southern Asia about 1956, bloc rivalry entered a new (and constructive) phase which continues with increasing intensity to the present day. By the end of 1957 United States economic aid to the new states of that area amounted to $765 million while Soviet bloc economic aid was $592·6 million.[2]

Viewed thus from the standpoint of bloc attitudes and actions, the new states seemed intimately involved in the bloc struggle. Seen in terms of their response, however, the role of these states is marginal to the outcome of that conflict. There are three distinct orientations to the cold war. North Vietnam is linked to the Sino-Soviet bloc by military alliance, economic aid, and ideological affinities.[3] Four others are associated with the West—Pakistan and the Philippines (and Thailand) in SEATO (Pakistan is in CENTO as well), South Vietnam through military arrangement with the United States, and Malaya in the form of Commonwealth bases and troops. Seven states are non-aligned, some also being neutralist and one, Laos, being neutralized since 1962.[4] The new states of Asia are therefore either aloof from entangling alliances with the blocs or, if they participate at all, they are members of a peripheral collective security organization and/or receive military support. Their own power is sufficiently limited to be unimportant, except in some contiguous

[1] For an informative, early account see Klaus Knorr, *Ruble Diplomacy*, Princeton 1956.
[2] The recipient states were Afghanistan, Burma, Cambodia, Ceylon, India, Indonesia, and Nepal. The United States statistics are for the period 1955–7, Soviet bloc figures are for 1954–7 inclusive. Taken from Charles Wolf Jr., *Foreign Aid: Theory and Practice in Southern Asia*, Princeton, 1960, p. 390.
[3] See Bernard B. Fall, *Le Viet Minh* (2nd ed.), Paris 1960.
[4] For the distinctions among these terms see pp. 111–12 above. See also Ernest W. Lefever, 'Nehru, Nasser, and Nkrumah on Neutralism', in Laurence W. Martin (ed.), *Neutralism and NonAlignment*, New York 1962, pp. 93–120, for a thoughtful comparison.

areas as with North Vietnam in the Laotian conflict. Certainly none of the new states has the military strength to protect itself against a massive invasion of bloc power or to contribute substantially to the inter-bloc balance of power. Even India, the largest, most populous, economically most developed, diplomatically most influential, and militarily strongest among them revealed grave weaknesses and limited capability during the border war with China in October–November 1962.[1]

One lesson of that confrontation between the Asian giants will not easily be forgotten—the security of the new states rests ultimately with Great Powers outside the region of Southern Asia. Conversely, the influence of these states in the world balance of military power is at most marginal and will continue to be such in the foreseeable future. This cardinal truth was also revealed in 1960–1 at the height of the Laotian civil war. The bloc leaders became increasingly committed. Soviet aid was flown in to the Pathet Lao while American financial assistance, weapons, and military advisers kept the Royal Army and Government in being.[2] The outcome of that struggle was due entirely to a tacit and then formal agreement of the bloc leaders to disengage and to guarantee the permanent neutrality of the land-locked kingdom.

Laos also pointed up the marginal role of SEATO. By the spring of 1961 Pathet Lao advances gave them almost two-thirds of the territory of Laos—and SEATO stood by: its contribution to the cease-fire agreement was peripheral. It was American not SEATO power that prevented total military disaster in Laos. And it was American and British diplomacy which helped to find a settlement at Geneva. SEATO as such was a virtual onlooker, although four members made a timely show of force in Thailand in May 1962 when the Geneva Conference seemed to be foundering.[3]

[1] For a detailed, day-to-day account of that conflict see the *New York Times*, 21 October–23 November 1962. Of special interest are Hanson Baldwin's articles, 'Measuring the Armies', *New York Times*, 20 November 1962, and 'Assessment of the Indian Army', *New York Times* Service, in the *Montreal Star*, 15 December 1962.

[2] A sensitive account of war in that area is to be found in Bernard B. Fall, *Street without Joy: IndoChina at War*, Harrisburg, Pa. 1961. See also the notes on p. 58 above.

[3] An account of SEATO's role during the 1959 crisis is to be found in Norman J. Padelford, 'SEATO and Peace in Southeast Asia', *Current History*, vol. 38, February 1960, pp. 95–101, 109. For the 1961 crisis see *The Times*, London, 24–30 March 1961. A valuable account and analysis of the 14-Power Conference is George Modelski, *International Conference on the Settlement of the Laotian Question 1961–2*, Canberra 1962.

An almost exact replay of this drama occurred a year later, with SEATO once more on the periphery.

It could not have been otherwise. SEATO has no armed forces or operational staff. Indeed its organizational structure is too rudimentary for a positive role. There is a Council—of Foreign Ministers or their deputies—which meets once or more a year, a small secretariat in Bangkok under a Secretary-General, and three committees—Military, Economic, and Anti-Subversive. In all these respects it is incomparably weaker than NATO. Moreover, its obligations are vague—'to act in accordance with constitutional processes' or 'to consult' (article 4).[1] As one observer remarked, SEATO military planning is 'highly theoretical because the committee has no standing army to play with, because in any serious war the puny land forces of which SEATO might immediately dispose could be swamped by the Chinese, and because the Americans refuse to tell SEATO what action they would take in such an emergency. . . .'[2] SEATO's utility is as a potential channel and instrument of Western power rather than as an autonomous actor in Southern Asia.

The new states continue in the roles of: (a) objects of bloc rivalry, courted and pressured by the bloc leaders with economic aid and prestige, sometimes with arms as well; or (b) military satellites, dependent on their bloc patrons and without any real initiative or influence in the bloc conflict. The only major exception is India. Indeed the effect of New Delhi on the bipolar bloc system was disproportionately great considering its paucity of military power, under-developed economy, and the deep schisms within Indian society. Whatever the reasons—its potential Great Power status, its position of democratic alternative to Communist China and/or its acknowledged leadership of the non-aligned states—India was assiduously cultivated by the bloc leaders and its views carried great weight. Here are but a few examples of India's influence on the bloc struggle: a decisive role in breaking the stalemate over the question of repatriation of prisoners-of-war, leading to the Korean truce in 1953; a strong initiative for a settlement of the Indo-China war in 1954; selection by both blocs for the delicate and vital posts of chairman of both the Neutral Nations Repatriation Commission in

[1] See pp. 100–1 above.
[2] Dennis Bloodworth, 'Real Achievements of SEATO Should Lessen Asian Fears', *Observer* Service, in the *Montreal Star*, 25 April 1959.

Korea (1953–4)[1] and the International Commissions in Vietnam, Laos, and Cambodia (1954–); and a little-known but important influence in the 'package deal' admission of sixteen new members to the United Nations in 1955.[2] Other new states of Asia exert some influence through collective action, as in the Asian–African bloc at the United Nations, to be noted later, and in the Commonwealth, of which Pakistan, India, Ceylon, and Malaya are members.

Despite their penetration of the region, neither bloc leader appears to be genuinely feared by the new states. Those that are aligned with the West certainly do not fear the United States of America. Nor is there evidence that they fear the Soviet Union as a direct threat to their security. Some neutralists, notably India and Indonesia, seemed at times to identify America as the natural successor to British–French–Dutch imperialism.[3] But this is no longer true of India, at any rate, after the Chinese assault in 1962. As for Moscow, the neutralists were always well-disposed, perhaps because it was physically remote, untarnished with the brush of colonialism, and seemingly more sympathetic to their aspirations and policy.

The new states are involved in the bloc struggle but for the most part as reluctant actors. Their real interest is twofold, a negative-positive compound. First is the fear of war between the super-powers, a major cause of their pleas and pressure for disarmament. Although the non-aligned are more vociferous on this theme, all the new states are concerned. Second is the desire for capital and technical assistance. All desperately need aid and all realize that, if the bloc struggle could be diverted to peaceful competition among the uncommitted, they would be the beneficiaries. An open conflict in bloc relations would lead to an aid drought. These are the key self-interest motives in the bloc system. There is, in fact, no genuine ideological involvement among the aligned states of the area. For Pakistan the main stimulus to alliance with the West is fear of India and the expectation of greater bargaining power from an American 'presence'. The evidence of ideological non-involvement

[1] India's role in the NNRC is carefully examined in B. S. Steinberg, *India's Neutralism in Theory and Practice* (unpublished Ph.D. thesis, McGill University, 1961).

[2] Prime Minister Nehru personally intervened with Khrushchev who was in Delhi and successfully urged Soviet acceptance of the package without Outer Mongolia. Related to the author in Delhi in 1958 by a senior official in the Indian Ministry of External Affairs.

[3] See note on p. 98 above for an Indian reaction to Western motives in SEATO.

is periodic threats to leave SEATO and CENTO because of alleged indifference to Pakistan's claims, the latest being at the end of 1962.[1] For the Philippines, South Vietnam, and Malaya, the principal motive is also fear—of China, the Viet Cong and North Vietnam, and of the local Chinese minority, respectively.

All this points up the salient conclusion about the new states and the bloc struggle: except for Pakistan, their main focus is Communist China not the bloc leaders; and that interest spills over from the Dominant (bipolar bloc) System of inter-state politics to the Subordinate System of Southern Asia, for China is a leading member of both.[2]

THE SUBORDINATE SYSTEM:
THE NEW STATES AND CHINA

An acute awareness of Communist China is evident in all the new states. Some are hostile, others friendly, and still others are cordial. None is indifferent to the 'awakened dragon' which has begun once more to 'shake the world'.[3] For some, notably Malaya, there is concern over a large Chinese minority of uncertain loyalty. For others, such as Laos, India, Nepal, and Pakistan, China's 'presence' takes the form of territorial contiguity and/or border disputes. Some, especially Vietnam, Thailand, and Burma, lie under the spell of history and the long tradition of Chinese suzerainty over lands on the periphery of the 'Middle Kingdom'. Only the Philippines has a marked ideological aversion to Peking. For India there is the added feature of rivalry for the leadership of Southern Asia. Thus China looms large on the political horizon of the new states.[4]

This is inevitable. There are more Chinese than any other nation on earth, about 700 million. In fact, the Chinese outnumber the peoples of the Western Hemisphere and Africa combined and are more than three times the total population of South-East Asia. Their

---

[1] The catalyst was Anglo-American arms shipments to a beleaguered India. Pakistan feared these arms might be used against it in Kashmir later or, at least, that they would alter the balance of power in the sub-continent, an ironic reversal of the situation and attitudes of India and Pakistan in 1954, when the latter received American arms aid. See the *New York Times*, 19, 23, and 24 November 1962.

[2] See pp. 95–6 above.

[3] Napoleon was reported to have said of China, 'Let the dragon sleep. For when it awakes it will shake the world.'

[4] For a lucid survey of China's relations with Southern Asia to 1959 see A. Doak Barnett, *Communist China and Asia*, New York 1960, ch. 11.

net annual increase is approximately 15 million. Barring war or pestilence or effective birth control there will be one billion[1] Chinese by 1980 and 1·6 billion at the end of the century. That fact alone gives China a major role in contemporary world politics.

In geographical size China ranks second to the Soviet Union. A glance at the map reveals a great land basin in East Asia cut off from the rest of the continent by deserts and mountains on the western periphery. China's territory of $3\frac{3}{4}$ million square miles extends from the north-eastern tip of Manchuria to the Indian frontier and from the East China coast to the innermost recesses of Asia's heartland, a distance of 2,700 miles. The 'land of the five races' is bounded on the east by Korea, the Yellow Sea, and the East China Sea. To the south lie North Vietnam, Laos, and Burma, and to the west India and the Hill States of Nepal, Bhutan, and Sikkim. Still further west lie Pakistan and the Soviet Union, and to the north Outer Mongolia and Soviet Siberia. This location, too, gives China a pivotal role in Asia and the world.[2]

The history of relations between China and her neighbours adds a further dimension to the portrait of a giant. Two examples will suffice. From the third century B.C. until 1885 part of Vietnam was either under direct Chinese control or acknowledged China's suzerainty for all but six centuries; Chinese colonization and culture also penetrated deeply into northern Vietnam. In Burma the impact has not been as great but the Chinese threat has recurred. The principal ethnic groups themselves, Burmans, Chins, Kachins, and Shans, were forced south by Han population pressure. There were vassal Burmese states to the T'ang Dynasty, between the seventh and tenth centuries. The Mongols invaded the territory of the Burmese Pagan Dynasty twice. The Mings asserted their suzerainty whenever their power permitted, and the Manchus attempted to do so in the late eighteenth century. Even the British, in a treaty with China (1886), acknowledged the historic vassal status of Burma. No wonder the Burmese have trodden carefully in their dealings with Communist China.[3]

Two other features accentuated the awesome fact of China for the new states. One was unity, the other ideology. As long as China was

---

[1] United States usage: billion = a thousand millions.

[2] On the geography of China see George B. Cressey, *Asia's Lands and Peoples* (2nd ed.), New York 1951, ch. 4, 6–8.

[3] See John F. Cady, *A History of Modern Burma*, Ithaca 1958, ch. 3.

weak and fragmented the border peoples were safe, but when the 'Middle Kingdom' was strong and united there was danger on the periphery. This old adage, valid for Vietnam and Burma for millennia, took on a new meaning in 1949 when the communists came to power after four decades of warlordism and civil war. If one adds the confusion in the downswing phase of the Manchu Dynasty, more than a century of internal turmoil now came to an end. To unity were added military strength—the largest, most disciplined, battle-tested army in Asia—and an ideology, Marxism–Leninism, ideally suited to reinforce and validate traditional Chinese chauvinism and expansionism *vis-à-vis* the territories to the south and west. It was in this setting that the new states had to adjust to Communist China. The historic pattern had always been thus: China took the initiative and the territories of the Monsoon Coastland responded. On this occasion the power difference seemed even greater than in the past, for most of them were in the throes of transition from colonialism to independence. Some, like Vietnam, were engaged in protracted civil war. Others like Burma and Malaya were beset with crippling rebellion. And even the rival giant, India, had not yet recovered from the trauma and the legacies of Partition.

Like most of the preceding Chinese dynasties, the communist régime was quick to assert its power in Southern Asia. The aim— hegemony—has been constant since 1949, but the techniques and tactics have varied. Three distinct stages are apparent. At the outset, flushed with victory, Peking adopted a hard line of military and ideological activism, similar to Trotsky's policy of 'permanent revolution' in Europe during the twenties. Armed revolt against non-communist governments was the order of the day. The 'two camp' thesis was rigidly defined and all the new Asian leaders were lumped together as 'running dogs of imperialism'. Neutralism was termed an illusion and all but the faithful adherents of Marxism–Leninism were considered enemies. This was the period of the occupation of Tibet, the Korean War, and military assistance to the Viet Minh, the Huks in the Philippines, and the 'People's Liberation Army' in Malaya.

A new approach gradually took shape under the impact of the truce in Korea, a more pragmatic leadership in Moscow, and China's economic difficulties. The new line stressed the virtues of 'Asian solidarity' and 'anti-colonialism'. The once-despised policy of non-

M

alignment now became the hallmark of genuine independence. Governments long scorned were now courted in a calculated effort to reduce Western bloc influence in Southern Asia and to lure the new states to the communist camp. Disputes and ideological differences were concealed while the common legacy and aspirations were projected to the centre of the stage. All this crystallized in the joint sponsorship by China and India of the *Panch Sheel* or Five Principles of Peaceful Coexistence, first enunciated in the agreement on Tibet early in 1954. Soon after, Chou En-lai journeyed to Geneva and provided an object-lesson of moderation on the Indo-China settlement. Indeed this second phase of China's policy towards Southern Asia was closely identified with Chou's 'personal diplomacy'.

He entered the Asian stage officially at Bandung in 1955, spoke gently and proved to be a suave, elegant, persuasive spokesman for Peking.[2] In 1956-7 he carried the soft line to most of the new states. Everywhere he invited his hosts to see 'new China' at first hand and many of them came. He made conciliatory gestures, calling on the 12 million (now 15 million) Chinese in South-East Asia to obey the laws of their lands of residence and to choose one nationality. Everywhere, too, he offered friendly negotiation of existing frontier disputes. In Delhi he told Nehru that China accepted the McMahon Line as the legal frontier between India and China, without saying that there was a dispute as to where the Line lay![3] This was also a period of trade expansion. The result was that by 1958 Communist China had established diplomatic relations with all the new states except the Philippines, South Vietnam, and Malaya. From a pariah it had become a member in good standing and a recognized leader of Afro-Asia.

In view of that striking success, the reversion to a hard line is difficult to fathom. Whatever the reason(s)—fear of a Soviet–Ameri-

[1] The Five Principles are: (1) mutual respect for each other's territorial integrity and sovereignty; (2) mutual non-aggression; (3) mutual non-interference in each other's internal affairs; (4) equality and mutual benefit; and (5) peaceful coexistence. For a clear exposition of the Indian view of *Panch Sheel* see two of Nehru's speeches in 1955, in Jawaharlal Nehru, *India's Foreign Policy*, New Delhi 1961, pp. 99–102.

[2] The Bandung Conference is examined on pp. 174–5 below.

[3] Related by Nehru to Chou En-lai in a letter dated 14 December 1958. Government of India, *Notes, Memoranda and Letters Exchanged and Agreements Signed Between the Governments of India and China 1954–1959*, White Paper I, Delhi 1960, pp. 49–50: China's maps show the McMahon Line farther west than the watershed used in India's maps.

can *rapprochement*,[1] an extension of the tough internal Commune policy, and/or anger at the Tibetan Revolt—Peking reversed course. It began with the eruption of new hostilities in Laos in 1959. But the policy shift became clear only after Chinese probes on India's Himalayan frontiers during the autumn of that year. There have been some deviations from the first stage; not all new states have been subjected to threat and intimidation; neutralism remains in vogue; trade continues; there have even been conciliatory gestures such as aid to non-communist Cambodia, the agreement on Laos, and border settlements with Nepal, Burma, Outer Mongolia, and Pakistan. Nevertheless, the dramatic sundering of the Five Principles of Peaceful Coexistence marks a turning point in China's policy towards Southern Asia with grave consequences still to unfold.

What has been the response to the challenge of Communist China? Among the five states aligned with the West only Pakistan has recognized Peking.[2] Relations remained correct for a decade, even after Karachi became a member of SEATO. Then during the Chinese border conflict with India they reached agreement on the frontier between China and Pakistani-occupied Kashmir. There was much talk about withdrawal from SEATO and CENTO in 1962–3 when Pakistani public opinion became incensed over Anglo-American arms aid to India. The press adopted a virulently pro-Chinese tone; and the overwhelming majority of politicians spoke out in support of Peking.[3] Among the other four pro-Western states there is diversity in tone. The most militant is Thailand which took the lead in forming a collective security organization (SEATO) and pressed for a strong line on Laos in 1959, 1961, and 1963. South Vietnam is no less hostile but pressure from the north and preoccupation with guerrilla war have dictated prudence in declarations about China. In Malaya there are the stern facts of the Chinese minority, 90 per cent of the population of Singapore and 38 per cent of the Malaya Federation, and their position of economic power. One consequence was to exclude Singapore from the Federation of

---

[1] It is generally believed that Mao vetoed a proposed summit conference during the Lebanon–Iraq crisis, at a secret meeting with Khrushchev in Peking in August 1958.
[2] This was in 1950, four years before Pakistan became aligned with the West through SEATO and the Baghdad Pact, later CENTO.
[3] It was reported that, in the foreign affairs debate in the National Assembly in December 1962, almost all participants spoke in favour of China and against the West—and 90 of the 153 members spoke. Rawle Knox, 'British-American Gamble on Kashmir', *Observer* Service, in the *Montreal Star*, 18 December 1962.

Malaya in 1957. Another has been a policy of non-recognition of Peking. A third has been a complicated electoral roll in the proposed state of Malaysia which will include Malaya, Singapore, and the Borneo territories; only thus can the Chinese 'presence' be controlled.[1]

Among the non-aligned new states of Southern Asia only Cambodia has had a record of friendly ties with Communist China. Prince Sihanouk, the dominant personality in that Buddhist land, visited Peking in 1956, 1958, and 1960, each time with results beneficial to Cambodia. These included a trade agreement, the first Chinese grant of aid to a non-communist state, and a Sino-Cambodian friendship treaty.[2] The rationale for this policy of friendship with Peking was stated with refreshing candour in mid-stream: 'If I have no particular liking for communism, neither have I any cause or means to join a crusade—even a moral one—against the nations that have adopted that ideology and which since 1954 have not given my country sufficient grounds for complaint. It would be absurd to suppose that a tiny country like mine, geographically situated as it is, would risk provoking the Chinese and Soviet colossi. . . . I maintain that we are merely being realistic. By practising genuine neutrality which eliminates any pretext for aggression we have a chance of not bringing down a storm on our heads. . . .'[3]

Burma shared these sentiments and had further reasons to tread carefully in matters concerning Peking. One, already noted, was a history marked by long periods of Chinese suzerainty. Another was the presence of 10,000 Nationalist troops who had fled to Burma in 1949. A third was a complex border dispute. The question of Nationalist soldiers was perhaps the most vexed. Their refusal to disarm aggravated an already serious problem of law and order in the face of many-sided insurrection. It marred Burmese–American relations—Washington was blamed for continued Taiwan support to these forces. Peking was also given a pretext for intervention if it

[1] A perceptive analysis of Malaysia was offered by Frank H. H. King in a paper read to the 14th Annual Meeting of the Association of Asian Studies in April 1962 (unpublished). For a comprehensive, informed analysis see Willard A. Hanna, 'Malaysia: A Federation in Prospect', American Universities Field Staff, 1962–3, parts 17–18.

[2] Bernard B. Fall, 'Cambodia's International Position', Current History, vol. 40, March 1961, pp. 164–70.

[3] Prince Norodom Sihanouk, 'Cambodia, Neutral: The Dictate of Necessity', Foreign Affairs, New York, vol. 36, July 1958, pp. 585–6.

were so inclined. The issue came before the United Nations in 1953 and led to the evacuation of most Nationalist troops. Peking stood by patiently and reaped the benefits.

The border problem dates from an Anglo-Chinese treaty of 1886 calling for demarcation of the boundary. Efforts to settle it were made in 1894, 1897–1900, 1934, and 1941, but with only partial success. Soon after coming to power the Chinese Communists re-asserted traditional Chinese claims. These concerned four areas: a territory leased to the British known as the Namwan Assigned Tract, three Kachin villages, the Wa state area, and the northern frontier above Myitkyina. After protracted negotiations a settlement was reached in 1960. Burma conceded the first two claims and China abandoned the others.[1]

India's relations with Communist China have run the gamut from warm friendship to dismay and anger. Nehru himself had set the tone of admiration and goodwill in his diary of a 'voyage of discovery' to China in 1939: 'A new China is rising, rooted in her culture, but shedding the lethargy and weakness of ages, strong and united.'[2] India was the second non-communist state (after Burma) to recognize the Peking régime. It was India's ambassador, Sardar Panikkar, who (correctly) warned the world of dire consequences should United Nations forces cross the 38th parallel. It was Indian pressure that brought a Peking observer to the Security Council's deliberations in 1951. And it was India that played a crucial, friendly role during the debate on the prisoner-of-war issue leading to the truce. Then, with much fanfare, came the joint sponsorship of the *Panch Sheel*, the Five Principles, in the 1954 Agreement on Tibet. Nehru and Chou En-lai exchanged visits the same year. At Bandung the Indian leader eased the path of Communist China into the Afro-Asian community. And for more than a decade Delhi had taken the lead in pressing Peking's claim to China's seat in the United Nations.

There were, of course, disquieting incidents: the rude rejection of Delhi's mild protest at the manner of Tibet's absorption by Peking in 1950; a Chinese probe on the Uttar Pradesh frontier in

[1] For the background see Richard J. Kozicki, 'The Sino-Burmese Frontier Problem', *Far Eastern Survey*, vol. XXVI, March 1957, pp. 33–38, and Hugh Tinker, 'Burma's Northeast Borderland Problems', *Pacific Affairs*, vol. XXIX, December 1956, pp. 324–46.

[2] For Nehru's account of his visit to China on the eve of the Second World War see his *China, Spain and the War*, Allahabad 1940, pp. 11–53.

1954; the continued circulation of Chinese (Nationalist) maps by the communist régime, showing large slices of Indian territory on the Chinese side of the border—accompanied by Chou's deceitful remark that his government had not yet found the time to revise them; and the Indian discovery in 1957 of a road built by China across the Aksai Chin area of Ladakh (Kashmir) in order to link Tibet and Sinkiang. Yet these incidents were few in number and seemingly inconsequential in the larger context of Sino-Indian friendship. Delhi thought so, with the result that the incidents were ignored, even concealed for years from the Indian public. It was only the drama of revolt in Tibet in 1959 and the border incidents which followed that shattered the illusions of a decade.[1]

There seemed to be good reasons for friendship with China. One was geography, a common border of 2,500 miles, and India's military weakness which dictated prudence in dealing with an assertive, powerful neighbour allied to a super-power. Another was history, the fact of 2,000 years of peace and friendly cultural ties between Asia's two greatest civilizations. A third was emotion, the force of anti-colonialism. To Nehru and others the communist triumph in 1949 was simply the culmination of a century-old process of revolution. This was welcomed as part of the decline of Western colonial influence all over Asia. Nationalism was in any case considered a more potent force than Communism in the 'new China' and Peking was not, in the Indian view, rigidly tied to the Soviet bloc. It was clearly in India's interest to weaken the Sino-Soviet axis. This would ease the pressure of that bloc on the sub-continent. It would also raise Asia's prestige and power and might lead to an expanded 'third area of peace' based on Sino-Indian leadership.

There was one (disastrous) error in the assessment—the belief that Peking would not be a threat to India for at least a generation. China, it was argued, would be too immersed in internal problems to indulge in foreign adventures. India need not reckon with this remote contingency. In any event much could happen in the interval —and so it did.

Until 1950 India's Northern Wall was secure since there was no direct contact with China proper. But with the occupation of Tibet the strategic map of Inner Asia was transformed. Chinese troops now stood at the gates to the Indian plains and a powerful China

[1] For a perceptive analysis of the shortcomings of India's policy towards China see P. C. Chakravarty, *India's China Policy*, Bloomington, Indiana 1962. See also Frank Moraes, *Revolt in Tibet*, New York 1960.

could once more lay claim to large stretches of territory in the borderlands on the 'Roof of the World'. To Peking expansionists these are the 'Five Fingers of Tibet': the North-East Frontier Agency (NEFA), Bhutan, Sikkim, Nepal, and Ladakh—areas which at different times have been under Chinese influence or control. Together they comprise the Himalayan frontier between India and China, a 2,500-mile arc of Central Asia from Sinkiang to the northern tip of Burma.

Peking moved slowly in the fifties, concentrating on the effective absorption of the fabled land of the lamas. The clash between communism and a feudal theocracy led to mounting resentment, exploding in the Tibet Revolt of 1959 and the flight of the Dalai Lama and 13,000 refugees to India. Peking turned its venom on its erstwhile friend. China accused India of complicity in the revolt and warned the Indian parliament not to discuss Tibet. Nehru's daughter and sister were openly attacked in the Chinese press. Even the Indian Prime Minister was not spared Peking's anger. Soon after, in August-September, Chinese patrols made symbolic probes in the north-east while Chinese troops quietly occupied large chunks of Ladakh. At the same time the old maps reappeared showing 51,000 square miles of territory on the Chinese side of the border—all of NEFA and 15,000 square miles of Ladakh.

The events of 1959 turned out to be a prelude to a dramatic border war three years later.[1] A front-line joint Sino-Indian inquiry was held in the interim period of uneasy calm when both sides also made preparations for the next phase of a protracted struggle. The Chinese prepared aggression much more efficiently than the Indians prepared their defences. Indeed, India talked tough in September–October 1962 while her defences were poorly manned. When the Chinese renewed hostilities on 20 October 1962, India's military weakness was laid bare before the world. Chinese troops swiftly occupied the remaining territory claimed in Ladakh and cut through Indian defences all along the NEFA. A month later, when they unexpectedly invoked a unilateral cease-fire, their forward troops had reached the densely-populated Assam plains and were a few days' march from India's major oil centre.[2] Uncertainty of their being in a

---

[1] For an analysis of the 1959 phase of the border conflict and its long-term implications see the author's 'Five Fingers of Tibet', *The Nation*, New York, vol. 189, no. 10, 3 October 1959, pp. 183–6 and 'Trouble on the Roof of the World', *Saturday Night*, Toronto, 21 November 1959, pp. 19–21.

[2] *New York Times*, 23 November 1962.

military position to consolidate and improve these swift advances may well be the key to their 'magnanimous' cease-fire.

Of the two areas in dispute Ladakh is strategically more important for China and NEFA for India, but Peking and Delhi have persisted with claims to both. In essence the Chinese contend that the frontier between Ladakh and Sinkiang has never been demarcated on the ground and that the line claimed by India is simply the furthest point of British imperial expansion in Central Asia. All this merely masks their determination to retain Aksai Chin, the Ladakhi bulge which contains a strategic military road the Chinese built a few years ago to link Tibet and Sinkiang. The Indians have denied the Chinese contention but have shown much greater interest in the north-east. There the nub of the dispute is the legality of the McMahon Line which extends 800 miles from Bhutan to Burma. It was drawn in 1914 to demarcate the frontier between India and Tibet and was 'formalized' by the Simla Convention, an agreement between British India, Tibet, and China. Peking's present case arises from the fact that, while the Chinese delegation initialled the Convention, no Chinese Government has ratified it. Almost half a century later Communist China now terms the McMahon Line 'an historic leftover', a product of 'British aggression against the Tibet region of China'. Ironically the Nationalist Government on Formosa declared in favour of its ideological enemy on the mainland! India's view has been consistently expressed by Nehru with the words: 'The McMahon Line is right by usage, right by treaty and right by geography.'

The most puzzling feature of the 'Himalayan Affair' has been China's motives. Why should Peking so brazenly antagonize its leading friend in the non-communist world? The Chinese were clearly annoyed at Delhi's kindness to the Dalai Lama and the Tibetan refugees in 1959. At the same time that incident provided an opportunity to revive the then dormant dispute over the frontiers. In 1962 there seem to have been short-term and long-run goals. The first was to establish a 'position of strength' for the negotiations which Peking was certain would follow. Closely related was the attempt to force India to the bargaining table—nothing else had succeeded in three years. That China's aims are limited to territory on the frontier is apparent from the reiteration of its 1959 offer of a mutual withdrawal to a point $12\frac{1}{2}$ miles from 'the point of actual control' on 7 November 1959. In any case, no sane Chinese leader would contemplate the conquest of all India, for the cost would exceed any possible advantage. In the short-run military victory is also a useful diversion from internal difficulties, especially on the economic front, and there have been many during recent years.

In a broader perspective other motives are apparent. First Peking desires to keep the international situation in turmoil lest an irritated ally, the Soviet Union, make concessions at China's expense and even come to terms with the 'imperialist enemy', the United States. Secondly China seeks to tarnish India's image in the new states of Asia and Africa by making it look weak, a goal apparently achieved.[1] Thirdly China wishes to compel India to divert limited resources from economic development to wasteful military activity. Both of these are really efforts to cripple India's challenge for Asian leadership. There was also a calculated effort to force Russia off the fence, to compel Moscow to side with an ally against a friend. The Chinese have not enjoyed watching the Soviets supply greater economic aid and weapons to their rival for leadership in Southern Asia. Peking was also motivated by chauvinism and irredentism, the urge to reclaim 'lost territory'. To any Chinese régime NEFA and Aksai Chin were 'lost' to British imperialism when China was weak. Nor has it been forgotten that Ladakh belonged to Tibet until 1840 and that the majority of its people are Buddhists who look to Lhasa for cultural inspiration; or, for that matter, that Nepal paid an annual tribute to Peking until the middle of the nineteenth century; or, indeed, that Bhutan was long a tributary of China. But these 'fingers' can be reclaimed later. For the moment the thumb and index finger of Tibet are uppermost in Peking's strategic plans. Another probable motive is the Chinese desire to undermine neutralism and thereby to embarrass the Soviet leadership. Less likely but not inconceivable was the hope of toppling Nehru and causing grave instability in India.

Whatever the motives, the effect on Sino-Indian relations was unmistakable. The last vestige of illusion vanished. No longer did one hear the long fading symbolic cry, 'Hindi-Chini Bhai Bhai'— 'Indians and Chinese are brothers'. India felt betrayed. *Panch Sheel* was consigned to the dustbin of history as far as Sino-Indian relations were concerned. Six new Afro-Asian states met in Colombo in December 1962 to attempt mediation.

[1] Paul Grimes, 'Asian-African Solidarity a Myth', *New York Times* Service, in the *Montreal Star*, 19 December 1962.

The Colombo Proposals were as follows: in the Western Sector (Ladakh), (*a*) Chinese forces were to withdraw 20 kilometres from the actual line of control on 7 November 1959 (both India and China accepted), and (*b*) pending final solution of the border dispute, the area of Chinese withdrawal was to be a demilitarized zone, to be administered by civilian posts of both sides, without prejudice to claims (India accepted but China insists on Chinese posts only in the demilitarized zone); in the Eastern Sector (NEFA) the line of actual control in areas recognized by both Governments was to serve as a cease-fire line to their respective posts, the remaining areas to be settled in future discussions (India accepted, the Chinese insist that Indian troops do not return to the McMahon Line).

During the first half of 1963 the positions were frozen. Delhi accepted the Colombo Proposals, with clarifications, *in toto,* and insisted on unqualified Chinese acceptance as the prerequisite to any direct negotiations. Peking first accepted the Proposals 'in principle', then made known 'reservations', as above, later termed the Colombo intervention merely 'good offices', not a solution, and finally saw it as a barrier; the way out, said Chen Yi, China's Foreign Minister, was direct talks between the interested parties without pre-conditions. A Sino-Pakistani boundary accord in the Kashmir-Sinkiang region early in 1963 made the Chinese position, if anything, more rigid.

THE SUBORDINATE SYSTEM: REGIONALISM AND BILATERAL DISPUTES

An adverse legacy of the colonial era was the artificial isolation of the peoples of Southern Asia from one another. There were few active ties within the region. The economy of each dependent territory was linked indissolubly to the metropolitan economy in the West. The new élites were educated in the language, culture and often in the universities of the 'Mother Country'. Political association, too, was 'vertical'. Each colony was attached to an imperial power far removed from the area. Indeed, until 1940 there was no real contact among the movements for national self-determination. Each focused on the local scene and the colonial enemy, none on the regional front.

Inevitably the colonial division of Southern Asia has had a deep, continuing effect on the new states. Like all states they are prisoners of their past. One result has been high barriers to effective regional integration. As noted elsewhere,[1] Southern Asia is the least developed of all subordinate state systems in this respect, lacking security, judicial or political organs embracing all or even most members of the region. Nor has this been due to want of interest. The history of the past fifteen years is full of attempts at integration, most abortive and none successful except in the sphere of economic consultation.

Talk of a security pact dates to the summer of 1949 when Chiang Kai-shek and President Quirino of the Philippines called for collective action to meet the danger from Communist China. After much quiet diplomacy and the enforced exclusion of Nationalist China and South Korea, five new states, India, Pakistan, Ceylon, Indonesia, and the Philippines, met with Thailand and Australia at the Baguio Conference in May 1950 to consider matters of common interest. Security issues were studiously avoided and no organization was formed. It was only under the impact of French defeat in Indo-China that a military dyke was established—SEATO. Even this included only three states in the region. The initiative and control remains with the West, especially the United States.

There is no judicial body in Southern Asia comparable to the European Court, the court of the Arab League, or the earlier Central American Court of Justice. And in the economic realm one organ is a United Nations commission, ECAFE, without binding authority on its members, many of whom are outside the region. The other—the Colombo Plan—is an agency for channelling aid.[2] Indeed the most dramatic, though the least tangibly impressive, efforts at integration have been in the political sphere.

These may be grouped into two categories—sub-regional and all-Asian. The French proposed a Pan-South-East Asia Union of Thailand and Indo-China in 1947. In the same year an enterprising Viet Minh agent succeeded in forming a South-East Asia League with unofficial representatives from Vietnam, Laos, Cambodia, Indonesia, Burma, Malaya, and Thailand. It proved to be merely a short-lived pressure group in favour of Ho Chi Minh. A promising development was the formation of the 'Colombo Powers' in 1954, consisting of India, Pakistan, Ceylon, Burma, and Indonesia. But this too was short-lived with only one real contribution, namely the preparations for a mammoth conclave leading to Bandung. First conceived as a neutralist group in Southern Asia, the Colombo Powers

[1] See pp. 100–101 above.   [2] See p. 101 above.

disintegrated in the face of Indo-Pakistani disputes and Karachi's adherence to the Western bloc. From time to time there had been talk of a Pan-Malaya Union or South-East Asia Union. More promising was the high-level agreement among Malaya, Indonesia, and the Philippines in 1963 for close co-operation in matters of security, economic development, and social and cultural affairs. A *de facto* mutual defence pact was formed against 'subversion in any form or manifestation', a thinly-disguised reference to Peking expansionism. Differences over Malaysia were resolved by a diplomatic formula, including an ultimate 'confederation of nations of Malay origin', and a central secretariat was created to handle problems between the three countries.

On the all-Asia level the Delhi Conferences of 1947 and 1949 have already been noted.[1] One of the more striking efforts at integration along special-interest lines was the Organization of Asian Socialist Parties formed at the first Asian Socialist Conference in Rangoon in 1953. Delegates attended from Egypt and Israel, Pakistan and India, Burma, Indonesia and Malaya, and Japan, with observers from other states. A Bureau and Secretariat were established and another conference was held but the organization remained moribund, largely because nationalism was a far more potent force in Asia than socialism.

The most revealing event in the unfulfilled quest for integration was the Bandung Conference of 1955, one of the greatest international gatherings in non-Western history. Disunity was evident throughout the proceedings, even before the assembly convened. First came the 'horse trading' among the Colombo Powers on the vexed issue of whom to invite. Communist China and Israel dominated the debate at the preparatory Bogor Conference. Ultimately Israel, the Koreas, and Formosa were denied invitations.

A second major cleavage concerned conference procedure. India, Burma, China, and Egypt wanted to reduce the expression of anti-communism and to omit controversial issues like Formosa and China's seat at the United Nations. Thus they pressed for the exclusion of current diplomatic matters and for the circulation rather than the oral delivery of opening policy speeches. Pakistan's Prime Minister, arriving late, objected to these restrictive provisions and secured two major changes—a daily as well as a final communiqué and the right of each delegation to present its policy statement orally.

[1] See p. 100 above. For concise accounts of regionalism see note on p. 100 above.

A third source of discord was the meaning of 'colonialism'. India, Burma, and Indonesia, among others, expected unanimity on a vague condemnation of colonialism, by which they meant Western control in Asia and Africa. But this line was dramatically challenged by Ceylon's Kotelawala who pressed for 'opposition to all forms of colonialism . . . to Soviet colonialism as much as to Western imperialism'. After much haggling an Indian compromise was accepted, referring to 'colonialism in all its manifestations'.

A fourth disagreement centred on the conditions of world peace. Nehru proposed general acceptance of the Five Principles. Pakistan's Mohammed Ali offered the Seven Pillars of Peace, the crucial addition being the right of collective self-defence. Again a compromise was accepted—Ten Principles, including the Pakistani addition (providing it was not inspired by the Great Powers). Compromise was also evident behind the scenes on the Formosa problem. Indeed, much of the communiqué was vague on highly controversial issues in an effort to create the image of unity. Such unity was at its highest on matters of little direct concern or when special national interests were involved; hence a strong pro-Arab resolution on 'Palestine', a condemnation of the Dutch on West New Guinea (West Irian), the French on North Africa, and the British on Aden, and a severe attack on *apartheid* in South Africa. On the desirability of ending nuclear tests agreement was also reached.

Three distinct groups emerged on the communist-colonialist issues: two communist states including North Vietnam; nine neutralists including Burma, Cambodia, India, Indonesia, Laos, and Nepal; and fifteen anti-communists including Ceylon, Pakistan, the Philippines, and South Vietnam. All the others were 'old' states, like Thailand, or new ones outside Southern Asia. Bandung revealed deep fissures. However, it also expressed one of the fundamental traits of the contemporary global political system—the 'anti-colonial revolution' and the (re)birth of some 60 new states in Asia and Africa with influence in and on the United Nations and the balance of military and political power.[1]

In the years since Bandung intra-area disputes have mounted in frequency and intensity. Some of these have already been sketched, notably the Sino-Indian conflict in the Himalayas and the Sino-

---

[1] A perceptive analysis of Bandung is to be found in Mary Knatchbull Keynes, 'The Bandung Conference', *International Relations*, London, Vol. I, 1954–1959, pp. 362–76. For a detailed daily account see the *New York Times*, 18–25 April 1955.

Burmese border problem. Others are continuations of the struggle for independence, like the tension between North and South Vietnam[1] and the complex battle over Laos. Still others are active, such as the Thai–South Vietnam–Cambodia frontier dispute, the position of Ceylon residents of Indian origin, and Indo-Pakistani legacies of Partition, particularly Kashmir.

A brief reference is appropriate for the most recent of these sources of disharmony, the Philippines' claim to British North Borneo. Manila remained silent until 1962 when plans were completed for the merger of British North Borneo with Brunei, Sarawak, Malaya, and Singapore into a new state of Malaysia. Then the Philippines espoused a private claim for the first time. This dates to an agreement of 1878 between the then Sultan of Sulu and a group of merchants, later to become the British North Borneo Company. In the summer of 1963 this dispute appeared on the verge of solution following an accord reached by Malaya, Indonesia and the Philippines. The face-saving formula provided for: the U.N. Secretary-General ascertaining the wishes of the people of the Borneo dependencies before Malaysia came into being at the end of August of that year (thereby permitting the federation to be formed); consideration of the Philippine claim by the new state; and the prospect of confederation among the signatories. In this manner, the three Malay states received 'satisfaction'.[2]

Preoccupation with bloc politics has concealed deep-rooted tension between Cambodia and her neighbours. Early in the nineteenth century, 'Cambodia was little more than a Siamo-Vietnamese condominium . . . completely split up into Siamese and Vietnamese provinces with colonial governors of the neighbouring nations directly administering them. . . .' Laos was under even more direct subjugation. Indeed, it was the coming of the French that saved both these communities from total conquest by more powerful neighbours. To the present day fear of Thailand and South Vietnam is the key factor in Cambodian foreign policy, explaining both its neutralism and its request, in 1962, for a 14-nation conference on the Geneva-Laos model to guarantee its integrity and neutralization. As paraphrased by his interviewer, Prince Sihanouk remarked in that year, 'It has been our observation that in the case of a communist

---

[1] A comprehensive analysis of that conflict is to be found in Bernard B. Fall, *Two Viet Nams: Background of Conflict*, New York 1963.

[2] *New York Times*, 12 and 16 June 1963, and editorial on 15 June 1963.

take-over, be it in Eastern Europe or in Asia, the national *entity* of the country thus taken over is preserved. . . . If we were to be swallowed up by the Thai and Vietnamese tomorrow, we would purely and simply disappear as a *people*, not to speak of Cambodia as a national unit . . . even our language and culture would be wiped out. . . .' Set against the possibility of genocide, communist control is not an unbearable thought.[1] Sihanouk himself later wrote that the ultimate Thai–South Vietnamese goal is to establish a common frontier on the Mekong River, obliterating Cambodia from the map.[2] History suggests that this is not an unreal fear although Ngo Dinh Diem is at present too busy at home. Certainly the Thai reaction to the World Court decision in 1962 awarding Cambodia ownership of the long-disputed Temple of Preah Vihear on the Thai border— including talk of withdrawal from SEATO—has not eased the strain between these traditional foes.[3] Continuing Cambodia–South Vietnam frontier incidents, caused mainly by over-zealous South Vietnamese security operations along an uncertain border, are a serious irritant and source of Cambodian suspicion and fear.

Of Ceylon's ten million people about two million are of Indian descent. These fall into two groups of equal size—the Ceylon Tamils (Dry Zone Tamils) and the Ceylon Indians (Estate Tamils). The former are really indigenous to Ceylon, having arrived between the tenth and thirteenth centuries, A.D. Their rights as citizens are not contested and they hold important positions in the country's economic life. The Ceylon Indians, by contrast, came to the island in the past century as indentured labourers to work the vast tea and coffee plantations, and later, rubber plantations as well. On the whole they have remained a distinct community with strong family and economic links with South India. The overwhelming majority are not recognized by Ceylon as her nationals although many desire Ceylonese citizenship. Colombo insists that they are really citizens of India. Delhi, on the other hand, asserts that they have been in

---

[1] A succinct account of this conflict, from which these quotations are taken, is to be found in Bernard B. Fall, 'Southeast Asia: The West at Bay', *Current History*, vol. 43, November 1962, pp. 296–8. For a more comprehensive analysis see Michael Leifer, 'Cambodia and Her Neighbours,' *Pacific Affairs*, vol. XXXIV, No. 4, Winter 1961–62, pp. 361–74.

[2] In *Realités Cambodgiennes*, as reported by John Stirling, *Observer* Service, in the *Montreal Star*, 23 November 1962.

[3] The text of the Court decision is in the *New York Times*, 16 June 1962. See also L. P. Singh, 'The Thai-Cambodian Temple Dispute', *Asian Survey*, II, No. 8, October 1962, pp. 23–26.

Ceylon for a long time and must therefore be regarded as Ceylon citizens or, at worst, stateless persons. This in essence is the problem.

Before independence Ceylon Indians were protected by the foreign ruler. Both Sinhalese and Indians were British subjects and the suffrage (there had been universal adult franchise since 1931) was based on that fact. From 1948 on, however, the right to vote was tied to Ceylon citizenship. Much of the conflict and controversy has raged around the question of who are to be considered citizens of Ceylon. Sinhalese and Ceylon Indians disagreed on the answer. And there was ominous evidence from the past that the former would impose restrictive legislation once in power.[1] This was not long in coming.

Within a year of independence the new state enacted three crucial pieces of legislation. The Ceylon Citizenship Act of 1948 effectively barred most Ceylon Indians by requiring three generations of domiciled ancestors as a condition of citizenship by descent. The Ceylon (Parliamentary Elections) Amendment Act of 1949 held that only citizens of Ceylon could vote and thereby deprived most Ceylon Indians of the franchise. And the Indian and Pakistani Residents' Citizenship Act of the same year enumerated stiff qualifications to be met by prospective Ceylon Indian applicants for citizenship. Those who applied for citizenship within two years, i.e., by 6 August 1951, would be allowed to vote in the 1952 elections. But this pledge was broken. Reversing its earlier boycott the Ceylon Indian Congress persuaded its supporters to register *en masse* at the last moment. By the deadline some 237,000 applications were filed, covering 650,000 persons. Processing was painfully slow so that on the eve of the elections only 7,500 Ceylon Indians had been granted citizenship. There followed a bitter exchange between the principals and token civil disobedience.

Various attempts were made at the highest level to solve the dispute, with only minor success. The first and most noteworthy was at a meeting between Nehru and Prime Minister Senanayake in 1953. Senanayake offered to grant citizenship to 400,000 Ceylon Indians and permanent residence permits to another 250,000 provided the

---

[1] In 1939, John (later Sir John) Kotelawala, a member of the Board of Ministers, proposed that all daily paid non-Sinhalese workers in government departments be repatriated to the country of their birth with gratuities and thereafter prevented from re-entering Ceylon for employment. It is worth noting that Nehru was involved in negotiations on this problem as early as 1939 when he was sent as a special delegate of the Indian National Congress to discuss the matter with the Ceylon Board of Ministers.

remainder, some 300,000, were compulsorily repatriated to India over a ten-year period. Nehru rejected the compulsory character of the scheme. The next year Nehru and Prime Minister Kotelawala reached an accord on various points which eased the tension. By 1956 the problem became enmeshed with the broader issue of language and there the interests of Ceylon Tamils and Ceylon Indians merged.

With the approach of elections both the United National Party and the leftist Sri Lanka Freedom Party appealed to Sinhalese nationalism and pledged a 'one language' policy. Tamil speakers protested vigorously and inter-communal tension mounted. The result was severe riots in 1956 and 1958, causing a thousand dead and many more injured. Only the use of emergency powers restored order. Similar violence occurred in 1960 with almost as heavy a toll. Mrs. Bandaranaike, who succeeded her assassinated husband as Prime Minister in 1959, exchanged visits with Nehru. But while the tension between Delhi and Colombo has eased in recent years, the ugly scars of the past are still in evidence in relations between Sinhalese and Ceylon Indians (and Ceylon Tamils as well). As long as this continues it will mar the otherwise friendly ties between these two new states.[1]

The gravest discord between any two new states in Southern Asia is that between the successors to the British Raj. The story of their tragic enmity is too well known to bear repetition here.[2] Suffice it to note that Partition produced violent emotion and bitterness, along with many complex problems, and that as a result India and Pakistan have looked upon each other as enemies since independence. Some of the disputes have been settled: all territorial claims but two, the Chad Bet area in the west and the transfer of the Berubari and Cooch-Behar enclaves in the east; some financial questions such as

---

[1] Accounts of this problem may be found in W. Howard Wriggins, *Ceylon: Dilemmas of a New Nation,* Princeton 1960, pp. 399–403; K. P. Mukerji, 'Indo-Ceylon Relations', *Indian Journal of Political Science,* vol. 18, January–March 1957, pp. 41–54; I. D. S. Weerawardana, 'Minority Problems in Ceylon', *Pacific Affairs,* vol. XXV, September 1952; pp. 278–87; and K. P. Krishna Shetty, 'The Law of Citizenship for Indian and Pakistani Residents in Ceylon', *The Indian Year Book of International Affairs,* Madras 1958, vol. VII, pp. 165–85.

[2] See Michael Brecher, *The Struggle for Kashmir,* Toronto 1953; J. Korbel, *Danger in Kashmir,* Princeton 1954; Sisir Gupta, *India's Relations with Pakistan 1954–1957,* New York 1957; and Sisir Gupta, 'The Kashmir Question 1947–60' (survey of source material), *International Studies,* Delhi, vol. III, No. 2, October 1961, pp. 184–93.

the value of defence capital works and the extent of income tax arrears at the time of Partition; and the vital issue of control over the Indus valley canal waters. But many remain to plague all efforts at *rapprochement*. Most are of minor importance such as the disposition of pre-partition assets and military and railway stores of the Government of undivided India, the use of the Ganga (Ganges) River waters north of Calcutta, and the border disputes noted above. One involves billions of rupees but is technical in nature, namely, compensation for the property left behind by some 14 million refugees. But all these are dwarfed by the supreme barrier to friendship—Kashmir.

The facts concerning this dispute are straightforward. The princely State of Jammu and Kashmir, the largest of the 600-odd 'Indian' states before 1947, was ruled by a Hindu Maharaja. Its population of about four million was 77 per cent Muslim at the time of Partition. Under the impact of a tribal invasion across Pakistani territory (probably with support from some Pakistani officials) the Maharaja of Kashmir acceded to India in accordance with procedures laid down by the departing British. Pakistan termed the accession a fraud. Indian troops, invited by the Maharaja, repelled the tribesmen. At the end of 1947 India raised the issue in the United Nations Security Council to secure the withdrawal of the tribesmen and, later, of Pakistani troops who joined the battle in the spring of 1948. The United Nations is still seised of the issue.

Both India and Pakistan have accepted the two resolutions of UNCIP, the United Nations Commission for India and Pakistan, one dated 13 August 1948, the other 5 January 1949. Together they laid down the procedure for realizing the goal of a plebiscite in which the people of Kashmir would determine their future—as part of India or Pakistan. A truce came into effect at the beginning of 1949. Since that time a stream of United Nations representatives have attempted to implement the resolutions, so far without success: General MacNaughton of Canada and Sir Owen Dixon, an Australian jurist, during 1950; Dr. Frank Graham, an American educator, from 1951 to 1953; Gunnar Jarring, a Swedish diplomat, in 1957; and Graham again in 1958. During the mid-fifties (and again in 1963) there were direct negotiations between Delhi and Karachi and since 1958 debates in the Security Council, all without any end to the impasse. Graham continues as (inactive) United Nations Representative for India and Pakistan.

Every proposal for a plebiscite has been eagerly accepted by Pakistan and rejected by India on the grounds that Pakistan had never fulfilled the first requisite of the procedure laid down in the United Nations' resolutions, namely, the withdrawal of Pakistani forces from all Kashmir. From 1957 onwards India even rescinded its approval of a plebiscite, asserting that much had happened in the intervening decade, that conditions were settled and that a plebiscite would only arouse latent unrest. In Nehru's words, in October 1960, 'Kashmir is a pandora box which, if opened, might produce dangerous consequences.' To which President Ayub replied, 'It is a time bomb never far removed from the flash point.'[1]

Delhi's adamant stand is due in part to a strong desire to retain an attractive territory. But it is also influenced by the fear that a plebiscite would exacerbate communal tension and would have grave consequences for India's internal stability. There would be a strengthening of Hindu communal forces, increasing distrust of the Muslim minority—of fifty millions—and a challenge to the secular foundations of Indian life. Pakistan would undoubtedly like to secure control of the Vale. But for her too there is an important ideological factor. Kashmir is in a very real sense the final test of the validity of the two-nation theory, the *raison d'être* of Pakistan. The danger of communal conflict is less—there are few Hindus left in West Pakistan and the East Bengalis feel little attachment to Kashmir. But Kashmir dominates discussion in the public life of Pakistan. Every government, civil or military, democratic or authoritarian, must press the claim on all fronts at every opportunity.

The cost of Kashmir has been enormous. Both states have felt compelled to devote a large portion of their budget to defence—an annual average of 75 per cent for Pakistan and over 50 per cent for India. This in turn has slowed down economic development in both states. It has also reduced trade between complementary economies and has wasted valuable foreign exchange. Kashmir has also stimulated—and has been aggravated by—propaganda of the most vicious type, heightening the sense of insecurity among the minorities on both sides of the border. No less costly have been the strategic consequences. The sub-continent is a natural military unit. Its security depends on joint defence arrangements. But instead of co-operation these countries have prepared for war with each other, defying the lessons of history and the realities of the contemporary world.

[1] *Pakistan News Digest*, Karachi, 15 October 1960.

Some hope for a settlement appeared in the aftermath of China's move into Ladakh in the autumn of 1959. Only after renewed Chinese incursions into Ladakh and NEFA, however, did prospects for a Kashmir settlement improve.

There were six rounds of negotiation between December 1962 and May 1963. Zulfikar Ali Bhutto represented Pakistan, and Sardar Swaran Singh, India. The first two sessions were exploratory, with both parties clinging to their time-encrusted 'solution', for Pakistan a plebiscite in the entire state, for India acceptance of the cease-fire line with minor revisions. In the third session, as they moved towards a 'political', i.e. a realistic, settlement, Pakistan apparently laid claim to the entire territory, except for $1\frac{1}{2}$ districts of Jammu Province, while India reportedly offered to partition the Vale—in such a manner as to give Pakistan control over the headwaters of rivers whose water was vital to West Pakistan.[1] The fourth round took place in the aftermath of the Sino-Pakistani border agreement, the timing of which suggested doubts about Pakistan's interest in a compromise solution; at Pakistan's own admission, out of a difference of 3,400 square miles between the Pakistani and Chinese claim lines, Pakistan received 1,350 square lines and the Chinese 2,050.[2] The fifth round bogged down at the point reached in the 'political' approach of round three. And the last session proved abortive, terminating abruptly on 16 May, the day they were resumed. Both parties naturally blamed the other for the failure.[3] Only one thing is clear: it will not be easy for Nehru to make concessions or for Ayub to accept anything less than a plebiscite.

One possible way out of the deadlock has commended itself to this writer and was proposed at a conference in Pakistan in 1958.[4] The compromise would be an internally autonomous Vale of Kashmir jointly guaranteed by India and Pakistan, with the remaining four areas of the state divided thus: Gilgit and Poonch to Pakistan, Jammu and Ladakh (what is left of it) to India. This would require a willingness on the part of Delhi and Karachi to lift themselves out

[1] The Indian delegate revealed, at the end of the talks, that the Indian offer would have given Pakistan 34,000 of a total area of 85,000 square miles, while the Pakistani offer would have left India with only 3,000 square miles.

[2] See *Pakistan News Digest*, Karachi, 15 March 1963.

[3] The Pakistani version of the 1963 negotiations is set out in seven special issues of *Pakistan Affairs* (Washington). The Indian version is to be found in the near-daily *Indiagram* (Ottawa).

[4] The proposal was contained in the author's data paper for the 13th Conference of the Institute of Pacific Relations, Lahore, February 1958. See the author's *India's Foreign Policy: An Interpretation*, New York 1957.

of the rut of charge and counter-charge. Its merits are many. Neither side would 'lose' Kashmir nor suffer loss of face. It is more important to the contestants that the opponent should not gain control over Kashmir than that either should do so. This solution would give the two states free economic and tourist access to the Valley. India would be able to remove the one major blot on its foreign policy in the view of many sympathizers abroad. And while it is true that India has physical control over the most valuable parts of the territory, the continuing price of its retention is exorbitant. In practical terms this would involve the presence of Indian and Pakistani special commissioners in Srinagar, with an election commission comprising officials of both supervising elections in the Vale of Kashmir. A special High Court would be established to deal with inter-communal and other vexed cases. And a joint Indo-Pakistani military force would safeguard the Vale's physical security.

Such a settlement would relieve the oppressive tension which hangs over the sub-continent, now confronted with a massive challenge from the north-east. It would ease the tremendous economic and financial burden of defence. It could pave the way for broader military and economic co-operation, so vital to both states. India's fear of dangerous internal repercussions arising from the loss of Kashmir would be substantially alleviated. Pakistan would be greatly relieved of the commitment to 'liberate' Kashmir. The contest over the two-nation theory would end in stalemate, the most desirable outcome from a political point of view. The first step, a recognition of the Vale of Kashmir's autonomy with a joint guarantee, would be all-important, for it would clear the air of mistrust. It would also pave the way for a psychological reconciliation. One thing is certain. If some such solution is not found soon both India and Pakistan will pay an even more exorbitant price than in the past—to an expansionist, powerful neighbour who can benefit from the deep fissures within the sub-continent.

Two conclusions flow from these explorations of bilateral relations. The first is that, despite appearances to the contrary at times, the new states of Southern Asia have many important disputes with their neighbours. The second is that these disputes, and intra-area relations in general, are more important to the foreign policy of these states than the bipolar bloc struggle.[1]

[1] For an informative analysis of the role of India and Pakistan in each other's foreign policy see M. S. Rajan, 'India and Pakistan as Factors in Each Other's Foreign Policy and Relations', *International Studies*, Delhi, vol. III, No. 4, April 1962, pp. 349–95.

THE NEW STATES AND THE UNITED NATIONS

The number of Southern Asian new states in the United Nations increased gradually over a decade. Only two, India and the Philippines, were charter members of the world organization. Pakistan was added in 1947, Burma in 1948, and Indonesia in 1950. Five years later the 'package deal' included Cambodia, Ceylon, Laos, and Nepal. The last to join was Malaya in 1957, making a total of ten.

Thus far in this chapter it has been feasible to analyse these new states in world politics apart from larger groupings. In sketching their role at the United Nations, however, this would be artificial. There is no group, caucus, or bloc comprising only these states. There are basic schisms among them which prevent unity of action on many issues. And thirdly their common feature of 'newness' is shared by some fifty other states in Asia and Africa with whom they are members of the largest caucus in the United Nations. In short their attitudes and roles tend to merge with a definable group and to gain importance thereby. Thus the focus will be on 'the new states' in the largest sense and on the bloc most closely identified with them, although some overlapping to 'old states' will occur. Wherever possible the role of Southern Asian new states will receive special attention.

The analysis falls logically into three periods: 1946–54; 1955–60; and since 1960. The dividing points are the inception of the United Nations, the formal organization of the Asian–African caucus at the 10th Session, and the mass influx of African states, making the African caucus a potent instrument in its own right. During the first stage there were 19 members from Asia and Africa but only 12 worked together as a group—six Arab states, two 'old' Muslim Middle East states, Afghanistan and Iran, and four new states of Southern Asia—Pakistan, India, Burma, and Indonesia. The 'Arab–Asian' bloc did not come into existence even on an *ad hoc* basis until the 5th Session, 1950. But its roots and stimuli lie deeper and to a large extent outside the United Nations. The Arab caucus had operated continuously since the San Francisco Conference in 1945. The Asian Relations Conference in 1947 had brought the leaders of many new states together. And the Asian Conference on Indonesia in 1949 explicitly recommended co-operation at the United Nations. The stimuli were common experience and aspirations. Their position as a distinct minority within the organization was an added inducement.

During the first few sessions of the General Assembly these states were occasionally brought together by a colonial or racial theme. Thus in 1946 all Asian and African members except Turkey joined with the Soviet bloc and others to win a majority for the Assembly's competence to deal with the treatment of Indians in South Africa. Similar co-operation was in evidence during the 3rd and 4th Sessions on the question of the disposition of former Italian colonies, leading to a compromise in the form of a pledge of independence for Libya in 1952 and Somaliland in 1960. By the 5th Session, 1950, the influence of these states was recognized, especially by the Soviet bloc, always in a minority of five at that stage. However, it was not until the Korea crisis that the Arab–Asian caucus met formally on 5 December 1950 under the guidance of the Indian delegate Sir Benegal Rau. Its initial efforts at a compromise settlement failed but an important precedent had been set. From that first venture onwards the bloc met more frequently and on a wider range of issues.

Year after year the bloc pressed successfully for stronger resolutions on discrimination against Indians in South Africa and in 1952 it added *apartheid* as a separate item. Much attention was also devoted in the early fifties to Morocco and Tunisia. In due course its pressure contributed to French withdrawal from these North African protectorates. It also hastened the end of United Nations trusteeship over Togoland and the Cameroons. There was some division on cold-war issues. All supported the historic 'Uniting for Peace' Resolution in 1950 but India and Indonesia abstained on the recommendations of the Collective Measures Committee the next year. Most abstained on the Soviet Korean proposals in 1950 and moved skilfully between the giants during the next three years.[1]

By the end of the first stage there were four additional members of the bloc—the Philippines, Thailand, Ethiopia, and Liberia. Only Turkey among the Asians had never been a member, and Israel had been denied membership from 1949 to 1951 when it voted the same way on some issues. Thereafter Israel veered towards a pro-West posture. At no time during that period did the bloc have a one-third

---

[1] No member of the group supported the Soviet bloc on more than 15 of the 65 General Assembly roll-call votes on Korea taken between 1950 and 1953. Reported in Mary Knatchbull Keynes. 'The Arab-Asian Bloc', *International Relations*, London, Vol. I, 1954–59, pp. 238–50, on which the analysis of the first stage has relied.

veto in the Assembly. Thus it sought and found allies—sometimes the West and Latin America, as in the collective security resolutions of 1950 and 1951, sometimes the Soviet bloc and some Latin Americans, as on colonial issues.

The formal organization of the bloc as the Asian–African caucus occurred at the 10th Session, 1955, in accord with a recommendation of the Bandung Conference: 'The problem of peace,' said the communiqué, 'is correlative with the problems of international security. In this connection, all states should co-operate, especially through the United Nations. . . .' At the outset all 17 United Nations members who attended Bandung belonged to the caucus, including Turkey. With the 'package deal' 10 more were added. By 1959 there were 29 members. Then came the massive influx of 1960, increasing the Afro-Asian caucus to 46. By 1963 it had grown to 58, more than half the total membership of the world organization. Africa alone had experienced a twelve-fold increase in just six years, from three in 1957 to 36 at present!

During the second stage of the bloc's evolution, 1955–60, there emerged three broad voting groups although much overlapping existed: a pro-West group based largely on participation in military pacts; a non-aligned group, led by India; and a floating group consisting of Lebanon, Jordan, Laos, and Japan, with Libya, Tunisia, and Morocco from Africa. Colonial (or self-determination) issues continued to be the bloc's major concern during those years. The bloc focused particularly on Africa and pressure on the Western colonial powers to hasten their withdrawal. On the great crisis of the middle fifties, Hungary and Suez, the new states tended to adopt a double standard. Without exception they called for withdrawal, some condemnation as well, of the United Kingdom, France, and Israel. And most were unwilling to consider any conditions or safeguards against further Egyptian misdeeds. On Hungary, however, their voices were softer, many even muted, and some—Afghanistan, Ceylon, India, Indonesia, Saudi Arabia, the United Arab Republic, and Yemen—consistently abstained from voting. As for disarmament, all favoured it in principle. Many of the non-aligned states supported the Soviet position and many abstained. On the perennial issue of China's representation in the United Nations the breakdown was roughly as noted earlier. For example, in 1955, 1956, 1957, the votes were 42–12–6, 47–24–8, and 48–27–6 against considering the question. The big increase among those opposed to the resolution, from 12 to 24, reflected the 'package deal'. Greater unity was demonstrated on a wide range of economic questions, notably the increase of capital and technical assistance to be made available by the United Nations and the richer members to the underdeveloped lands through such schemes as SUNFED and the International Finance Corporation. Here there was no clash.[1]

A careful study of the Asian–African voting record during the first two stages reveals a striking growth of cohesion following the formation of the caucus. Thus, before 1950 members voted against each other 53·9 per cent but thereafter only 23·6 per cent. Similarly their identical vote increased threefold from 11·4 per cent to 33·4 per cent and solidarity voting rose from 34·6 per cent to 43 per cent. Noteworthy changes in voting patterns on specific subjects are as follows: 2·9 per cent to 34·2 per cent on pacific settlement; 14 per cent to 39·5 per cent on self-determination; and 18·2 per cent to 35·8 per cent on collective measures. Despite its growing numbers and heterogeneity, the Asian–African caucus increased its alignment with the majority of the General Assembly from 77·1 per cent to 84·8 per cent. The conclusion drawn by Professor Hovet is that 'the organization of the Asian–African caucusing group has made significant changes in the relations of its members with the Assembly. . . . Considering the multitude of divisive forces in the group [some neutralist, others in military alliances, some in the Arab caucus, others in the African caucus and others in the Commonwealth, and many having disputes with each other] the extent of identical votes is significant; and it would be misleading to assume that the large size and varied membership of the group render it ineffective.'[2]

More recent evidence tends to support that observation. The Asian–African caucus was greatly enlarged in 1960 with the admission of many new African states. This meant more divisive forces and greater heterogeneity. It also meant the formalization of an autonomous African caucus.[3] Nevertheless the overall Asian–

[1] For a succinct survey of the United Nations and South-East Asian states, including frequent references to other new states in the Asian–African group, see Fifield, op. cit., ch. 11.

[2] Thomas Hovet, Jr., *Bloc Politics in the United Nations*, Cambridge, Mass. 1960, pp. 87–90.

[3] For an analysis of the African record at the United Nations from 1960 to 1962 see John H. Spencer, 'Africa at the U.N.: Some Observations', in Norman J. Padelford and Rupert Emerson (eds.), 'Africa and International Organization', special issue of *International Organization*, Vol. XVI, No. 2, Spring 1962, pp. 375–86.

African caucus has remained an effective force, perhaps more power-ful in this third stage than ever before. This was revealed on various occasions: the condemnation of Portuguese action in Angola; the call for French withdrawal from Bizerte; the virtual veto on any United Nations action following India's occupation of Goa; the cen-sure vote (67–1–36) against the remarks of South Africa's Foreign Minister; and the successful insistence on an Afro-Asian consultation committee on Congo affairs to guide the (Asian) Secretary-General.

They were not, of course, always united. There was disagreement on such cold-war issues as Tibet, Hungary, and Cuba. Even on the Congo and Algeria some divisions were evident. Yet on a matter of decisive importance to the future of the United Nations—the office of the Secretary-General—the bloc stood fast and ultimately com-pelled the Soviets to abandon their *troika* proposal. As in the past they joined hands in pressing for larger economic and financial aid from the developed member-states. Perhaps their most dramatic set-back was the failure to win adequate support for a five-member Afro-Asian neutralist proposal in September 1960 for a summit conference between Khrushchev and Eisenhower.

Some insight into the behaviour of this group at the United Nations is afforded by a recent analysis of 80 important roll-call votes by 50 'non-aligned' states at the 15th and 16th Sessions, 1960 and 1961.[1] Where the super-powers differed, 26·1 per cent of the votes cast by these states, of whom 43 were Afro-Asian, coincided with those of the United States, 29·2 per cent with those of the Soviet Union. The corresponding figures for the Asian states were 19 per cent and 34·2 per cent; for the Africans, 30·7 per cent and 24·4 per cent; and for the Arabs, 11·6 per cent and 40·5 per cent in agreement with the United States and Soviet votes respectively. Among the 10 states having the highest coincidence with the United States were Malaya, 47·5 per cent, and Laos, 42·4 per cent. Among the 11 states having the highest coincidence with the Soviet Union were Indonesia, 53·7 per cent, Ceylon, 41·8 per cent, and India, 41·2 per cent; India's vote coincided with that of the United States only 10 per cent of the time. Other new states of Southern Asia, notably Pakistan and the Philippines, had a much higher coincidence with the votes of the United States. It must be added that these statistics may conceal the crucial fact that coincidence is not synonymous with stimulus; very

[1] Francis O. Wilcox, 'The Non-Aligned States and the United Nations', in Laurence W. Martin (ed.), *Neutralism and NonAlignment*, New York 1962, pp. 121–51.

often it was the Soviet bloc that aligned itself with the Asian–African neutralists. Another revealing fact is the high incidence of abstentions: 29 of these states abstained on at least 20 of these important votes. Very often some of them were absent from the vote. All this derives from a strong urge to compromise which, in turn, is a product of the deeply-rooted conception of a bridge and mediator between the two ideological blocs.

The Asian–African caucus meets regularly throughout the year and at the request of any member. Consultation takes place on all matters of special interest but not on issues in dispute between members of the caucus. Lebanon in 1958 was the only exception to this 'harmonizing' rule. Procedures are extremely informal—monthly rotation of chairmen, occasional non-binding votes, free and frank discussion directed to the maximum solidarity consistent with 'national interests'. Meetings are open to senior members of delegations. Agreements are by consensus and views are presented by each member to the General Assembly or other United Nations organ without formal co-ordination in the caucus. In this as in many other respects this group is more flexible than either the Soviet bloc or the Latin American caucus.[1]

There is ample evidence of the high regard with which the United Nations is held among the new states. This is natural because the United Nations has great value for these states. In some cases it hastened the coming of independence, as with Israel and Indonesia, Libya and Somalia, Togoland, the Cameroons and Tanganyika, perhaps with Tunisia and Morocco as well. Almost certainly the United Nations has kept the Congo in being. More generally the new states are weak and fearful, especially of nuclear war or super-power conventional war. To the non-aligned, at least, only the United Nations can provide adequate protection against these hazards. In case of a threat to their territorial integrity the United Nations is a shield, as the Congo demonstrated. This role as defender of small states led, in return, to the defence of a strong Secretary-General's Office. Aside from these two functions, the United Nations is a valuable and untïed channel for economic and financial, as well as technical assistance. No less important, perhaps, is the sense of dignity derived from equal membership in a world organization along with old and powerful states. And in co-operation with other new states they can wield disproportionate influence. They have supported United

[1] See Hovet, op. cit., pp. 47–56, 64–69.

Nations intervention in crisis areas but with a strong preference for small-state contingents, as in Suez and the Congo. However, where vital interests have been involved they have resented intervention, e.g. Kashmir, Goa, and West New Guinea. The United Nations is for the new states first and foremost an agency to end the epoch of colonialism and to achieve racial equality.

What is the influence of the new states of Southern Asia? This is difficult to measure, for they function as part of the much larger Asian–African caucus. Outside that caucus they comprise only 9 per cent of the total United Nations membership. Within the caucus they constitute a crucial segment of more than half the membership of the organization. Despite the numerical predominance of African states, the predominant influence remains Asian because of their greater experience. If the caucus is united it can not only block any resolution on an 'important subject', which requires a two-thirds majority, but can, with the support of a few extra votes, secure the necessary majority for a resolution of its choice. Perhaps the most dramatic illustration was the General Assembly resolution of November 1962 (67–16–23) which called on all members to impose economic sanctions on, and break diplomatic relations with, South Africa. This unity is very rare but the very size of the Asian–African caucus enables it to deny an overwhelming majority to anyone. This gives the caucus great bargaining power. In that sense the new states can paralyse the United Nations. They can also elevate the organization to new levels of achievement as a result of their dependence on, and attachment to, its principles and purposes.

Recent events have cast a cloud over the paths likely to be taken by the new states in the near future. On the one hand, they have received recognition as a possible conciliating force in the appointment of four of their number—India, Burma, Egypt, and Nigeria—to the 18-member Committee on Disarmament in 1962. On the other, the Sino-Indian border conflict has undermined the policy of non-alignment for its leading exponent and thereby raised serious doubts about its efficacy for many other new states. Nehru, it is true, has affirmed his determination to remain non-aligned and has maintained the fiction of equal Western and Soviet aid in India's 'time of trouble'. But the impact of China's assault is already evident. India adopted a more pro-West view on the need for effective inspection in any disarmament agreement and voted with the West to bar Communist China from an international atomic energy conference in 1964. Moreover, the vote on China's representation in the United Nations in 1962 went more heavily against Peking. Eight new states shifted from abstention to opposition.

It is difficult to see the future clearly but nothing has occurred to alter this writer's view that the new states, and especially the non-aligned among them, perform functions necessary to general inter-state stability. At times they can mediate between the blocs. On other occasions they can provide the small contingents of troops for the United Nations' peace-keeping function. At all times, in the foresee-able future, they offer an enormous area for genuine peaceful com-petition between the blocs to the advantage of all concerned. And, as one former American official remarked, 'If they use their influence wisely and well, they might even prevent nuclear war.'[1] Most of all, the new states are concerned with problems within their own subordinate systems, Southern Asian or African. The vast majority want to reduce their involvement in and intrusions from the bloc struggle.

[1] Wilcox, op. cit., p. 149.

TALKS WITH NEHRU

Selections from the author's interviews with Prime Minister Nehru
6 June and 13 June 1956

ON GANDHI

BRECHER. On many occasions, Mr. Prime Minister, as related in your Autobiography and elsewhere, you found yourself profoundly disconcerted by Gandhi's decisions. Yet, ultimately, you followed his course of action. I find it difficult to understand this apparent duality and would therefore appreciate your reflections on these events years after they occurred.

NEHRU. It is rather difficult to discuss these matters. There was this apparent duality and, to some extent, it continues even today, in regard to certain aspects of Mr. Gandhi's thinking or action. But the duality did not really come in very much on the political plane. It was other matters which impinged on politics. . . . Primarily, it was my lack of understanding of, well, what he called his inner voice. He would go on a fast. I didn't understand that—and I don't understand it still. Again, he referred to the Bihar earthquake [1934] and said that it was because India had the sin of untouchability. I didn't understand that and I don't understand it still. But, on the political plane, and I would say also to a considerable extent on the moral plane, he attracted me a great deal. Also, it's always difficult to describe a man who is rather unusual and a tremendous personality, and who gave an impression of enormous strength and inner reserves of power. I don't think his books or his writings bring it out; to some extent they do but not very much. . . . And then his career was one of success. Not success on normal standards which you may have to apply, success in moulding the Indian people, in affecting the Indian people, in making them better than they were, stronger, braver, more disciplined. One saw that happening and that affected one.

BRECHER. What was it that attracted you initially to Gandhi?

NEHRU. I think I met him first at the end of 1915. But before that, of course, I had heard a great deal about his activities in South Africa . . . so that he was known to us a great deal by reputation and he was already a hero, in our minds. Then he came nearer to us. . . . We saw him functioning, functioning with success. It was so different from our method, the normal political method of a nationalist movement, which shouted a great deal and did little. Here was a man who didn't shout at all. He spoke softly, gently, and put forward what he thought were his minimum demands and stuck to them. There was an element of great strength about it.

BRECHER. Some years ago, I believe it was in 1942, Mr. Gandhi expressed the view that after his death you would follow his message more closely. I think it's fair to say that his prediction has come to pass. I would appreciate it very much if you could explain this metamorphosis.

NEHRU. Whose metamorphosis?—in whom? In me, or in somebody else?

BRECHER. In your own change with regard to certain issues about which there may have been disagreement before, whereas now you find yourself speaking his language more closely and following his message in a way that wasn't true in the thirties or forties?

NEHRU. I don't think that is so. Mr. Gandhi was an extraordinarily generous man. He had a remarkable capacity for winning over people, even opponents. If he couldn't win an opponent over, he somehow dulled his antagonism and his hostility, because, fundamentally I think, he just praised a person. That's too simple a thing, he didn't do that, but he spotted the good points in a person and laid stress on them, and rather slurred over the bad points. . . . Mr. Gandhi said that I would speak his language more. I don't think that has any very special meaning except that he always managed to induce a person to behave in a particular way by expecting him to do so. There was that in him. And he pulled out a person—he was by no means a soft person with his colleagues or others. He was a very hard task-master, but at the same time one could see his friendship and affection. Now, I don't think, myself, that I have changed my mind at all about violence or non-violence during the last 35 years—basically, I don't think so. I should imagine, indeed, that in the early twenties . . . I was much more powerfully influenced by him; in fact, to the extent, if I may say so, that my mind was sort of under his—not under his control, that's not right, but still more so than I was a few years later when I started questioning about violence and non-violence. . . . I just cannot imagine him as a leader in any other country but India.

BRECHER. In the sense that he gave expression to the traditional values of India?

NEHRU. Yes, that is, he gave expression, he appealed to something in the minds of Indians. He would be out of place elsewhere, that is to say, he would be respected, maybe admired, but he never would have political power which he got through his affecting the mass mind here. Remember this, that when he started his big movement here, in 1919 and 1920, almost every political leader of the Congress, leave out the others, opposed him. . . . He went ahead in spite of them and it was the success he obtained in those three or four months [the boycott of elections] that convinced all these people. . . . It was his success and his demonstration of his strength with the Indian people, and how he could discipline them and make them act in a particular way.

ON THE PARTITION OF INDIA

BRECHER. What were the circumstances which compelled you to accept Partition, particularly in view of your dedication to a united sub-continent all during the Freedom Movement?

NEHRU. Well, I suppose, the compulsion of events, and the feeling that we couldn't get out of that deadlock or morass by pursuing the way we had done; it became worse and worse. Further, a feeling that even if, somehow, we got freedom for India, with that background, it would be a very weak India, that is, a federal India with far too great power in the federating units. . . . A larger India would be weak and would have constant troubles, disintegrating pulls; and, also, the fact that we saw no way of getting the freedom too— in the near future, I mean. And so we accepted this, we said, let us build up a strong India. And, if the others, the Muslim League leaders and those who do not want to be in it, well, how can we and why should we force them to be in it?

BRECHER. Would you say, in the perspective of 1956, that the partition of India was inevitable?

NEHRU. The partition of India became inevitable, I should say, in less than a year before it occurred. It wasn't inevitable till the last year.

BRECHER. Could you recall for me, very briefly, the crucial acts or sequence of events which, in your opinion, sealed the issue of a divided or united India?

NEHRU. I don't think that preceding the war they [the British] had any clear ideas about partition or, indeed, wanted it. But obviously throughout that period, and long before, the British Government's policy, as the policy of any such governing authority in a colonial territory, was to weaken the national movement. And the major way of weakening it was to play up the Muslim League and other dissident elements. . . . I think now, looking back, that Partition could have been stopped if the British Government's policy had been different, about a year or, say, eighteen months before the partition.

BRECHER. From what you say, Mr. Prime Minister, it would appear that in your opinion the onus for the partition of the sub-continent must rest ultimately on the then-existing Government of India.

NEHRU. Yes, the chief men here.

ON NON-VIOLENCE

BRECHER. To what extent would you say that a statesman who is responsible for the welfare of his people can rely on non-violence as an approach to the settlement of disputes? What constitutes, in your opinion, the boundary line beyond which resort to violence is justifiable and perhaps necessary?

NEHRU. Mr. Gandhi once said that he believed completely in non-violence, but he said cowardice is worse. And he said, 'I prefer you to fight with arms than to run away.' He said that. 'I do not want the non-violence of the coward. I believe in the non-violence of the brave man.' He said that repeatedly. But there is no great difference in that, because slavery is not non-violence, according to him. It is submission, it is submission to an evil which is not non-violence,

o

according to him. You should not submit to an evil . . . that is sub-
mitting to violence. But he used to say, really, that the way to get rid
of that evil is the non-violent method, both on grounds of principle
and in practice. . . . It's very, very difficult to draw a line. It's really
one's motive and one's desire to avoid violence.

BRECHER. Some people have expressed the view to me that the
police in this country are too prone to use violence to meet violence.
Would you care to comment on this with particular reference to the
larger question of violence as a technique of social action and as an
instrument for the maintenance of order in a state?

NEHRU. It's rather difficult to say anything general about police
firings in India. It's quite possible that some of them could have
been avoided, that some of them were wrong. But I think that, putting oneself in the place of the policemen, they are usually a small
number and they are surrounded by a stone-throwing crowd, well,
it's difficult to keep one's nerve. . . . After all, merely saying that
the police have fired is a bad thing. . . . If they had not fired, on
many occasions the situation would have been infinitely worse.

ON PREVENTIVE DETENTION

BRECHER. Some have expressed misgivings in this country and elsewhere about the continuing need for a Preventive Detention Act in
a flourishing democracy. Granted that such an Act has a place during an emergency, what is the justification for its perpetuation in
normal conditions?

NEHRU. Have you seen the figures? . . . 150 in the whole of India.

BRECHER. But doesn't it suggest that if the number is so small this
particular group in a population of 370 millions can be dealt with
under the ordinary laws which are available to the Government?

NEHRU. That's a valid argument. On the other hand, there is
another argument; the Act being there and not being used much is
itself a deterrent; both ways. And you see, of the 150 or so I doubt
if more than perhaps 10 were political people. The rest were just
gangsters and goondas in big cities. It is very difficult to convict
them.

BRECHER. Would you say that, in theory, such an Act has a place
in a democratic state except in time of national emergency?

NEHRU. Surely that is a theoretical question. I don't like that Act and I hope it won't continue. But I do say that when there are all kinds of violent elements and people who create a good deal of mischief it is helpful, at least sometimes. Suppose we know that there is going to be a big communal riot, well, if we arrest a dozen persons, the riot doesn't take place. You may let them off a month later but it just suppresses the riot. . . . It can't be done under the ordinary law. . . . There are plenty of political opponents cursing us all over. The only ones that have been put in prison have been persons indulging in violence. . . .

BRECHER. But you would hope that by 1957, unless there is a fundamental change in conditions in this country, there would not be a need to continue this Act?

NEHRU. I hope not.

ON THE PRESS

NEHRU. Criticism was made about our dealing with the press . . . I don't know if you have seen the worst part of the press, in Hindi and Urdu and these languages. . . . Terrible, something terrible, and we found it did little good. We put an end to it.

BRECHER. That gave rise to the Press Objectionable Matter Act?

NEHRU. Yes. That we are suppressing the press, it is absurd.

ON INDIA'S ACHIEVEMENTS SINCE INDEPENDENCE

BRECHER. Moving to a somewhat different plane, Sir—since Partition, India has attained an honoured place, both in terms of world prestige and internal stability. Viewing this period as a whole, what do you consider to be the significant achievements of independent India since 1947?

NEHRU. First, the Indian States, the absorption of the Indian States into the Union of India. Secondly, our meeting the tremendous problems following Partition, including the, well, not only the killing, etc., but in a sense a kind of rebellion. . . After the partition we had to contend against two forces. One was the powerful reaction, communal reaction, which affected both sides, Pakistan and here. . . . The other was advantage taken of the situation by all the reactionary elements in India who did not like . . . a progressive, independent government, and they wanted to break it, taking advantage of the communal situation. Well, we controlled it. And then the third biggest thing was, I think, our dealing with the refugees, a pretty big task, seven or eight million coming over in two or three months' time, a tremendous task, not only then but in subsequent years. I rather doubt if anywhere else such a major problem of refugees in the conditions we had in India . . . was tackled so successfully, practically without any foreign assistance, United Nations or other. Then I would refer to our economic front because, at that time, we had suffered a great deal of inflation. . . . The food question. We had to import vast quantities of food and it was a constant difficulty in reaching a place (with the food); because it was really a ship-to-mouth kind of thing. . . . Then, broadly, our general economic rehabilitation, with big schemes (the Five Year Plans). And finally, something that I think is bigger than all, the community schemes, the Community Development projects, which are really, I think, revolutionary in their context. The fact is that they are changing the villagers, and they are the great majority of the Indian population.

BRECHER. What would you consider the principal obstacles, institutional and other, to more rapid and far-reaching change in the social and economic spheres?

NEHRU. Well, the principal obstacle is a tendency to disruption . . . whether it is on the communal plane, whether it is on the caste plane or on the provincial plane—they are all coming in the way of the basic unity of India. Of course, the forces in favour of unity are also very strong . . . but when there is no apparent danger to it people forget this (the need for unity) and go off into these factions, and that affects even our parties, whether it is the Congress or whether it is the Socialist Party and even, to some extent, the Communist Party—which is very, very disciplined! And, unfortunately, if there is an election, there is no doubt that when the area of the constituency is a small one, probably the dominant caste will get its man in. Mind you, caste is rapidly ceasing to be. . . .

BRECHER. But there is still caste consciousness?

NEHRU. Very much so. Marriage (on caste lines) still continues very largely even though it is getting less. But a certain political aspect of caste comes in, that is, a man would vote for his caste—in that sense—and if the Communists put up a candidate in a particular constituency, they take jolly good care that he belongs to the dominant caste of that constituency. . . . Social customs also come in the way.

BRECHER. Would you say that, in a sense, poverty itself is a great barrier?

NEHRU. Poverty is a barrier and a certain inertia which comes from poverty—these are tremendous barriers.

ON ECONOMIC PLANNING, DEMOCRACY, AND
INDIA'S 'HOPE LEVEL'

BRECHER. While talking about economic affairs, Mr. Prime Minister, you used the interesting expression 'hope level' as the minimum objective of planning; and added if this could not be maintained in India the process of peaceful transformation would be jeopardized. Does not the maintenance of the 'hope level' depend, at least in part, on external considerations? . . . If the 'hope level' cannot be maintained, then much of the structure of the new India is threatened. What is your priority of values here—is it social and economic change to achieve your conception of the good society, or is it the preservation of the existing (democratic) methods of achieving such change?

NEHRU. I think it is quite essential for any country to have a certain confidence in itself. This is basic. The moment that that confidence goes down, it becomes weak progressively. The big lesson that Gandhi taught us was to rely on ourselves and no others. . . .

BRECHER. But if . . . this 'hope level' cannot be maintained by the use of democratic methods, what then becomes the primary objective, the preservation of existing methods or the use of other methods in order to carry through the programme of a new society in India?

NEHRU. There is no absolute choice between two extremes. There are many middle ways. You can keep the democratic method. What does it consist of? Many things, of course, but essentially, your giving a chance to every opposing idea and party to function and ultimately, the majority of the people supporting you. Well, if the majority of the people do not support you I don't think any other method is going to tell—in India certainly, I can't speak for others. And Gandhi has increased the individuality of the Indian so much. All this satyagraha business—everybody wants to fast for something. You see, all this is increasing the individual consciousness of a person and it will be exceedingly difficult, and I doubt if it will be possible, for the normal type of authoritarian government to come in. I can conceive —in theory—a military dictatorship. I don't think it is likely. That does not matter but I can theoretically conceive of it, that the army is strong and powerful and imposes itself, but it would have a lot of trouble, all over the place.

ON LAND REFORM

BRECHER. You once expressed to me, Sir, your view that the pace of land reform is not as rapid as you would like it to be and that Bhoodan [voluntary land-giving] is not really a solution to the land problem in India. Yet the Congress has often gone on record in support of Bhoodan. What function do you think Bhoodan can perform, if any? And if Bhoodan cannot solve the land problem, why is there no other positive approach?

NEHRU. During the last six or seven years there has been any amount of legislation in regard to land problems. . . . The abolition of the Zamindari [absentee landed estates], and the limitation of estates in the future, the limitation in the present, too. I think the record is a fairly good one. It hasn't gone far enough. Much remains still to be done.

BRECHER. What represents the next stage in the land reform programme?

NEHRU. Well, although the Zamindari is gone, there are individual proprietors, not Zamindars as such, who have fairly large estates, hundreds of acres. Maybe they are not too many but they are there. Then, in the peasant proprietorship provinces there are fairly large peasant holdings. . . . Theoretically we would like to make them smaller and then have co-operatives among them. The difficulty comes in, first of all, we don't want to do anything which might result in reducing production. This is most important. Secondly, when we do all these things we give compensation to the land-owners and it is hardly possible for us to give compensation again on this vast scale. . . . So far as Bhoodan is concerned, I don't think —and I doubt if even the chief supporters of Bhoodan think—that by itself it will solve the land problem in India. But it creates a tremendous atmosphere which helps in its solution and partly solves it, in a small way. But really, it is the atmosphere that helps in bringing in laws and other things.

BRECHER. But ultimately it is the legislative approach which you consider to be the most effective approach to its solution?

NEHRU. Yes, it is.

ON SOCIALISM

BRECHER. I know of your own socialist convictions dating back to the thirties, but why was [the Congress Party's official] move to socialism taken only last year; why not earlier or why not later?

NEHRU. ... We [had] talked about socialism throughout, and as long ago as twenty-five years the Congress said that the chief industries, heavy industries and basic industries, should be owned and controlled by the State. ... The Congress, being a vast organization, had all kinds of people in it, anti-socialists, socialists, but we could always get through a resolution on socialism when we wanted it. The majority would welcome it. But in consideration, really, of many of our senior colleagues, who didn't like to go that far, we didn't press it. Now, after the coming of Independence, gradually, there was a tendency to go a little further. It developed gradually and ultimately it came out. Nothing special happened last year.

BRECHER. A suggestion has been made that perhaps the impact of your own experience and the impressions during your China tour [in November 1954] which occurred just two months before the Resolution was passed. ...

NEHRU. Absolutely nothing to do with it ... I hadn't even thought of it but, since you mention it, I think of it. It has nothing to do with it. But I might tell you, I had very little to do with that Resolution. It was the new Congress President [Mr. Dhebar]. .... I approved, of course, heartily, but it was the new Congress President who took the initiative in the matter.

ON CHINA

BRECHER. I wonder if you could tell me briefly your basic impressions during this tour [of China in 1954].

NEHRU. My major impression was one of the enormous basic strength of the Chinese people. Of course, even in the old days [tour of China in 1939] I had that sensation but it was spread out. They are amazing workers and they work together and that itself gives strength. And now, with a centralized government and all that, it gives them really a terrifying strength, I may say, these masses of people all working together and each person capable of working hard. I do not think there is any person in the wide world who works as hard as a Chinese, individuals apart, I mean. The average Chinese is a harder worker, certainly, than the average Indian.

BRECHER. Would you say that the rate of progress has been very considerable?

NEHRU. Now, I can't judge of that. One's impressions are mixed, derived from statistics, from what one sees, what one reads and all that. And I think that the progress has been very considerable. I may say, production, food production and even industrialization are going ahead pretty fast.

BRECHER. One question that has often been raised is whether it would be correct to say that there is in reality a peaceful economic and cultural competition between India and China?

NEHRU. There is no competition as such, but it is, perhaps, inevitable for people to compare, from time to time, the progress made because the two countries are alike in that they are big, with large populations, industrially undeveloped, and also very ancient countries. We have many similar problems.

BRECHER. Would you be inclined to say that in a sense the future course of events in South-East Asia depends very largely on the degree to which either India or China or both succeed with their development programmes?

NEHRU. Yes, they are bound to influence other countries. . . . As a matter of fact we are constantly sending groups of experts and delegations to study conditions there. . . . The Chinese have sent two or three teams to study some aspects of what we are doing. It is a mutual thing, of course. Quite apart from communism, more than anything, there is a way of doing a thing, and we can learn from it. Take flood control. There are problems that face us and face them. . . . We learn from each other.

ON POPULATION CONTROL

BRECHER. You have frequently indicated your conviction that [India's population problem] is not a pressing issue; that its solution is possible only within the framework of general economic improvement and higher literacy. . . . However, even after the

Second Plan there will be twenty million new mouths to feed in this country. . . . Is this not a pressing economic problem which develops into a vicious circle, the larger population hindering economic development which, in turn, makes it more difficult, as you suggest, to solve the population problem? . . . Would you say that if experiments in simple methods of birth control prove to be effective, the Government of India would have any objections to giving its full support and publicity to these methods of family planning?

NEHRU. Well, I should like to limit the population of India or, if I may say so, to prevent it from growing too much. It is obvious that the larger it grows the more difficult the economic problems become—and I am personally in favour of methods of family planning and birth control. As a matter of fact, broadly speaking, our Government has been helping, not in a major way, but in experimentation. And if the experiments succeed, we are likely to do much more. Having said that, I should like to say also that in the near future I think the question of limiting the family is not the primary question. . . . We have to make economic progress much more rapidly, and we cannot wait for family planning to bring about results. I am all in favour of family-planning work being done, but I think it is all wrong for people to say that our economic problems depend on family planning. . . . Also the rate of population growth in India is not a high rate. . . . The point is that India can support a larger population given economic growth.

ON FOREIGN POLICY, WAR, AND NON-ALIGNMENT

BRECHER. As one of the most prominent practitioners of the art of diplomacy in this century, what would you consider to be of primary importance in the decision-making process with regard to foreign affairs? Is it the consideration of power or material factors, or is it, rather, ideological urges?

NEHRU. Ideological urges obviously play some part, though not so much the ideological urges of the individual. But, if they become part of the common thinking of the people, then they play an important part—especially in a democracy, because, unless the common people have those urges, they are not reflected in their representatives in Parliament; and no policy can go very far if it is quite divorced from the people's thinking. However, in the final analysis, all foreign policy concerns itself chiefly with the national interest of the country concerned. National interest can be seen in two ways, that is, rather narrow national interest, temporary national interest— and most people see it that way—or a long-term view of national interest, which may well lead one to the conclusion that a country's national interests are served, let us say, by peace in the world, or by friendship with other nations, or by the well-being of neighbouring countries. So it becomes an intelligent long-term interest . . . en- lightened self-interest. But obviously in a democracy no government can take any step which is patently, from the point of view of public opinion, against national interest.

BRECHER. Does it suggest that if the Soviet Union possessed insti- tutions and an ideology comparable to those of the United States and the West generally, the mere fact that these were two Great Powers would itself constitute a significant source of conflict or friction?

NEHRU. I think that the conflict in the past few years has been essentially due to political reasons, not communist or anti-com- munist, the main reason being two Great Powers whose national interests appear to come into conflict. And, therefore, they do not like each other, or are apprehensive of each other . . . it is essentially a conflict on the political plane that separates countries. . . .

BRECHER. As regards India's foreign policy, Mr. Prime Minister, would you sum up briefly the primary considerations which give rise to the policy of non-alignment?

NEHRU. Yes. During the last thirty years, I should say, that is in the Indian National Movement, we gradually developed a foreign policy of a kind, though we were not a Government. If you study that, you will see that whatever we have done is essentially a continuation of it. . . . So that, first of all, the background and the conditioning factors are there. Secondly, apart from our desire for peace, which is there, is our feeling that peace is absolutely essential for our progress and our growth. And if there is war, big or small, it comes in the way of that growth which is for us the primary factor. Thirdly, with the coming of nuclear weapons, war seems to us—and seems to most people everywhere—as extreme folly, that is, it has ceased to promise what you want. People have had war in the past because they expected to get something out of it; it may have been a gamble but anyhow there was a chance of something. Now, you know the result of the gamble. There is not even the slightest chance of attaining what you want through a war. Therefore, war is sheer folly. . . . One may say, of course, 'what are we to do if some mad person or some mad bull comes in and we have to deal with him?' That is a different matter; that is, if some mad country attacks us, what are we to do? Are we to go down? Well, I have no answer to that except that you must defend yourself, and if you have to defend yourself you have to be prepared to defend yourself. That is true, but, apart from that, war should be ruled out. And I believe there is widespread recognition of this fact both among leaders of nations and among the common people. It's only a measure of fear that comes in the way, that the other party might take advantage of us if we do this or that. Well, the only way to get over that fear is for some common steps to be taken so that this fear of the other party having an advantage does not come in the way. That means disarmament, etc.

BRECHER. Given the state of technology at the present time, would you say that a state which can remain non-aligned with either bloc in time of peace can also remain non-aligned if the Great Powers are at war with each other?

NEHRU. That depends so much on the geographical position of the state. . . . A small country, surrounded by warring nations, will be in a more difficult position, undoubtedly. But India is big and India is happily situated. And I do not conceive of any kind of, let us say, invasion or attack on India—not because of other countries' love of India but because it will bring them no profit and it will only give them trouble, whether it is a world war or any major conflict of that type. India does not come into the picture. It does not help. Any country attacking India merely adds to its troubles.

BRECHER. But supposing such an attack on India should take place?

NEHRU. Well, of course, if it takes place it is obvious that the people of India will fight that attack and defend themselves. But again, who was it who said 'a wise general is a person who wins battles without fighting'; that is, why create enemies who will be induced to attack you? Why not have friendly relations, for when there is no particular inducement to attack, there is less likelihood of attack.

BRECHER. Would you say, then, that India's unique geographical position makes it possible for it to be non-aligned whereas this would be exceedingly difficult for other countries?

NEHRU. I would say that non-alignment is a policy which is nationally profitable for any country. But in some cases there is danger—because of the smallness of the country or because of its geographical position—that, whether it is aligned or non-aligned, it may suffer from the war. It may even be somehow involved in it. Other countries which are geographically better situated do not face that big risk. In a big war every country will suffer. In modern war no country can escape suffering.

BRECHER. I wonder how one should distinguish non-alignment from the concept of a Third Force.

NEHRU. Non-alignment is a negative word and only partly explains the position. What is much better is a positive policy for peace. That positive policy will be successful, not because of pressures nor because of sanctions, military or other. I do not think that a real policy of peace can be furthered by military threats. It can only succeed if it responds to the reality of the situation and therefore finds an echo in people's minds. If it does, then even a small voice is heard, a voice, I mean, that is not backed by power. It is heard. If it does not fit in, then it is a voice in the wilderness and just does not count. You talk about a Third Force. That simply means you are trying to create another force to counter the forces or as a balancing factor but you are thinking still in terms of force. I think that this thinking in terms of force really puts you in that vicious circle of force. I can understand an area which wants to keep out of war. That is a different matter or rather a state of men's minds which may exist anywhere.

ON WORLD FEDERATION

BRECHER. For a long time, Mr. Prime Minister, you were, I believe, a very staunch advocate of a world federation as the ideal to which states should aspire. Do you consider the cleavages that exist today in social, economic, and political systems to be too great and too rigid to conceive of this in practical terms in the foreseeable future?

NEHRU. I think it is quite inevitable in the long run for some kind of world organization to come into being. . . . It will have to be a loose federation but I just do not see it in the foreseeable future. I can see, perhaps, steps towards it but I think just talking about world federation now is totally artificial and unreal. . . .

ON THE UNITED STATES AND THE SOVIET UNION

NEHRU. Take the two most powerful countries in the world today, the United States and the Soviet Union. I don't think that they are as terribly far apart as they themselves or other people imagine. I think there are quite remarkable similarities between them despite their different systems. And I am inclined to think that the gap between them will lessen. And it might even lessen with fair rapidity once the present climate of fear and war is removed.

ON KASHMIR AND INDO-PAKISTAN RELATIONS

BRECHER. In view of the Pakistani rejection of your proposal to negotiate a solution of this problem on the basis of partition along the cease-fire line, where do we go from here?

NEHRU. There are only three ways of dealing with the Kashmir problem. One, if you like, is war. We rule it out. The others are a legal approach, legal and constitutional, or, if I may use the word, a practical approach, not quibbling about legal points and taking things as they are. . . . If you want a practical approach to this problem, my practical approach would be governed, first of all, by no war of course. Secondly, by accepting things as they are, in the main, because any other approach leads to some kind of conflict.

BRECHER. What makes Kashmir so important to India? Does it have any implications for India's efforts to establish a secular state and to maintain communal harmony in this country?

NEHRU. Yes, that is probably the most important aspect of it. . . . Probably in Kashmir more than anywhere else in India there has been less of what is called communal feeling, and Hindus and Muslims and others have very rarely quarrelled. And even if they have quarrelled, it has been of short duration. . . . Now, we have never accepted, even when Partition came to India, the two-nation theory, that is that the Hindus are one nation and the Muslims are another. . . . I say we cannot accept that because once we accept that nationality goes by religion, we break up our whole conception of India . . . 35 million Muslims remained in India [after Partition]. Today, there are more Muslims in India than there are in West Pakistan. . . . The National Movement of Kashmir deliberately rejected the Muslim League idea of the two-nation theory . . . and,

when Kashmir joined India . . . it was very important for us because it helped our thesis of nationalism not related to religion. If
the contrary thesis were proved in Kashmir, it would affect somewhat—I don't say it would break up India—but it would have a
powerful effect on the communal elements in India, both Hindu
and Muslim. That is of extreme importance to us—that we don't,
by taking some wrong step in Kashmir, create these terribly disruptive tendencies within India.

BRECHER. If one assumed for the moment—it is largely hypothetical, very remote indeed—but if one assumes that Pakistan with-
draws all of its forces from Kashmir and fulfils all of its obligations
under the United Nations resolutions, as India interprets these
resolutions, would India then be prepared to reconsider the question
of a plebiscite under international supervision? Or is a plebiscite, in
your opinion, no longer a valid approach to the settlement of the
Kashmir problem under any conditions?

NEHRU. You are asking me a hypothetical question. I cannot rule
out a plebiscite under any conditions. . . . But if you put this question to me, that if every condition is fulfilled, then am I to refuse a
plebiscite? I say no. But, in practice, we have been considering this
matter for the last seven or eight years and even the first condition
has not been fulfilled, leave out many others.

BRECHER. You mean the withdrawal of all Pakistani forces?

NEHRU. Yes, the withdrawal. But I will tell you this, that we have
always attached great importance to one factor in a plebiscite, that is,
we have said that if there is a plebiscite, it should be a fair political
plebiscite and not one in which wildly religious passions are roused;
and, by bringing in religion, making it impossible for people to
decide really on political and economic issues.

BRECHER. That would be one of the conditions of such a plebiscite
if it were ever to be held?

NEHRU. We have said that right from the beginning, repeatedly.
How to bring that about I don't know.

BRECHER. In view of the tragic aftermath of Partition, Mr. Prime
Minister, in the form of communal riots, the Kashmir problem and
other unresolved issues between India and Pakistan, is it visionary,

do you think, to expect a genuine *rapprochement* between the two countries in the foreseeable future?

NEHRU. Many people think and say that the Kashmir problem is a major problem which comes in the way of good relations between India and Pakistan. That is true, in a sense, but not basically true. What I mean is this: the Kashmir problem is a result of other conflicts between India and Pakistan, and even if the Kashmir problem were solved, well, not in a very friendly way, those basic conflicts would continue.

BRECHER. But what are these basic conflicts?

NEHRU. I should say, basically, they are ideological. And we go back again to what I was just talking about, this business of the two-nation theory, what is nationalism. . . . I would also say that so far as the people of Pakistan and the people of India are concerned, they are in a much better and more friendly frame of mind today than they were some years ago at Partition time. Conditions have improved very greatly. There really is hardly any prejudice against each other *qua* individuals or *qua* groups. . . . You see, we have the same language, so many things in common. . . . But Pakistan is afraid and has fed itself on fear of India. This is totally unjustified because under no circumstances whatever, even from the view of the narrowest national interests, do we wish to interfere in Pakistan. We want them to be an independent country and a flourishing country.

BRECHER. Is it possible that instead of tackling these vexed issues separately, more positive results might flow from a larger approach . . . to secure an agreement in principle on the entire gamut of disputes between the two countries? Many people refer to this as a package deal.

NEHRU. We have no objection at all to considering all the issues. . . . The major ones at the present moment, apart from Kashmir, are supposed to be canal waters, evacuee property and, well, this exodus from East Pakistan. We have been dealing with each one.

BRECHER. On principle . . . you would have no objection to considering all of these disputes in conjunction with one another rather than separately?

NEHRU. Not at all, not at all.

ON THE BANDUNG CONFERENCE, ISRAEL, AND THE ARABS

BRECHER. Would you sum up briefly your view of its significance [the Bandung Conference] in terms of the renaissance of Asia and . . . of world politics at the time it occurred [Spring of 1955]?

NEHRU. The mere fact of all these countries meeting and officially, as Governments, was itself a recognition of a fact we know of course, but there it was—a significant illustration of it. Secondly, that with our very different problems there was so much common ground between us that we could ultimately produce a document which was unanimously agreed to. And there was a psychological feeling of commonness, in spite of our differences, common objectives, common—if you like—adversaries. And that in itself gave one a feeling of strength and created a feeling of comradeship and friendship among those countries. Practically, as you know, nothing much was decided, apart from these things. We said something about economic matters and the rest. Something has been done but not very much because there is no common economy from the Gold Coast to Indonesia.

BRECHER. May one look upon it as the first step in the direction of a more cohesive group of states in Asia and Africa?

NEHRU. Well, it is too widespread for it to develop into a cohesive group. . . . But you can say that it may develop into something which holds together.

BRECHER. There is one aspect of the Bandung Conference which perturbed many people and that was the exclusion of one sovereign Asian state, namely Israel. . . . How can this be justified in terms of the criteria set up by the five sponsors? Is it likely that this act of exclusion will be repeated at the next Afro-Asian Conference, if one is ever held?

NEHRU. I don't know what will happen at the next Conference but conditions were and still are that the Arab nations and Israel don't sit together. They do sit at the United Nations, but apart from that, they just don't sit. And one is offered this choice of having one or the other. It is not logical, my answer, but there it is. When the proposal was made for Israel to be invited . . . it transpired that if that were done the Arab countries would not attend . . . Our outlook on this matter was based on some logical approach. Our sympathies are with the Arab nations in regard to this problem. We felt that logically Israel should be invited but when we saw that the consequences of that invitation would be that many others would not be able to come, then we agreed. Our approach, obviously, if I may add, is that it is good for people who are opponents to meet.

BRECHER. Yes, but the Arabs have refused every invitation to sit and talk about the question of peace in West Asia.

NEHRU. It is obvious that there is the way of war to settle the question and, if you rule out war, then the only way is to meet—or allow things to drift.

BRECHER. But drift has the great risk surely that it may itself lead to war.

NEHRU. Yes, I know, but actually there is no other way.

ON INDIA AND THE COMMONWEALTH

BRECHER. What were the considerations which induced India to remain in the Commonwealth, particularly when set against the background of your many statements before 1947 that India would sever its connexion on attaining its freedom? Secondly, what positive contributions would you say the Commonwealth has made to the reduction of international tensions? And, thirdly, what benefits has India derived from its continued association with the Commonwealth?

NEHRU. I think you will find that in all the statements I made previously I said that India must be independent and an independent republic. We did not consider or rule out any kind of association with England or the Commonwealth. . . . When we became independent . . . the question arose: as a republic should we associate ourselves with the Commonwealth? It was a novel question, not only for us, but for the other countries as well. We decided that there was absolutely no reason why we should break an association which didn't come in our way at all, legally, constitutionally, practically, in any sense, and which merely helped us to co-operate in a measure, consult each other and maybe influence others and maybe to be influenced ourselves. In fact, I would like that type of association with every country in the wide world. It is far better than a treaty or an alliance where you undertake to do something. We have undertaken to do nothing in the Commonwealth and the Commonwealth

P

countries have undertaken to do nothing to us. We are freer than
two countries tied by an alliance. . . . The positive benefits are, I
say, that it is always a good thing for a number of countries to be
on friendly terms of consultation. . . . They accepted us as a republic.
Apart from being wrong, I think it would have been quite churlish.
There was absolutely no reason . . . why we should do it [leave the
Commonwealth]. And there were good reasons why we should be
there because it does help us in conferring with a number of
important countries . . . and, through them, to influence world
affairs to some extent.

ON CENTRALIZATION OF POWER

NEHRU. You talked about centralization and de-centralization.
There is a measure of de-centralization [in India]. Yet the Centre is
fairly strong. There is absolutely no suggestion that the Centre
should become weaker than it is. . . . I don't believe in a unitary
state. I don't believe that a large country like India can develop
in the way I should like it to develop and can be really democrati-
cally governed by a strong, by a central apparatus. I want the Centre
to be strong because there are disruptive tendencies in India and the
Centre must be strong enough to control them and to put them
down. . . . Nevertheless, we should develop as much local initiative
as possible.

ON COMMUNALISM AND THE PROTECTION
OF MINORITIES

BRECHER. Although many pay lip-service to the ideal of a secular
state, largely out of deference to you, there are many people within
the Congress, as well as in other parties, who retain a strong com-
munalist bias. Everyone with whom I have talked has stressed your
indispensable role as a barrier to the resurgence of communalism.
One wonders, therefore, what institutional safeguards there are for
the continued protection of minorities in this country?

NEHRU. Institutional safeguards we can have. We are going to have
some more—new changes in the Constitution. But really, no institutional safeguards can take the place of good will. No institutional
safeguards will protect isolated communities in the villages or towns.
They help, of course, the Constitution helps, the judiciary helps,

but in the final analysis people have to develop tolerance and respect for each other. Now they have got that basic tolerance. I would despair of India if I didn't believe that people have got that basic tolerance . . . and are friendly with each other in their normal lives. It is not that any group amongst them has got the spirit of a crusader to drive out the other. Odd individuals might be foolish enough. The difficulty only comes in when they can be excited on occasions. But they recover their balance a little after.

BRECHER. In the larger perspective of Asia, Mr. Prime Minister, do you think there is a rising tide of the power of religion or religious ways of thinking? If so, do you think this may be a serious threat to democratic institutions and a secular state?

NEHRU. I do not think there is any danger of religious revivalism coming in the way of social and economic progress or coming into conflict with each other. Basically that is so. It is true, however, that there are tendencies of religious revivalism. . . . I think they are the natural reactions of a country's freedom. But, after all, the basic problems are economic in every country.

ON 'AFTER NEHRU'

BRECHER. Everyone with whom I have talked, Mr. Prime Minister, has cited your presence as the greatest force for unity in India. They have also stressed your role as the initiator of policies which will transform Indian society. Some, of course, have criticized you for going too quickly, others for not moving fast enough. . . . I do not want to trouble you with a re-echo of 'after Nehru who?' but I am interested in knowing where to look for the institutional assurances for a continuation of your policies. The question of succession is important to many people in this sense. I have been particularly disturbed . . . by the evidence that many prominent persons in the Congress do not seem to share your fundamental ideology and policies, though they accept them for various reasons. Partly because of this and partly because one looks in vain for the semblance of a group who will faithfully continue your policies, there are many who wonder where to look for the safeguards that the policies and programmes associated with your leadership will be continued—in particular, socialism, democratic institutions, the secular state, and non-alignment in foreign affairs.

NEHRU. Well, that is a very long question!

BRECHER. It is indeed!

NEHRU. At the same time, it's difficult for me to answer except to say that the policies I have encouraged, advocated, sponsored, have not been just individual policies. There are many people, and important people, in the Congress and in the country, who believe in them. What is much more so is that they have, vaguely and broadly speaking, the backing of the masses in this country. And, as step by step we give effect to those policies, well, that is a step confirming a certain direction of growth. It is very difficult to go back from these things. . . . My chief business, in so far as the people are concerned, has been, if I may use the word, to speak to them as a schoolmaster, to try to explain things to them in as simple a language as possible and not to deliver, well I can't deliver them, fiery orations, but just trying to get them to think and to understand. . . . For the rest, well, really, one does one's best and one doesn't worry too much about the future.

BRECHER. But is it not very important that the policies which have been followed during the years since Independence should be continued in the future?

NEHRU. Yes, yes, certainly, and more. . . . Take the Planning Commission's report, the new one [for India's Second Five-Year Plan]. Now it is, if I may say so, a very good document—apart from the details of it. The broad approach of it. All of these sink into public consciousness. People discuss it. Almost everyone in India talks about planning. Their conception of planning may be very limited but they talk about it. And all this trains, educates people, makes them think in a particular way and drives all of them forward in a particular direction. Now, some of them may stop the pace, not going in that direction, or they may make it faster. But I don't think it is possible in the future for the mass of the people to be taken away, far away, from their moorings. . . .

ON THE GOOD SOCIETY

BRECHER. I have just one final question, Mr. Prime Minister. I don't propose to ask you to restate at great length your basic philosophy of life. But, in concluding these interviews, it would be appreciated if you were to sum up once again very briefly what, in your view, constitutes the good society?

NEHRU. I have written something about my philosophy in the early chapters of the 'Discovery of India'. Now, what constitutes a good society and the good life? Broadly speaking, apart from the material things that are necessary, obviously, a certain individual growth in the society, not only the corporate social growth but the individual growth. For I do believe that ultimately it is the individual that counts. I can't say that I believe in it because I have no proof, but the idea appeals to me without belief, the old Hindu idea that if there is any divine essence in the world every individual possesses a bit of it . . . and he can develop it. Therefore, no individual is trivial. Every individual has an importance and he should be given full opportunities to develop—material opportunities naturally, food, clothing, education, housing, health, etc. They should be common to everybody. The difficulty comes in about the moral aspect, the moral aspect of religion. I'm not at all concerned about the hereafter. It doesn't worry me; I don't see why it should worry people whether the next world is or is not there. And I am not prepared to deny many things. I just don't know! The most correct attitude, if I may say so, is that of the Buddha who didn't deny it and didn't assert it. He said 'this life is enough for me and when you don't know about something why talk about it!' I do believe in certain standards. Call them moral standards, call them what you like, spiritual standards. They are important in any individual and in any social group. And if they fade away, I think that all the material advancement you may have will lead to nothing worthwhile. How to maintain them I don't know; I mean to say, there is the religious approach. It seems to me rather a narrow approach with its forms and all kinds of ceremonials. And yet, I am not prepared to deny that approach. If a person feels comforted by that, it is not for me to remove that sense of comfort. I don't mind— I think it's silly for a man to worship a stone but if a man is comforted by worshipping a stone why should I come in his way. If it raises him above his normal level it is good for him. Whatever raises a person above his normal level is good, however he approaches that—provided he does not sit on somebody and force him to do it. That is a different matter. So while I attach very considerable value to moral and spiritual standards, apart from religion as such, I don't quite know how one maintains them in modern life. It's a problem.

INDEX

ADAMS, Brooks, quoted, 17–18
Addis Ababa Conferences, 148, 150–2
Aden, 175
Afghanistan, 1, 48, 184, 186
Africa:
  Colonialism, 3, 4, 21, 122
  Conferences, 148–52
  Israel, and, 135, 138–52
  Partition (1880–1914), 2
  Retreat from democracy, 73
  Technical assistance, 135, 139–45, 148
  United Nations caucus, 100, 160, 184–91
  Zones of influence, 107
Afro-Asia:
  China and, 167
  Conference: see Bandung Conference
  Economic development, 124
  Israel and, 123–52
  Literacy rate, 124
  Nehru's views, 210–11
  Solidarity Conference (Conakry), 148–9
  United Nations bloc, 100, 148, 160, 175, 184–91
Afro-Asian Institute, 143
Agadir, 21
Agriculture, unemployed labour's drift to, 16
Ahmad, Mushtaq, cited, 52
Air transport, 107
Akaba, Gulf of, 132, 135
Aksai Chin, 168, 170, 171
Albuquerque, Alfonso d', 4
Algeciras, 21
Algeria, 20, 105, 152, 188
Ali, Mohammed, 50, 51, 175
Alimin, 29
All-Asian integration, 173–5
All-India Muslim League: see India: Muslim League
Almond, Gabriel A., cited, 124
Amboina, 5, 52
America: see United States
American Subordinate System, 93, 95, 99–109
Amritsar Massacre (1919), 31
Andhra, 60, 86
Anglo-Chinese Treaty (1886), 167
Angola, 188
Annam, 7, 11, 26, 27, 38, 39
Apartheid, A., cited, 100, 134
Apartheid, 175, 185
Appadorai, A., cited, 100, 134
Arab League, 102–3, 137, 173
Arab States, core in Middle East, 99, 103, 104, 106–8; and United Nations, 125, 184–6, 188; Nehru's views, 211
Arabic language, 107
Arabs, and Israel, 105, 127–38, 144–5, 148–9, 150–1, 210; Bandung Conference resolution, 133–4; and Palestine, 175
Arakan, 9
Arcot, 7

Armed forces, 97
Army influence on politics: see Military influence
Asian Games, 137
Asian Relations Conferences (1947 and 1949), 44, 100, 174, 184
Asian Relations Organization, 107
Asian Socialist Conference (1953), 134, 174
Asian Socialist Parties, Organization of, 174
Asian Studies, 88, 92, 95, 166
Asian System, Southern: see Southern Asian Subordinate System
Assam, 9, 35, 60, 86
Atjeh, 13
Attlee, C. R. (later Lord Attlee), 36
Aurobindo, 23
Austria, neutrality, 111, 112
Austrian Succession, Wars of the, 7
Authoritarianism, 47–49, 62, 108–9
Autocracy, 64, 65, 68, 109
Ayub Khan, Mohammed, 51–52, 70, 74–75, 77–78, 181, 182
Azad, Maulana, 130

Badgley, John H., cited, 56
Baghdad Pact (later CENTO, q.v.), 137, 165
Baguio Conference (1950), 173
Bailey, Sydney D., cited, 5, 10
Balance of power, 89, 91, 121
Baldwin, Hanson, cited, 158
Balfour, Arthur (later Lord Balfour), 126
Balfour Declaration (1917), 127
Balkans, 110
Bandaranaike, S. W. R. D., 57, 74
Bandaranaike, Mrs. S., 179
Bandung Conference (1955), 53, 100, 103, 105, 132–3, 164, 167, 172–5, 186; Nehru's views, 210–11
Bao Dai, Emperor, 27, 38, 40, 41, 58
Barnes, H. E., cited, 2
Barnett, A. Doak, cited, 161
'Basic Democracy', 74–79, 82, 85
Batavia, 5
Belgium, 3, 4, 111
Ben Bella, 151
Ben-Gurion, David, 131–2, 143, 146–8, 151–2
Ben-Zvi, Izhak, 135
Bengal, 7, 15, 23–24, 35–37; East, 49, 50, 70, 181
Berlin, 105
Berubari, 179
Bhave, Vinoba, 86
Bhoodan, 86, 200
Bhutto, Zulfikar Ali, 182
Bihar, 36, 84; earthquake, 192
Binder, Leonard, cited, 52, 92, 103, 107
Bipolar bloc system, 89–94, 99, 100, 105, 113, 122
Bizerte, 188

Black Star Line, 139
Bloc formation, 90–92, 98, 110–14, 155–61
Bloodworth, Dennis, cited, 159
Bogor Conference, 174
Bolitho, Hector, cited, 65
Bombay, 6, 32, 60, 86
Bondurant, Joan V., cited, 60
Boorman, Howard L., cited, 80, 103
Borneo (British), 1, 166; Filipino claim to, 176
Borneo (Indonesia), 13, 43, 52
Boxer Rebellion, 14
Braibanti, Ralph, cited, 101
Brazil, 107
Brecher, Michael, cited, 37, 60, 65, 85, 156, 169, 179, 182; selections from talks with Nehru, 192–215
British (see also under country and subject headings throughout the index):
  China concessions, 14
  Colonies in Asia, 1, 3, 4, 19, 175
  France, rivalry with, 6–7
  India, in: see under India
  Indies, and, 5, 6
  Indo-China, and, 40, 41
  Indonesia, and, 43
  Second Empire, 7–11
  Zionism, and, 127
British Commonwealth, 104, 157, 160; Nehru's views, 211–12
British North Borneo: see Borneo (British)
Brunei, 1, 176
Brzezinski, Zbigniew, cited, 102
Buddhism, 41, 107, 116
Budi Utomo (High Endeavour), 28
Budiardjo, Miriam S., cited, 54
Bulganin, N. A., 156
Burma:
  Anti-Fascists (AFPFL), 55–56, 66, 73
  Border dispute, 105, 165–7
  Boundaries fixed, 10
  British rule, 7, 9–10, 14, 17
  China, relations with, 10, 105, 161–7
  Chinese Nationalist troops in, 166–7
  Communists, 55
  Independence (1948), 1, 10, 20, 46, 155
  Indians, 67, 105
  International relations, 95, 96, 103–5, 109, 173
  Israel, relations with, 125, 134–5, 138–40, 142–3
  Leadership, 65, 73
  Minorities, 67, 73
  Nationalists, 55
  Political system, 48, 49, 108; record since independence, 55–56, 62, 64, 73
  Soviet Union, relations with, 156
  United Nations, and, 184, 190
Burmese Wars, 9
Burns, Sir Alan, cited, 18
Butwell, Richard, cited, 56, 154

Cady, John F., cited, 10, 12, 162
Calcutta, 6, 24, 36
Callard, Keith, cited, 52, 109
Calvocoressi, Peter, cited, 125

Cambodia:
  China, relations with, 165, 166
  French rule, 11, 39, 41
  Frontier disputes, 176, 177
  Independence, 38, 39, 41, 155
  International Commission, 160
  International relations, 95, 103, 104, 173, 176–7
  Political system, 48
  United Nations, and, 184
Cameroons, 185, 189
Canada, 121
Canyes, Manuel S., cited, 102
Cao Dai, 38, 41, 58
Cape of Good Hope, 4, 7
Carnatic, 7
Carr, Edward Hallett, cited, 89
Casablanca 'Summit Conference' (1961), 149
Castro, Dr. Fidel, 105, 106
Celebes, 52
CENTO (earlier Baghdad Pact), 105, 157, 161, 164
Central American Court of Justice, 173
Centralization of power, Nehru's views, 212
Ceylon:
  British rule, 5, 7, 10, 17
  Early history, 4–6
  Independence (1948), 1, 5, 20, 46, 155
  Indians, 105, 176, 177–9
  International relations, 95, 96, 98, 103, 104
  Israel, relations with, 135–6
  Language dispute, 56–57, 67, 106, 179
  Nationalism, 46, 56
  Political system, 47, 108; record since independence, 56–57, 62, 66, 67, 73, 82
  United National Party, 56, 66
  United Nations, and, 184, 186, 188
Chad Bet area, 179
Chakravarty, P. C., cited, 168
Chao Kuo-Chun, cited, 80
Cheng Chu-yuan, cited, 82
Chen Yi, 172
Ch'en Yün, 80
Chiang Kai-shek, 173
Ch'in, 96, 99
Chin Hills, 10
China:
  Ancient, distribution of power, 95–96, 99
  Border disputes, 105, 161
  Burma, relations with, 10, 105, 161–7
  Cambodia, relations with, 165, 166
  Communes, 80–82, 165
  Communism, 155–6, 163, 168
  Concessions, 14–15, 21, 39
  Economic difficulties, 163
  Geographical size, 162
  India, relations with, 100, 117, 161, 163, 167–72; border dispute, 105, 154, 158, 160, 164–72, 182, 190
  Indo-China, and, 11, 12, 37–40
  International relations, 103–5, 161–72
  Israel, relations with, 132–3, 137
  Laos, and, 161
  Malaya, relations with, 164, 166
  Nationalists (see also Formosa), 166–7, 173

China (*contd*):
Nehru's impressions, 201–2
Nepal, relations with, 98, 105, 161, 165, 171
'New Democracy', 41, 79–82, 85
Pakistan, relations with, 161, 165, 172, 182
Philippines, and, 161, 164
Political system, 47, 49, 79–82, 108
Population, 161–2
'Shaking the world', 161
Southern Asian System, inclusion in, 95–99; relations with new states in, 161–72
Soviet Union, and: *see* Sino-Soviet axis
Threat from, 100, 101, 105, 110, 114, 161, 173
Tibet occupation: *see* Tibet
Treaty Ports system, 14
Unification, 1
United Nations seat, 167, 174, 186–7, 191
United States, relations with, 131, 132
Vietnam, and, 161, 162, 164, 165
Western penetration, 3, 4, 7, 13–15
Chinese Eastern Railway, 14
Chinese in Asian countries, 6, 67, 96, 164
Chins, 67
Chou En-lai, 80, 164, 167, 168
Chou system, 96
Choudhury, G. W., cited, 52
Christian civilization, 108, 153
Ch'u, 99
Chundrigar, I. I., 51
Chu Teh, 80
Civil disobedience, 25, 31–35
Civil liberties, 47, 48, 83–84, 107
Civil servants, shortage of, 64–65, 70, 73
Civilian dictatorship political system, 48, 49, 108
Clive, Robert, 7
Cochin, 4
Cochin-China, 4, 11–12, 25–28, 38–40
'Coffee sergeants', 6, 9
Colbert, J. B., 6
Cold war, 100, 119–21, 156, 157, 185, 188
Coleman, James S., cited, 124
Colombo, 5
Colombo Conference (1962), 171–2
Colombo Plan, 101, 103, 104, 107, 173
Colombo Powers, 100, 173–4
Colonial empires, growth of, 1–15, 122
'Colonial' wars, 20–21
Colonialism, impact on colonies and colonial powers, 15–21; contains seeds of its own destruction, 19–22; neutralists' attitude, 115–16, 120, 121; Bandung resolution, 175
Coloured peoples, Western control over, 4
Cominform, 155
Comintern, 27, 29
Communalism, Nehru's views, 212–3
Communications, 17, 21–22, 106–7
Communes, 80–81, 165
Communist Party, 102, 104
Communist political system, 47–49, 79–81, 108–9
Compagnie des Indes Orientales, 6–7
Conakry Conference, 148–9
Concert of Europe, 101

Congo, 105, 115, 188–90
Cooch Behar, 179
Co-operation, International Seminar on (1958), 140–1
Corley, Francis J., cited, 59
Cressey, George B., cited, 162
Crick, Bernard, cited, 89
Cripps, Sir Stafford, 34
Cuba, 105, 106, 109, 110, 115, 116, 188
Cultural impact on colonies, 18–19
'Culture system', 12–13
Curzon, Lord, 23
Czechoslovakia, 116–18

Dairen, 14
Dalai Lama, 169, 170
Dalat Conference (1946), 40
Dalhousie, Earl of, 8
Danube Commission, 102
Dar-ul-Islam, 52
Datta, K., cited, 7
Dawn, cited, 51
Dayan, Moshe, 143
Dean, Vera Micheles, cited, 66
Deccan, 7
Delhi, 24
Delhi Conferences, 44, 100, 174, 184
Delhi Pact (1931), 32
Democracy, as political system, 47–49, 54, 108–9; causes of failure, 61–73; classic conditions, 68, 70; criticism of, 74; deviations from Anglo-American model, 74, 108–9; 'New Democracy', 41, 79–82, 87; 'Guided Democracy', 54, 109; 'Basic Democracy', 74–9, 82, 87; Indian form, 82–87; Nehru's views, 199
Denmark, 3
Diaz, Bartholomeu, 4
Diem, Ngo Dinh, 27, 42, 48, 58–59, 65, 177
Dien Bien Phu, 41, 156
Digby, William, cited, 16
Diplomatic incidents and crises, 21
Disarmament, 105, 160, 186, 190
Disputes, mediation in, 120–22, 172, 189; regional and bilateral, 175–83
'Divide and rule' policy, 5
Dixon, Sir Owen, 180
Dizengoff West Africa, 141
Dominant System, 92–101, 104–5, 107–8, 110, 161
Donnithorne, Audrey, cited, 80
Donoughmore Constitution, 10
Dorsey, John T., cited, 59
'Drain of wealth', 15, 17
Dravidistan, pressure for separate state of, 60
Du Bois, Cora, cited, 153
Dupleix, Marquis de, 7
Dutch colonialism, 1, 3, 5–6, 12–13, 19, 20, 42, 175
Dutch East India Company, 5, 6, 12
Dutch East Indies (*later* Indonesia, *q.v.*):
History, 1, 5–7, 12–13
Impact of colonialism, 12–13, 16–18
Independence, 42–46
Japanese control, 42–43
Nationalism, 28–30, 42–46

Dutch East Indies (*contd.*):
  Second World War, 42–43
  Volksraad, 30
Dutch New Guinea: *see* New Guinea, West
Dutch West Indies, 43
Dutt, R. Palme, cited, 16
Duy Tan, Emperor, 26
Dyarchy, principle of, 25

East India Company, 4, 6–10, 15
ECAFE, 101, 103, 107, 173
Economic impact of colonialism, on
  colonies, 15–17, 21; on colonial
  powers, 17–18, 21
Economic motives for Western expansion,
  2–3, 5, 6
Economic Mutual Assistance, Council for,
  102
Eden, Sir Anthony, cited, 156
Education, Western, 3, 22, 28, 69
Egypt:
  International relations, 99, 105, 109,
  186, 190
  Israel, attitude to, 131, 134
  Political system, 109
  Soviet arms, 105
  Suez crisis: *see* that title
Eilat, 135
Eisenhower, President D., 188
Elsbree, Willard H., cited, 61
Elysée Agreements (1949), 40–41
Emerson, Rupert, cited, 11, 13, 19, 46, 61,
  68, 91, 187
Ethiopia, 124, 139–40, 142–3, 150, 185
Europe:
  Change in, 73, 90
  Common market, 102, 148, 151
  Eastern, 155
  Economic organizations, 102
  Expansion overseas, 2–3, 7
  Israel's status in, 147–8, 151
  Nineteenth-century, 98–99, 101, 108,
  109, 121, 122
Europe, Council of, 102
European Court, 102, 173
Exchange economy, 16–17
Eytan, Walter, 129–30

Fairbank, John K., cited, 15
Fall, Bernard B., cited, 58, 59, 157, 158,
  166, 176, 177
Fashoda, 21
Federated Malay States, 4, 10–11
Feith, Herbert, cited, 54
Feldman, Herbert, cited, 52
Fenwick, C. G. cited, 102
Fifield, Russell H., cited, 100, 187
Fischer, Louis, cited, 54
Fishel, Wesley R., cited, 59
Fisher, Margaret W., cited, 60
Five Principles of Peaceful Coexistence,
  164–5, 167, 171, 175
Flugel, F., cited, 2
Fontainebleau Conference (1946), 40
Food from colonies, 17, 18
Forced labour, 6, 13, 15
Foreign Affairs, cited, 74
Foreign aid (*see also* Technical assistance),
  115, 122, 124, 145, 157, 182

Foreign policy, 88, 94, 105, 109, 110
Formosa, 14, 105, 170, 174, 175
Fox, William T. R., cited, 89, 92
France:'
  British rivalry with, 6–8
  Colonial power, as, 1, 3, 4, 6–8, 18, 20
  Communists, 28
  Indo-China: *see* that title
  Israel, relations with, 152
  Political system, 74
  Second World War, 37–39
  Union, 39–41
Friedman, Harry J., cited, 74
Furber, Holden, cited, 8
Furnivall, J. S., cited, 10, 13, 46

Gama, Vasco da, 3, 4
Gamba, Charles, cited, 61
Gandhi, Mahatma, 24, 25, 30–32, 34, 37,
  126, 129, 131; Nehru's views on,
  192–4
Ganges waters, 180
Gapi, 30
Garratt, G. T., cited, 16
Geneva Conferences (1954), 41, 57, 164;
  (1962), 58, 158, 176
Gerindo, 30
German reparations, 124
Germany, 14, 94
Ghana, 133, 139–40, 145
Gilkey, Robert, cited, 58
Gledhill, Alan, cited, 56
Global Political System, 91, 93–95, 104,
  105, 175
Goa, 4, 105, 188, 190
Gokhale, G. K., 23
Good society and good life, Nehru's views,
  214–15
Government, antipathy to, 20, 63–64, 69,
  71
Government of India Acts (1919), 25;
  (1935), 10, 32–33, 76
Gracey, Gen. D. D., 38
Graham, Dr. Frank, 180
Greek city-state system, 95–96, 99, 112
Greene, Fred, cited, 17, 154
Grimes, Paul, cited, 171
Gross national product in Afro-Asia, 124
'Guided Democracy', 54, 74, 79, 82, 87
Gupta, Sisir, cited, 179

Ha'aretz, 151
Haas, Ernest B., cited, 91, 102
Hague Agreement (1949), 45
Hague Conventions (1907), 113
Haiphong, 39, 40
'Hair-cutters', 26
Hall, D. G. E., cited, 6
Hamashbir, 134
Hammer, Ellen J., cited, 28, 42
Handicraft industries, 16
Hanna, Willard A., cited, 166
Hanoi, 11, 25, 26, 38, 40
Harrison, Selig G., cited, 67, 156
Harvey, Godfrey E., cited, 10
Hastings, Warren, 8
Hatta, Mohammed, 29, 42–44, 53, 54, 72
'Haves and Have-nots', 21
Hazard, H. W., cited, 18, 46

Henderson, William, cited, 100
Henry the Navigator, 4
Herz, John H., cited, 89, 90, 91–94
Herzl, Theodor, 126
Hi, Gen. Pak Chung, 79
Hindus (*see also* under India; and Pakistan), 19, 107, 116, 153
Hindustan Standard, 137
Hinton, Harold C., cited, 80, 82
Histadrut, 140, 141, 143
Hoa Hao, 38, 41, 58
Ho Chi Minh, 26, 27, 37–41, 173
Hodgkin, Thomas, cited, 92
Hoffmann, Stanley H., cited, 89, 90, 92, 94
Hokokai, 42
Holland: *see* Dutch
Hong Kong, 1, 7, 10
Hovet, Thomas, cited, 187, 189
Hudson, G. F., cited, 80
Hukbalahap movement, 61, 163
Hume, A. O., 22
'Hundred Years' Peace', 122
Hungarian revolution, 105, 116, 118–21, 186, 188
Hyderabad, 60, 82, 84, 85

Ideologies, 91, 105, 108, 113, 163
Illiteracy, 68, 69, 71, 124
Imperialism, 119, 127
Independence (*see also* under name of country), viii, 1, 21, 30–46, 96, 155; U.N. help, 189
India:
  'After Nehru', Nehru's views, 213–14
  Agriculture, dependence on, 16
  August Revolt, 35
  British rule, 3, 4, 6–9, 32–37, 46; Nehru's views, 195
  Cabinet (British) Mission (1946), 35–36
  Capital moved to Delhi, 24
  Ceylon, relations with, 176–9
  China, relations with, 100, 117, 161, 163, 167–72; border dispute, 105, 154, 158, 160, 164–72, 182, 190
  Civil disobedience, 25, 31–35
  Civil liberties, 83–4
  Commonwealth, and, 211–12
  Community schemes, 198
  Congress, National, 22–25, 31–37, 59, 66, 83, 178; and socialism, 201
  Constitution, 25, 32–34, 82–85
  Economic development, impact of colonial rule, 9, 15–18; Nehru's views, 198–200
  Elections, 82–3, 85
  Famines, 16, 17, 23
  French settlement, 6–8
  Goa, occupation of (1961), 1, 105, 188, 190
  'Great Power' status, potential, 97–99, 159
  Great Rebellion (1857), 8
  Hindu–Muslim tension, 23, 31, 36, 70, 130, 181; Nehru's views, 207–8
  'Hope Level', 199
  Hungary, attitude to, 118–21
  Independence (1947), 1, 20, 22–25, 30–37, 46, 155; Nehru on achievements since, 197–9

India (*contd.*):
  International relations, 95–99, 103–5, 159–60; Nehru's views, 203–6
  Israel, attitude to, 128–33, 137–8
  Korean war, and, 116–21
  Land reform, Nehru's views, 200–1
  Languages, 67–68, 86, 105
  Leadership, 65, 213–14
  Local councils, 85
  Military aid from America and Britain, 161, 190
  Muslim League, 24, 31, 33–35, 37, 194–5
  Muslims (*see also* Hindu-Muslim tension, above), 24, 33–37, 67, 130, 138, 180, 181
  Nationalism, 22–25, 30–37, 46
  Neutralism, 112–22, 204–6
  Non-violence, 30–31, 195–6
  Pakistan, relations with (*see also* Kashmir), 103, 105, 130, 156, 160–1, 165, 172–6, 179–83; Nehru's views, 207–10
  Panchayati Raj, 85
  Paramount Power, 4, 8–9, 11, 35
  Parliament, 83
  Partition, 23, 24, 34–37; Nehru's views, 194–5
  Political system, 47, 82, 108; record since independence, 59–60, 62, 66, 68, 82–87, 197–9
  Population, increase, 16; Nehru's views, 202–3
  Preventive detention, 84–5
  'Quit India' campaign (1942), 31, 34–35
  Refugees, 71, 180, 198
  Salt tax, 32
  Second World War, attitude to, 31, 33–35
  Soviet bloc, relations with, 156–7, 190
  States, Princely, 4, 8–9, 33, 35, 60, 67–68, 86, 197
  Suez crisis, and, 118–20
  Taxes, 15
  Technology, 15
  Terrorism, 23, 24
  Union, 34, 197
  United Nations, and, 116–21, 184–6, 188, 190
  United States, relations with, 161, 172
  Viceroy, 32, 36
Indian Councils Act, 24
Indian Express, 137
Indo-China:
  Burma boundary, 10
  China and, 11, 12, 37–40
  Communists, 25–28, 37, 39, 41, 42
  Federation, 39, 40
  French rule, 4, 7, 11–12, 17–18, 20, 22, 25–28, 37–42, 46, 57, 173
  Geneva Agreements (1954), 41, 57, 164
  Independence (1954) (*see also* under names of new states), 1, 22, 37–42
  Japanese occupation, 37–39
  Leaders, 65
  League of National Union, 40–41
  Nationalism, 25–28, 37–42
  Political system, 64

Indo-China (*contd.*):
  Second World War, 37–39
  United States and, 40–42
Indonesia (*earlier* Dutch East Indies, *q.v.*):
  Chinese, 6, 67
  Communists, 29, 53
  Delhi Conference (1949), 100, 174, 184
  Dutch rule (*see also* Dutch East Indies), 20, 42–46
  'Guided Democracy', 54, 74
  Independence (1949), 1, 22, 42–46, 155
  International relations, 95, 96, 98, 103, 104, 109, 173, 174
  Leadership, 65, 72
  Masjumi, 52, 53, 73
  Nationalism, 28–30, 42–46, 53
  Political system, 48, 49, 64, 108; record since independence, 52–54, 62–66, 71–73
  Republic, 43–46
  Soviet bloc, relations with, 157
  United Nations, and, 184–6, 188, 189
  United States, relations with, 43–45
Indonesian Union, 29
Indus waters, 180
Industrial Revolution, 9, 17–18
Inter-American Conference, 102
International Finance Corporation, 187
International relations, 88–110; neutralism, 111–22; new states and, 153–91
International System, 89, 90, 92
Iran, 103, 107, 109, 184; relations with Israel, 130–31, 136–7
Iraq, 73, 99, 109, 137, 165
Israel:
  Africa, and, 135, 138–52
  Afro-Asia, and, 123–52
  Arab dispute with: *see* Arabs
  Asian attitude to, 125–52
  Asian Games, excluded from, 137
  Burma, relations with, 125, 134–5, 138–40, 142–3
  Ceylon, relations with, 135–6
  China, and, 132–3, 137
  Diplomatic recognition, 125, 132, 134–8, 140
  Economic development, 123–4, 135, 144, 145
  Foreign policy, five principles, 129
  France, relations with, 152
  Ghana, and, 133, 139, 140, 145
  Immigration, 124, 127, 128
  Independence (1948), 123, 125–6, 129
  Indian attitude to, 128–33, 137–8
  International relations, 94, 99, 103, 107, 174
  Iran, relations with, 130–31, 136–7
  Japan, and, 125, 132, 135
  Nehru's views, 210–11
  Nepal, relations with, 143
  Philippines, and, 135, 136
  Political system, 109
  Population, 124
  Racial composition, 124, 128
  Soviet Union, relations with, 129, 132
  Suez crisis: *see* that title
  Technical assistance, activities, 134–5, 139–48, 151–2
  Turkey, relations with, 125, 137

Israel (*contd.*):
  United Nations, and, 185, 186, 189
  United States, relations with, 129, 132, 147–8, 152
  Western orientation, 147–8
Israel Digest, cited, 124, 141, 143, 147, 149, 152
Italian city-state system, 112
Italian colonies, former, 185
Izvestia, 144

Japan:
  China, and, 14
  International relations, 96
  Israel, and, 125, 132, 135
  Korea, and, 1, 14, 19, 20
  Naval power, 3
  Political system, 47, 49
  Second World War, 22, 38, 155
  United Nations, and, 186
Jarring, Gunnar, 180
Java, 5–6, 9, 12–17, 28, 29, 42–44, 52–53, 72
Jennings, Sir Ivor, cited, 52, 57
Jerusalem Post, cited, 129
Jewish Agency, 124
Jewish link with Palestine, 125–8
Jewish National Home, 125–8
Jewish state: *see* Israel
Jinnah, Mohammed Ali, 24, 34, 36, 37, 49, 51, 65, 69
Jogjakarta, 44, 45
'John Company': *see* East India Company
Johore, 11
Jordan, 105, 109, 186
Judaism, 123, 126
Jumper, Roy, cited, 59

Kachins, 67
Kahin, George McTurnan, cited, 30, 46, 54, 56, 61, 80, 100, 134
Kandy, 10
Kaplan, Morton A., cited, 88–90, 92
Karens, 55, 67, 73
Kashmir, 71, 94, 104–5, 130, 138, 156–7, 161, 176, 190; facts of dispute, 180–83; proposal for autonomous vale, 182–3; Nehru's views, 207–10; Pakistani-occupied, 165, 172, 182
Kassem, Gen. Abdul, 109
Kantilva, 112
Keith, A. B., cited, 9
Kerala, 60, 82, 83, 86
Keynes, Mary Knatchbull, cited, 175, 185
Khan, Liaquat Ali, 37, 49–51, 65, 69
Khan, Mohammed Ayub: *see* Ayub Khan
Khrushchev, N. S., 156, 160, 165, 188
Kiaochow Bay, 14
King, Frank H. H., cited, 166
Klein, Wells C., cited, 59
Knight, M. M., cited, 2
Knorr, Klaus, cited, 89, 157
Knox, Rawle, cited, 165
Koirala, M. P., 143
Kong Le, General, 58
Korbel, J., cited, 179
Korea:
  Japanese rule, 1, 14, 19, 20
  North, 47, 96, 174

Korea (*contd.*):
    South, 48, 62, 79, 96, 174
    War (1950–53), 114, 116–21, 155–6,
        159–60, 163, 167, 185
Kotelawala, Sir John, 175, 178, 179
Kowloon, 14
Kozicki, Richard J., cited, 167
Kuomintang, 27
Kuwait, 105

Lach, Donald F., cited, 15, 21
Ladakh, 168–72, 182
Lagos Conference (1962), 150
Lambert, Richard D., cited, 52
Lancaster, D., cited, 42
Langer, W. L., cited, 2, 15, 21
Languages, 18–19, 21–22, 67, 106–7
Laos:
    China, relations with, 161
    French rule, 11, 15, 39, 41, 57
    Hostilities, 41, 57–58, 110, 115, 158,
        165, 176
    Independence, 38, 39, 41, 155
    International Commission, 160
    International relations, 95, 104–5, 120,
        173
    Neutralized, 110, 157
    Political instability, 57–58, 62
    United Nations, and, 184, 186, 188
Lasswell, Harold D., cited, 89
Latin America, 104, 186, 189
Lattimore, Owen, cited, 156
Leadership, 64, 65, 100
League of Nations Mandates Commission,
    127
Lebanon, 20, 73, 105, 109, 165, 186, 189
Lefever, Ernest W., cited, 157
Legal concepts and systems, 19
Legge, John D., cited, 54
Leifer, Michael, cited, 177
Liaquat Ali Khan: *see* Khan
Liberia, 185
Libya, 185, 186, 189
Linebarger, Paul M. A., cited, 155
Linggadjati Agreement (1947), 43–45
Liska, George, cited, 89
Little, T. R., cited, 103
Liu Shao ch'i, 80
London, Declaration of (1916), 113
Luard, D. E. T., cited, 80
Lucknow Pact (1916), 24
Luthy, Herbert, cited, 20, 46
Luxembourg, 111

Macao, 1, 14
Macao Conference (1936), 27
Macassar, 52
Macedon, 95–96, 99
MacFarquhar, Roderick, cited, 80
Mackinder, Halford J., 153
McLelland, Charles A., cited, 88
McMahon line, 164, 170, 172
MacNair, Harley F., cited, 15, 21
MacNaughton, Gen. A. G. I., 180
Macridis, Roy C., cited, 88
Madras, 5–7
Madura, 28
Magsaysay, Ramon, 61
Maier Brothers, 141

Majapahit, 5
Majumdar, R. C., cited, 7, 8
Malacca, 4, 10
Malay confederation, projected, 174
Malaya:
    British colonies in, 7, 10–11, 17, 18
    China, relations with, 164, 166
    Chinese minority, 67, 161, 165
    Federated Malay States, 4, 10–11
    Federation (1957), 11, 165
    Independence, 1, 4, 46, 155
    Indians, 67, 105
    International relations, 95, 96, 103, 104,
        157, 173, 174
    Nationalism, 20, 46
    Political system, 47, 108; record since
        independence, 61, 62, 64, 66
    Rebellion, 61, 163
    United Nations, and, 184, 188
Malays, 6
Malaysia Federation, 1, 166, 174, 176
Mali Republic, 143, 151
Manchu dynasty, 7, 13, 14, 162–3
Manchuria, 14
Mandalay, 9
Mangone, Gerard J., cited, 101
Manning, C. A. W., cited, 88
Mao Tse-tung, 37, 41, 79, 80, 165
Mapai, 134, 140
Maratha Confederacy, 8
Marchant, P. D., cited, 88
Maritime nations, as colonial powers, 3, 4
Marshall, Charles Burton, cited, 71
Martin, Laurence W., cited, 157, 188
Marxism-Leninism, 163
Meadows, Martin, cited, 61
Mehta, Pherozeshah, 23
Meir, Mrs. Golda, 140
Mekong River, 177
Menon, Krishna, 98, 131, 138
Menon, V. P., cited, 37
Middle class, 65, 68, 69
Middle East, 2, 73, 105, 121, 151
Middle Eastern Subordinate System, 93–
    95, 99, 102–9
'Middle zone' in politics, 48, 107, 108
Military influence in politics, 48, 62, 68–
    69, 73–74, 81, 108
Mills, Lennox A., cited, 11
Minorities, 66–68, 96; Nehru's views, 212–
    13
Mirza, Iskander, 50, 51
Modelski, George, cited, 92, 96, 102, 159
Moghul Empire, 6, 8
Mohammed, Ghulam, 50
Moluccas, 5, 52
Monarchies, 47–49, 108, 109
Monrovia Conference (1962), 150
'Monsoon Coastland', 153, 163
Montagu-Chelmsford Report (1918), 25
Montagu Declaration (1917), 25
Montreal Star, cited, 158, 159, 165, 171,
    177
Moraes, Frank, cited, 168
Morgenthau, Hans J., cited, 88, 89, 91, 154
Morley-Minto reforms (1909), 24
Morocco, 185, 186, 189
Morris-Jones, W. H., cited, 20, 60
Mountbatten, Lord, 36–37

Mukerji, K. P., cited, 179
Muslims (*see also* under India; and Pakistan), 19, 107, 128
Musso, 29

Namasivayam, S., cited, 10, 57
Nanking, Treaty of, 14
Naoroji, D., 23
Napoleon, quoted, 161
Napoleonic Wars, 6
Narayan, Jaya Prakash, 74, 79, 86
Nasser, Gamal Abdel, 109, 131, 136–7, 145, 150–1
Nasution, General, 72
Nation, The (New York), 169
Nation, The (Rangoon), 139
'National movements', 66
Nationalism (*see also* under names of countries), cultural values, 18–19; effect of colonial rule, 19–22; origins and formative stages, 21–30; character of, 46, 61; leaders, 64; Zionism and, 128
'Native values', 18–19
NATO, 101, 125, 159
Natsir, Mohammed, 53
Naval power and colonialism, 3, 4
Nazimuddin, Kwaja, 50
NEFA, 169–72, 182
Nehru, Jawaharlal, 65, 114, 160, 175; Author's interviews with, 192–215 (*see under* subject of interview)
Ceylon Indians, and, 178–9
China, and, 164, 167–9, 171, 190, 201–2
Hebrew translation of *Autobiography*, 129
Israel, attitude to, 126–33, 137–8
Kashmir, and, 181, 182, 207–10
Nationalist leader, as, 64
Partition, and, 36, 37, 194–5
Suez crisis, and, 119
Nepal:
China, relations with, 98, 105, 161, 165, 171
Independence, 155
International relations, 95, 104
Israel, relations with, 143
Political system, 48, 79, 108
United Nations, and, 184
Netherlands, Queen of the, 43, 45
Netherlands–Indonesian Union, 43, 45, 46
Neutral Nations Repatriation Commission, 116–18, 159
Neutrality and neutralism, 111–22, 128, 129, 157
'New Democracy', 41, 79–82, 85
New Guinea, West (West Irian), 1, 29, 45, 104, 175, 190
New Outlook, 143
New York Times, cited, 58, 134, 144, 149, 156, 158, 161, 169, 171, 175–7
Newman, K. J., cited, 52
Ngo Dinh Diem: *see* Diem
Nguyen Ai Quoc: *see* Ho Chi Minh
Nguyen Emperors, 26
Nguyen Thai Hoc, 27
Nigeria, 190
Nkrumah, Dr. Kwame, 139, 149

Non-alignment, 111–16, 122, 157, 163–4; in United Nations, 186–91; Nehru on India's policy, 204–6
'Non-identification', 129
Non-violence, 30–31; Nehru's views, 195–6
Noon, Firoz Khan, 51
North East Frontier Agency (NEFA), 169–72, 182
North West Frontier Province, 32, 49
Nu, U, 55–56, 73, 133, 134
Nuclear Research, Institute for, 102
Nuclear tests, 94, 175
Nuclear weapons and missiles, 90, 97, 113, 114

OAS, 102–4
Observer, cited, 159, 165, 177
Officer corps, role of, 62, 68–69
Oom, Prince Boun, 58
Opium War, 10, 14
Opposition, attitude to, 63, 68
Organization of American States (OAS), 102–4
Organizational integration, international, 100–3, 107–8
Orissa, 60
Outer Mongolia, 160, 165

Padelford, Norman J., cited, 158, 187
Pakistan:
Arms from United States, 156, 161
'Basic Democracy', 74–79, 82, 85
China, relations with, 161, 165, 172, 182
Civil servants, 65, 70, 71
Constitution, 33, 77–79
Councils, 75–77, 79
Geographical separation between East and West, 70–71
Hindus, 66, 70, 71, 130, 181
Independence (1947), 1, 33–37, 46, 155
India, relations with (*see also* Kashmir), 103, 105, 130, 156, 160–1, 165, 172–5, 179–83: Nehru's views, 207–10
International relations, 94–96, 98, 100, 103–4, 109, 157
Languages, 106
Leadership, 65, 69
Muslim League, 34–35, 49–50, 66, 69, 70
Muslims, 36, 69–71; Nehru's views, 207–8
Political parties, 78
Political system, 47–49, 77–79, 108; record since independence, 49–52, 62, 69–74
Presidential powers, 77–79
Refugees, 71, 180, 198
United Nations, and, 184, 188
Pal, 23
Palestine, 125–8, 133–4, 149
Palmer, Norman D., cited, 60
Palmier, Leslie H., cited, 66
Pan American Union, 102
Pan-Malay Union, 174
Pan-South-East Asia Union, 173
Panch Sheel (Five Principles), 164, 165, 167, 171, 175
Panikkar, K. M., 3, 167
Pantja Sila, 43

Park, Richard L., cited, 60
Parkinson, C. N., cited, 11
Parliamentary government, 47
Parmer, J. Norman, cited, 61
Parties, political, 66
'Partyless democracy', 74
Patel, Sardar V., 37
Pathet Lao movement, 57–58, 158
Pauker, Guy J., cited, 54, 69, 92, 154
Peace, World, 114, 121, 175, 185, 186
Peaceful coexistence, Five principles of, 164, 165, 167, 171, 175
Peasants, antipathy to government, 63–64, 69
Pegu, 9
Peking, 14
'People's Democracy': see 'New Democracy'
Permanent Court of Arbitration, 101
Pescadores, 14
Peta, 42
Philippines:
    China, relations with, 105, 161, 164
    Claim to British Borneo, 176
    Colonialism, 15, 18, 20
    Huks, 61, 163
    Independence (1946), 1, 46, 155
    International relations, 95–6, 98, 100, 103–5, 157, 174
    Israel, relations with, 135, 136
    Political system, 47, 108; record since independence, 60–62
    United Nations, and, 184, 185, 188
    United States occupation, 1, 15
Phouma, Souvanna, 58
Pirenne, Henri, cited, 2
Plamenatz, John, cited, 19
Planning, 17
Plassey, Battle of, 7, 8, 17
Poetera, 42
Poland, 116–18, 121
Politbureau, 79–80, 102
Political consequences, of Western expansion, 3–4; of colonialism, 19–21, 48
Political instability, the record, 47–61, 109–10; causes of instability, 61–73; the way out, 73–85
Political systems, 47–49, 61–64, 106, 108–9
Pondicherry, 6, 7
Population, of Asia, vii; increases in, 16, 97; Nehru's views on control, 202–3
Port Arthur, 14
Portugal, 1–5, 20, 188
Poverty, Asian, vii–viii; effect on government, 62–63, 69, 71
Power, distribution and level in Southern Asia, 97–99, 153–5; centralization, 212
Preah Vihear Temple, 177
Press, 106, 107; Nehru's views, 197
Preventive detention, 84–5; Nehru's views, 196–7
Previté–Orton, C. W., cited, 2
Prices and incomes, fluctuations in, 17
Punjab, 8, 36, 37, 49, 50, 60, 86
Purcell, Victor, cited, 67, 96
Pylee, M. V., cited, 60

Quirino, President Elpidio, 173

Racialism, vii, 4, 107, 115–16, 120, 121, 144
Radio, 106, 107
Raffles, Sir Stamford, 10
Rajan, M. S., cited, 183
Rangnekar, D. K., cited, 57
Rau, Sir Benegal, 185
Raychaudhuri, H. C., cited, 7
Regional integration, 100, 172–5
Rehovoth Conference on Science (1960), 136, 151
Religions, vii, 107, 108, 116
Renville Agreement (1948), 44
Revolutionary Youth Association, 27
Rhee, Synghman, 48
Roeslan, Abdulgani, cited, 54
Ronning, C. Neale, cited, 102
Rosenau, James, N. cited, 88, 89, 92, 94, 95
Roy, Ram Mohan, 22
Rudolph, Lloyd I. and S. H., cited, 60
Russia (see also Soviet Union), 2, 3, 14; Revolution, 22, 26, 29
Russo–Japanese War, 25

Sabry, Ali, 151
Saheb, Dr. Khan, 50–51
Saigon, 27, 38, 59
Saigon, Treaty of, 11
San, Gen. Aung, 55, 65, 73
San Francisco Conference (1945), 184
Sarawak, 1, 176
Serekat Islam, 28–29
Sastroamidjojo, Ali, 53
Satyagraha, 30
Saudi Arabia, 109, 186
Sayeed, Khalid bin, cited, 37, 52, 74
Schuman, Frederick L., cited, 21, 88, 96, 126
Science Conference (Rehovoth), 136, 151
Scigliano, Robert G., cited, 59
Seabury, Paul, cited, 103
SEATO, 98, 100–1, 103–4, 107, 156–61, 165, 172, 177
Senanayake, Dudley, 178
Seven Pillars of Peace, 175
Seven Years' War, 7
Shabad, Theodore, cited, 82
Shan States, 9
Shantung, 14
Sharett, Moshe, 134, 136
Shariat law, 170
Sherman, A. V., cited, 80
Shetty, K. P. Krishna, cited, 179
Shils, Edward, cited, 19
Sihanouk, Prince Norodom, 166, 176–7
Sikhs, 36, 60, 67, 68, 71
Silverstein, Josef, cited, 56
Simla Conference (1945), 35
Simla Convention, 170
Sinai Campaign (see also Suez crisis), 132, 135, 137–8, 148
Sind, 37, 49
Singapore, 1, 10, 11, 67, 165, 166, 176
Singer, David J., cited, 93, 94
Singh, L. P., cited, 177
Singh, Sardar Swaran, 182
Sino-Japanese War (1894–5), 14

Sino-Soviet Axis, 110, 114–15, 157, 168
Sjahrir, Soetan, 29, 42, 44, 72
Sjarifuddin, 42
Skilled man-power pool, 77
Smith, Adam, quoted, 15
Smith, Robert Aura, cited, 61
Smith, T. E., cited, 61
Smith, W. C., cited, 52
Social consequences, of Western expansion, 3; of colonial rule, 19
Social Democratic Association, 29
Socialism, Indian Congress Party and, 201
Socialist Conference (Rangoon), 134, 174
Soetardjo Petition (1936), 30
Solel Boneh, 139, 141
Somalia, 185, 189
Sondermann, Fred A., cited, 89, 94
South Africa, 149, 152, 175, 185, 188, 190
'South and South-East Asia', designation, 95
'South Asia' (area), 96, 97
'South-East Asia' (area), 96, 97, 153–4
South-East Asia, Association of, 107
South-East Asia League, 173
South-East Asia Union, 174
'Southern Asia' (term), definition, 95, 153
Southern Asian Subordinate System, 93, 94; definition, 95–96; inclusion of China, 95–99; date of origin, 96–97; structural features, 97–106; textural features, 106–9; conclusion, 109–10; power dispersion, 153–5; new states and China, 161–72; regional and bilateral disputes, 172–83; new states and United Nations, 184–91
Soviet bloc:
    Indian attitude to, 119–20
    Organizational integration, 102
    Southern Asia, and, 104, 106, 115, 156–7, 160, 163–4, 171–2
    United Nations, and, 185, 186, 188, 189
Soviet model of government: *see* Communist political system
Soviet Union:
    Arabs, attitude to, 132, 144
    Burma, relations with, 156
    China, and: *see* Sino-Soviet axis
    Colonialism, and, 3
    Economic aid to new states, 157, 158
    Indo-China, and, 40, 41
    International relations, 90, 100, 156
    Israel, and, 129, 132
    United States, relations with, 207
Spain, 2, 3, 15, 19
Spear, Percival, cited, 7, 8, 25, 37
Spencer, John H., cited, 187
Spice trade, 2, 4, 5
Stalin, Joseph, 156
Stalin School, 26
Stalinists, 28, 55
Steinberg, B. S., cited, 116, 160
Steiner, H. Arthur, cited, 80, 103
Stirling, John, cited, 177
Stokes, Eric, cited, 18
Straits Settlements, 11
Strausz-Hupé, R., cited, 18, 46
Subordinate State Systems, 92–95, 104–10; conditions, 95
'Substance of democracy', 74

Sudan, 73
Suez Canal, 135, 149
Suez crisis, 116, 118–21, 125, 132, 135–8, 148, 186, 190
Suhrawardy, H. S., 51
Sukarno, President Achmed, 29, 42–45, 53, 54, 65, 72, 74
Sukiman, 53
Sulu, Sultan of, 176
Sumatra, 13, 29, 42–44, 52–53
Summit Conference, 149, 165, 188
Sunda Islands, 13
SUNFED, 187
Super-powers, 90–92, 98, 99, 120–22, 155–6, 188
Surat, 6
Swadeshi (home-made goods), 23
Swaraj (self-government), 23
Sweden, 112, 113, 117
Switzerland, neutrality, 111–13, 117
Syria, 20

T'ai P'ing Rebellion, 14
Tamils, 56–57, 67, 177, 179
Tan Malaka, 29
Tanganyika, 189
Tannarive Conference (1961), 150
Tariff discrimination, 14, 16
Taxes, concealed, 15
Technical assistance, 134-5, 139-48, 151-2, 160
Technology changes, 90, 91, 97–98, 113–14
Telengana Rebellion, 82, 84, 85
Television, 106, 107
Ten Principles of Peace, 175
Tenasserim, 9
Thailand:
    Burma boundary, 10
    Frontier dispute, 176, 177
    International relations, 1, 95, 97, 100, 102–5, 158, 161, 165, 173–7
    Political system, 48, 49, 73, 108
    United Nations, and, 185
Tham, De, 25
Thomas, S. B., cited, 80
Thompson, Edward, cited, 16
Thompson, Virginia M., cited, 12
Thu Thau, 27
Thucydides, 112
Tibet, 105, 156, 163–71, 188
Tientsin Treaties, 14
Tilak, Lokmanya, 23, 24
Time and Tide, 145
Times, The, cited, 131, 151, 159
Times of India, 137
Timor, 1
Tinker, Hugh, cited, 56, 65, 69, 167
Tinker, Irene, cited, 54, 60
Tipu Sultan, 8
Togoland, 185, 189
Tongking, 11, 12, 14, 25–27, 38–39
Traditional political systems, 48, 62, 64
Trager, Frank N., cited, 56
Tran Cao Van, 26
Tran Van Giau, 27
Transport, 17, 21, 106, 107
Travis, Martin B., cited, 102
Treaty Ports system, 14
Trotsky, Leon, 163

Trotskyites, 27, 28, 38, 55–57
Tunisia, 151, 184, 186, 189
Turkey:
International relations, 99, 103, 107
Israel, relations with, 125, 137
Neutrality, and, 113
Political system, 109
United Nations, and, 186

Uganda, settlement offer to Jews, 126
United Arab Republic, 136–7, 149, 186
United Nations (see also under country and subject headings throughout the index):
African caucus, 184, 187
Arab-Asian bloc, 184, 185, 186
Asian-African caucus, 100, 148, 160, 175, 184, 186–91
China's seat, 167, 174, 186–7, 191
International Systems, role in, 89, 103, 105, 106
Neutralized states and, 111
'Package deal' of new members, 160, 184, 186, 187
Secretary-General, 188, 189
Southern Asian states and, 155, 184–91
Technical assistance, 141, 145–6
United Nations Economic Commission for Asia and the Far East: see ECAFE
United Provinces (India), 33, 36
United States:
China, and, 131, 132
Colonies, 2, 3, 15, 20
Europe, and, 98–9
Foreign aid, 157, 158
India, relations with, 161, 172
Indo-China, and, 40–42
Indonesia, and, 43–45
International relations, 101, 102, 106, 155, 156
Israel, relations with, 129, 132, 147–8
Neutrality, and, 111
Philippines, and, 1, 15
Power centre, 90
Southern Asia, and, 156, 160, 164, 171, 172
Soviet Union, and, 207
United Nations, and, 188
Vietnam (South), relations with, 59
Uruguay, 109
Uttar Pradesh, 84, 167

Vandenbosch, Amry, cited, 154
Van der Kroef, Justus M., cited, 54
Verba, Sydney, cited, 89
Victoria, Queen, 8
Viet Minh, 37–41, 163, 173
Vietnam:
China, relations with, 161, 162, 164, 165
French rule, 20, 41
Hostilities, 40, 110, 163
Independence, 39–41, 155
International Commission, 160

Vietnam (contd.):
Nationalism, 25–28, 37–41
North (Democratic Republic), 38–42, 47, 95, 104, 108, 155, 157–8, 161–2, 173–6
Partition, 41–2
South (Republic), 42, 47–48, 58–59, 62, 95, 104–5, 108, 155, 157, 161, 164–5, 175–7
Violence in politics, 63, 64, 71, 73; Nehru's views, 195–6
Vittachi, Tarzie, cited, 57
Vlekke, Bernard H. M., cited, 6
Vo Nguyen Giap, 38
von der Mehden, Fred, cited, 56

Walker, E. A., cited, 3
Walker, Millidge, cited, 54
Walker, Richard L., cited, 99
War, avoidance of, 113–15, 121, 122; fear of, 160; Nehru's views, 204–6
War, First World, 24, 26
War, Second World, 3, 22, 31–39, 42–43, 46, 64, 113, 155
Wared, 141
Warsaw Pact, 102
Weerawardana, I. D. S., cited, 10, 179
Weiner, Marjorie, cited, 59
Weiner, Myron, cited, 60
Weizmann, Chaim, 126
Welfare states, 65
Wellesley, Marquis, 8
West African Subordinate System, 93, 95
West European Subordinate System, 93, 95, 102, 104
West Irian: see New Guinea, West
Westerling, Captain 'Turk', 52
Whitaker, Arthur P., cited, 102
Wilcox, Francis O., cited, 188, 191
Wilopo, Dr., 53, 54
Win, Gen. Ne, 56, 135
Wint, Guy, cited, 100, 125
Wolf, Charles, cited, 157
Wolfers, Arnold, cited, 89
Woodward, Calvin A., cited, 57
World Court, 45, 177
World federation, Nehru's views, 206
World Political System, 93, 94, 104, 110
World politics, new states in, 153–91
Wriggins, W. Howard, cited, 10, 57, 179
Wright, Quincy, cited, 89
Wu, 99
Wurfel, David, cited, 61

Yangtse Valley, 14
Yemen, 109, 186
Yen Bay, 27
Yu-nan Chang, cited, 80
Yunnan, 14

Zauberman, A., cited, 80
Zim, 139
Zionism, 126–8, 138